AMALFI

edited by Robert Gathorne-Hardy

★

OTTOLINE

The Early Memoirs of Lady Ottoline Morrell

by Robert Gathorne-Hardy

FICTION

LACEBURY MANOR *(Collins)*
THE HOUSE BY THE BAY *(Collins)*
OTHER SEAS *(Collins)*
CORONATION BABY *(Collins)*
THE WIND AND THE WATERFALL *(Collins)*

BOTANY, GARDENING AND TRAVEL

WILD FLOWERS IN BRITAIN (Illustrated by John Nash) *(Batsford)*
THREE ACRES AND A MILL *(Dent)*
GARDEN FLOWERS *(Batsford)*
THE TRANQUIL GARDENER (Illustrated by John Nash) *(Nelson)*
THE NATIVE GARDEN (Illustrated by John Nash) *(Nelson)*
TRAVELLER'S TRIO *(Nelson)*

BIOGRAPHY

RECOLLECTIONS OF LOGAN PEARSALL SMITH *(Constable)*

POETRY

VILLAGE SYMPHONY AND OTHER POEMS *(Collins)*

1. The author walking below Furore (page 168)

AMALFI

*Aspects of the city
and her ancient territories*

by

ROBERT GATHORNE-HARDY

Doomsday, for Amalfitans who go to Paradise,
will be a day like any other

FABER AND FABER
24 Russell Square
London

First published in mcmlxviii
by Faber and Faber Limited
24 Russell Square London WC1
Printed in Great Britain by
R. MacLehose and Company Limited
The University Press Glasgow
All rights reserved

S.B.N. 5710 8576 8

DEDICATED
TO MY OLD FRIENDS AND
BROTHER ENTHUSIASTS
IN SO MUCH ITALIAN TRAVEL
ARTHUR PAYNE
AND
EDWARD HARVANE
WHOSE BENEFITS TO ME HAVE BEEN
TOO MANY AND TOO DEEP TO BE
COMPREHENDED IN THE BREVITY
OF A DEDICATION

Contents

PREFACE   *page* 13
PROLOGUE   15
MAP   20
I. THE BOUNDS OF AMALFI   21
II. INTRODUCTION TO
     ANTIQUITY   31
III. AROUND AMALFI   38
IV. THE BABE AND THE
     DEATH   108
V. PLANT HUNTING   114
VI. THE MIRACLE OF THE
     BLOOD   131
VII. EAST FROM AMALFI   143
VIII. WEST FROM AMALFI   160
IX. *I Promessi Sposi*   171
X. FEASTS OF THE SAINTS   182
XI. ULTRAMONTANE AMALFI   191
XII. AMALFI OUTREMER   210
XIII. GHOSTS AND LEGENDS   229
XIV. TWO BEETLES   240
XV. THE MIRACLE OF THE
     MANNA   248
EPILOGUE   255
APPENDIX I. Dates significant
in the history of Amalfi   257
APPENDIX II. The Maritime
Republic: a short history of
Amalfi   260
INDEX   281

9

Illustrations

1. The author walking below Furore
   frontispiece
2. 'That's pretty!' In the grotto-crypt of
   S. Maria de Olearia   *facing page* 17
3. Amalfi from the sea   32
4. Amalfi: thirteenth-century belfry of
   the campanile   32
5. Amalfi: figure of St. Andrew on the
   cathedral door   49
6. Atrani: figure of Christ on the door
   of S. Salvatore   64
7-8. Amalfi: fourteenth-century frescoes
   in the cloisters   64
9. Atrani: campanile of the Maddalena   81
10. Atrani: peacock panel in S. Salvatore   81
11. Ravello: cathedral door: St. George   96
12. Ravello: cathedral door: Madonna
   and Child   96
13. Ravello: cathedral: the larger pulpit 129
14. Ravello: church of the Annunziata   129
15. Minuto: church of the Annunziata:
   frescoes of about 1100   144
16. Scala: the cathedral   144
17. Atrani: procession of the *Battenti*   161
18. Atrani: procession of the *Battenti*   176
19. Giant Fennel (*Ferula communis*)   176
20. Maiori: S. Maria a Mare: English
   alabaster of the Assumption   193

II

Illustrations

21. Maiori: S. Maria de Olearia:
    eleventh-century frescoes *facing page* 193
22. Furore: S. Elia: altar-piece by Anton-
    ello da Capua 208
23. Furore: S. Elia: Roman cinerary urn 225
24. Atrani: festa of the Maddalena 225
25. Salerno: twelfth-century ivory in the
    cathedral museum 225
26. Below S. Maria dei Monti, to the
    south 240
27. S. Maria dei Monti on Easter Monday 240
28. Below S. Maria dei Monti, to the
    north 257
29. Léttere: the castle 257

Of the illustrations, 3, 4, 5 and 13 are published by courtesy of E.N.I.T., the Italian state
tourist department: 1, 2, 11, 15, 20, 21, 22, 23
and 25 are by Signor Samaritani of Naples and
Amalfi: 6, 7, 8, 10, 12, 17, 18, 19 and 29 are by
Mr. Edward Harvane: the rest are the author's.

Preface

Were I to thank by name all who have helped me with this book, my introduction would become longer than any chapter; many, parish priests, sacristans, local inhabitants, to whom I am indebted must, owing to the exigencies of space, remain anonymous. Some, however, I have to name. At their head is my old and close friend Signor Carmine Zuccaro, with whom I first visited the Amalfi coast; and in his name I pay homage to his brothers and sisters who, over many years, have made me as one of themselves, and above all to his father and mother, Antonio and Michele by name, whose kindness and hospitality to me have made inadequate any possible expression of gratitude. I must mention the Cavaliere Galileo Savastani of Vico Equense whose goodness to me has involved the transcription of essential documents: and Signor Roberto Romano, of Meta di Sorrento, from whom I have learnt much and whose hospitality I have often enjoyed. I must name, too, the Rev. Giuseppe Imperato, archpriest of Scala, not only for his helpful friendliness on my many visits to his church, but for the loan of his otherwise unprocurable book on Amalfi, Scala and Ravello, a work from which I have benefited. I am grateful to Signorina Nicky Mariano for permission to quote from *Sunset and Twilight* by Bernard Berenson. And I must thank Mrs. E. Lawrence, for her criticisms and for her help with the typing.

Many books which I have consulted are mentioned in the text. I list here those few which I have used on a larger scale; in my references to them I have used only the surnames.

FRANCESCO PANSA. *Istoria dell'antica republica d'Amalfi.* Two volumes. Naples, 1724.

MATTEO CAMERA. *Istoria della Città e Costiera di Amalfi.* Cava

Preface

dei Tirreni, 1955. This, a reprint of a nineteenth-century edition, was sponsored by the community of Amalfi, and may be bought at the Municipio.

Memorie Storico-diplomatiche dell'antica Città e Ducato di Amalfi. Two volumes. Salerno, 1875–1881.

LUIGI MANSI. *Ravello Sacra-Monumentale.* Ravello, 1887. This was the first, and very likely the only, book to be printed in Ravello.

Illustrazione dei Principali Monumenti di Arte e di Storia del versante Amalfitano. Rome, 1898.

Vita del giovane Medico S. Pantaleone Martire e Protettore di Ravello. Second edition. Amalfi, 1927.

PIETRO PIRRI. *Il Duomo di Amalfi e il Chiostro di paradiso.* Rome, 1941.

ARMANDO SCHIAVO. *Monumenti della Costa di Amalfi.* Milan-Rome, 1941. To this book I am profoundly indebted.

Visitors to Amalfi who cannot speak Italian will find useful Signor G. di Pino's little handbook on the place, of which an English translation is available.

Like many foreigners in Italy, I owe enormous gratitude to the guides of the Touring Club Italiano. It is a pity that these have not been translated into other languages. All English guides which I have seen are either out of date or inadequate.

In the appendix I have put a list of dates significant in the history of Amalfi; the curious reader may wish to examine this before beginning the book.

Prologue

It is now twelve years or more since I first visited Amalfi. I spent no more than ten days there and afterwards, at home in England, I was homesick. The lover postulates, though but in fantasy, possession of the loved one. I have been to many places which enchanted me and to which I have longed, often hopelessly, to return. Amalfi, almost from the first, I looked on as something to make my own. During the succeeding time I have passed at least two months every year, and sometimes more, in that neighbourhood, and the predatory spirit has possessed itself of much that is essential in the understanding of the country. History, legend, art and architecture, things of nature both living and inanimate, people and friendships, the thoughts and beliefs and activities of man, variations of the seasons — these are the headings under which I might file the spoils I have blamelessly ravished from the place.

Implicit in my record is a fragmented travel-story, a fusing of countless little excursions and passionate discoveries; but these had to be blended into a more shapely presentation; a chronological account would have turned progress into chaos. There is also, as I have discovered in retrospective glances, almost the basis of a love-story, a mazy journey in the mind like a mediaeval allegory of courtship, where each event — a dragon killed, a torrent crossed, a mountain climbed, an enchanter evaded — are all stages, possible of interpretation, towards the final and rapturous winning of the desired one. (I must interject that, although I have passed torrents and mountains, both metaphorical and real, very few have been the dragons or enchanters in my path.)

The lover and the curious traveller must, if his story is to be properly understood, make known something of himself. I will start with a disclaimer.

15

Prologue

Parts of this book, in particular the historical passages, might seem to claim a capacity for scholarship which, if carefully examined, I could not sustain. I have undertaken no original research, unless I may dignify by that term the careful reading of two books, difficult to come by, clumsily put together, and stodgily written in a language which twenty years ago was unfamiliar to me.[1]

Only in the chapter entitled *I Promessi Sposi* have I of intention evaded strict accuracy. Friendship and decency alike forbade the printing of records so that it could easily be discovered that this, for instance, had happened to Giuseppe, or that to Giovanni. The original events have been as it were taken to pieces and put together in a different setting; but each anecdote remains true in itself.

I will not be falsely modest. I will claim to be an amateur and a dilettante in the old and not in the modern pejorative sense of each word. Ever since I deeply attached myself to Amalfi, I have read much about the early and mediaeval art of Christian Europe. The subject in itself had obsessed me; yet always in my mind was the hope, often realised, of understanding a little more about the finer antiquities of the place. Humblingly enough, each book, while adding to my knowledge, made me ever the more aware of my own ignorance. Yet there has always been another, rather curious, consequence. In all matters which have greatly fascinated me and which I have studied, I have never read the work of an expert without discovering errors. This ever-recurring experience has made me the less timid in propounding heterodox propositions of my own.

[1] I am referring to the Amalfitan histories by Pansa and Camera. Pansa, who wrote about the turn of the seventeenth and eighteenth centuries, is particularly valuable for his descriptions of churches before they were gorgeously and often beautifully disfigured by Baroque work in the eighteenth century. I have also found him a pleasant source of legend. Historically he is not to be relied on and, where he differs from Camera, I have followed the latter, though even I have sometimes detected errors in his work. He is renowned for having printed many ancient documents, of which a large number has since disappeared; their insertion in the text does not make his book the more readable. Since the most scholarly books have errors, I myself must certainly have made mistakes in transcription or paraphrase. Any larger errors of history must be blamed not on me but on Matteo Camera.

2. 'That's pretty!' In the grotto-crypt of S. Maria de Olearia.
Old plaster-work can be seen (page 151)

Prologue

I realised very early that, although the city of Amalfi with the surrounding country was for centuries an autonomous republic, I should never understand her antiquities if I had not seen anything else of the kind. Though at one time great in commerce, Amalfi never produced her own school of art. Names are recorded of painters and architects from the coast, and anonymous work must often be by native hands; but in no case, whatever their merit, are they other than provincial members of a larger school, Byzantine, for instance, or Giottesque, or eclectic Renaissance, or Neapolitan Baroque. (With early work, the attribution to local artists may well be wrong.) Amalfitans of the great days were more notable as patrons than as creators of art.

To enlarge and enliven my understanding of local monuments, I have made many and diverse journeys in Italy. These excursions have not been pedantic and chiefly looked for expected beauties; yet always in my mind was the thought of Amalfitan treasure. Much have I seen in Campania and Lazio; Sicily and Apulia have enlightened me. In the huge artistic wealth of Naples I have often — too often, perhaps, and to the unwise neglect of other beauties — gone where I could train my eyes to a more perspicuous vision of art in Amalfi. Anywhere, in Rome or Umbria or Tuscany or Lazio, a mosaic pavement, or an old capital, has related itself to more familiar objects. In classic remains I have delighted to discover forebears of things especially known to me. In England itself I have come with joy on motifs related to southern work.

I have just observed that there are no works of art peculiar to Amalfi. In another province of my life, in the pursuit of botany, much the same proves to be true. There is no botanical species endemic in the ancient territories of Amalfi (one, claimed as such, I proved to be a ghost). Yet there are one or two plants more abundant there than in almost any other parts.

So might it be said of the people. The strain is mixed. Blond hair, not infrequently seen, suggests Norman blood; some faces reveal traces of Saracenic ancestry; abundant are the black hair and black eyes of Mediterranean stock. Yet, with all the mixture, there is something of uniformity, a corporate national character.

Prologue

For six centuries or more Amalfi, though formally vassal to the Byzantine empire, was a proud, prosperous and independent small nation. After her ultimate subjugation the power of an overlord was bitterly resented, and the sense of nationhood has not altogether faded away. Quite often I have heard pardonable boasting about the ancient glories and achievements of Amalfi — such as one would rarely hear in England of a city or a county. Her citizens have not lost all sense of an antique and lordly independence.

Chance has set me chiefly in the small area enclosing Amalfi, Atrani, Ravello and Scala. Here over the years I have gradually become familiar in a neighbourhood populated with friends. It is just here that would most probably survive a ghost of patriotism for the long-dead republic. Here was the rich heart of that venerable community, and here, in a space barely four miles by four, are all but a few of the greater works of art to be found on the Amalfi coast. The natural beauties of the country are not so restricted.

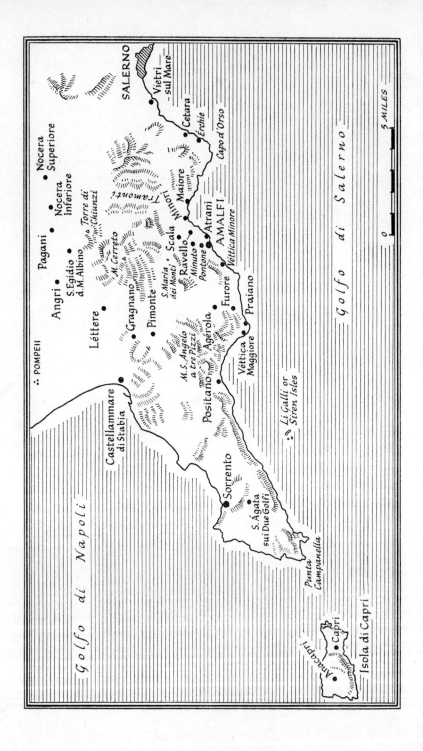

CHAPTER I

The Bounds of Amalfi

The Bay of Naples and the Bay of Salerno are divided from one another by the Lattari mountains. They, in their turn, are divided from the mainland proper by the valley which runs north from Salerno towards Pompeii. These mountains are the substance of the Sorrento Peninsula. On the north, at Castellammare, the Sorrentine coast merges with the Vesuvian plain, which stretches north as far as Naples. The south coast is about three times as long, ending at Vietri, not far from Salerno; this is known in Italian as the *Costiera Amalfitana*. The island of Capri is a mass broken off the same mountains; its highest point, M. Solaro, of just under two thousand feet, is the last westward peak of the vanishing range.

The Sorrentine and the Amalfitan coasts are different country. The north has been far more exposed, throughout thousands of years, to discharges from the volcanic regions of Naples, and over many parts of it fallen ash has hardened into tufa. In the south black volcanic sand appears on the beaches, but there are no substantial deposits of it such as are to be found on the other side of the peninsula. The northern climate would seem to be damper. Certain flowers, such as primroses, are abundant, although rarely to be found on the southern slopes. The steep hill-sides are thickly forested. Soil is far deeper. Sea-cliffs on the bay of Naples fall sheer from land that is no more than gently sloping. Utterly different is the Amalfitan coast.

The most pleasant way to reach Amalfi is by sea from Naples. The boat stops for a while at Capri, which was once subject to the Republic of Amalfi. For a short time after leaving Capri it is possible to see the south coast of the island where the broken, precipitous limestone formation is most fantastical with pillars, pinnacles, obelisks and arches.

Mountains of the peninsula fall away westward. Here their highest levels are close to the southern coast and ridges of a thousand feet or so drop to the sea over little more than a mile. The sea is correspondingly deep and the boat travels within about two hundred yards of the land. In summer I have heard, from on board, crickets singing on shore.

The boat rounds the extremity of the peninsula, the Punta Campanella (The Cape of the Bell). An ancient watch-tower is here, from which a bell was sounded in warning against the approach of enemy or pirate. There is also a lighthouse, with an older house in a style corresponding to our own Regency. It is approached from the village of Termini by a paved mule-track, dating in part from Roman times. I have walked along it only so far as to have a sight of Capri across the narrow strait. The disafforested hills, barren and grey, sweep down to the sea, where they break into low cliffs and jagged rocks, displaying, as Norman Douglas wrote of another coast, 'the sheer effrontery of their mineral charm'. In a short time the boat reaches a fishing village, where it sometimes stops, the Marina del Cantone; this is claimed to possess the most ample sandy beach on the coast.

From a little to the east of this, and ending about Positano, begins the most dramatic stretch of the coast. Cliff is piled upon cliff, in one part up to little less than two thousand feet. Nature has worked meticulously on this limestone. It is carved into precipitous wounds, then healed and adorned in many parts with stalactites, rendered smooth over the face of the rock, or pendulous in grace above high grottoes.

Southward are the isles of the sirens, usually referred to as the Galli. Landor had these in mind when he wrote, in his poem of compliment to Robert Browning:

> *The breeze*
> *Of Alpine heights thou playest with, borne on*
> *Beyond Sorrento and Amalfi, where*
> *The Siren waits thee, singing song for song.*

The Bounds of Amalfi

I am much subject to vertigo, except over cliff-ways which I have come, after much preliminary fear, to know well. I am afflicted when I see people walking fearlessly where I would never dare to go; I can even suffer sympathetic terror at the sight of places, although untrodden at the moment, where men must go at some time. Along this coast are well kept olive-groves on strange steep places, like islands in a vertical sea. At the sight of them I have wondered, with a faint, sick shudder, how can the cultivator ever get there, to prune the trees or to harvest their fruit: and, having collected it, how to get it away? As a vision they enhance marvellously the beauty of the coast, whose chief living adornment is the green-gold of tree spurge and the yellow-gold of Spanish broom. In calm summers the sea gently heaves in dark-blue translucence, broken sometimes by the leap and glitter and glide of flying fish. A butterfly may pass, most often a swallowtail, exquisite creature which seems to delight in the sea.

North of the Galli the road is first seen. This has been described as the most beautiful coast-road in the world, a proposition impossible either to prove or to controvert. It is not absurd. Huge deeps below it sometimes diminish the delight of those travelling that way for the first time. I have never, in ordinary travel, been so affected as not to feel its overpowering beauty. Once, in circumstances not ordinary, I did experience a terror as sharp as any I ever felt in my life before.

It was during a wintry month. After some exploration of the country, I was being driven back to Amalfi from Sorrento. A man with a flag stopped us. The road was being widened, and we were to wait while the rock was blasted. To my right (and I was sitting on the right) was a drop of about twenty feet: then a very steep slope: then a cliff which vanished into a depth of several hundred feet. There were trees on the seaward side of the road.

'I know what will happen,' I said to the driver; 'the road will be blocked with boulders, and we shall have to go back by a different way.'

Sure enough, there was a great *woof*, and a mass of large rocks fell all over the road! One of them knocked a tree upside-down, leaving its upturned roots level with the road. Others flew over and rolled down and fell into the sea. I was disturbed by the fact that, although I heard the heavy thump as they hit the slope, there was no sound at all of their falling into the water.

Workmen began rolling stones over the edge. One was too large to move. A hole was bored in it and dynamite inserted. The explosion shattered it into manageable pieces. While all this was going on, a motor-cyclist rode up. When he saw the heap of rocks he said to the workmen: 'The road is ruined. Make me another.'

At last enough space was cleared for one motor-car to pass at a time. We were beckoned forward with passionate gestures. We passed on to the narrow track, and I found that the outer wheels — and I, remember, was on that side — would have to go over the roots of the inverted tree. Nothing was visible to the right save the edge of the enormous cliff. My problem — and it was such as I never had to meet before — was whether to shut my eyes, or to keep them open. Fancy was fiercer than fact. With eyes momentarily closed, the imagined gulf became worse than reality. I looked at the workman who was directing us. The precision and violence of his gestures were not comforting. At one moment, a quick inward movement of his arms seemed to indicate a situation of peril. There was of course as, with shame, I afterwards realised, almost no danger at all. My driver was skilful; the roots of the tree were firm; the cleared track was perfectly passable. All the same, it was not a method of travelling I would often like to indulge in.

The cause of my terror signifies comfort of mind to those who now travel along that road. It has been adequately widened and, if you share my qualms, a *westward* journey will ensure that you travel on the inside of the road. The journey has drama hardly to be deduced from a sailor's view of it. At times the way curves into steep narrow valleys, where nothing is in sight save a narrow portion of sea, framed between mountainous walls. Then, on a promontory, long stretches of coast will imposingly appear, with glimpses of Capri, and its rocky pillars, the Faraglioni.

The boat anchors off Positano, with its comfortable hotels and every provision for the tourist, tastefully constructed over the

declivities of twin valleys. Eastward, a different country is revealed
to the voyaging ship. Much of the land is still propped on high
cliffs; in places overgrown steeps descend to the sea. The higher
slopes are habitable. Hamlets are on the hills, and many churches,
often with ancient towers. A small town swerves gradually into
sight, Véttica Maggiore, inextricably mingled with adjacent
Praiano. Next the promontory of Conca, with a round mediaeval
watch-tower on the tip of it, curves out as a hooked protection to
its bay.

Close by is a famous sea-cave, the Grotto di Smeraldo, the
Emerald Grotto. Inhabitants of the coast describe it as equal in
beauty to the Blue Grotto of Capri:— foolishly, it is probable,
I have never been there. The overbearing advertisements are too
much for me and I have sulkily resisted all their blandishments.
Photographs rebuke me; the scene of stalactites and glimmering
water must be well worth a visit.

Soon the city of Amalfi appears, covering the mouth and seaward flanks of its valley. It is impossible that a town so built
should not be wonderfully laid out, as may be seen also at
Atrani and, although architecturally less enticingly, at Positano.
These towns are spread like noble drapery over the declivities of
enclosing hills (Pl. 3).

Eastward of Amalfi the cliffs are less majestic than to the west,
yet the road preserves its drama, now hiding, now disclosing,
long stretches of the coast. Atrani is the first town; to ordinary
view it is divided from Amalfi only by a tunnel. It rises in the
mouth of the Valley of the Dragone. Up this valley, at about
twelve hundred feet, is the most important inland town, Ravello.

Minori and Maiori succeed Atrani. Beyond Maiori, the road
rises high to Capo d'Orso, with its rocks broken and pillared
and pierced into shapes of a rococo intricacy. Capri is visible
to the west; south is the Bay of Salerno bounded by the mountains
of the Cilento; south-east, between inland mountains and the sea,
is the plain, with its archaic, oriental buffaloes, and, glory above
all glories, the temples of Paestum. Near to Capo d'Orso is a
grove of stone-pines, grouped in accidental and felicitous perfection.

In this part of the coast, wooded and cultivated slopes rise to lower elevations than those eastward. Terraces enhance, with their firm edges, the flowing lines of the valleys. Vines and lemons alike are trained over pergolas about five feet in height, and always noticeable, even in seasons when the vines are leafless.

The town of Érchie comes next, with its large, dusty quarry, and boats always waiting for a cargo of limestone. Last of the eastward Amalfitan towns is Cetara, held, in the far past, for many years, by a colony of Saracens. Vietri is beyond the bounds, and now merges indistinguishably into Salerno.

This eastward road has some comical associations for me, connected with motor vehicles. On one occasion a friend and I had borrowed a motor-bicycle from Amalfi. At the time, owing to the reconstruction of a piazza, no petrol pumps were working in Amalfi. 'I shall have to take it to Minori,' said the owner of the bicycle, 'to fill up with petrol.'

'There is no need for that,' said my friend. 'We shall be going through Minori.'

'But,' came the answer, 'I don't think there is enough petrol to get to Minori.'

He was right. There was just enough to go about a hundred and fifty yards.

The other happening always comes to mind when I am passing through Cetara. A close friend, native of the coast, had arranged to take his sister on a day's visit to the family of her betrothed, far to the south of Salerno. A car had been lent to him. I was asked to be of the party.

When the day came, he did not want to go. I used what influence I had to show how disgraceful it would be to fail his sister. He yielded, at the expense of his temper, which simmered unceasingly, like a gently bubbling cauldron. The effect was to make him drive very fast. I did not enjoy myself. He would rush at a bend and, just when it seemed we would be over the cliff or into the hill, he braked violently. The overtried car revenged itself. Running down the hill towards Cetara, he braked, and the brakes stayed on. We got out and stared helplessly, but not silently, at the stubborn vehicle. Neither passionate talk, nor attempted manipulation, availed. Nothing would make the wheels turn. Anger and distress were evident in loud and hurried voices. I tried pouring the oil of reason on to the billows of agitation.

'It's not far to Cetara,' I said to my friend, 'let's walk there, and get help from a garage.'

The success of this plan was perhaps mortifying. Although within an hour we were on our way again, the driver regained nothing of calm. In Cetara there is a very sharp turn to the right. In his angry progress he scraped against a wall, damaging one panel of the borrowed car. Many grooves on that angle of wall showed he was not the first driver to have touched it. Shaken with increased agitation, he scraped the road-side wall a hundred yards or so farther on. Soon he complained that the mended brakes were not working properly, and suggested our turning back. It seemed wise to agree, although I doubted his premises.

I considered what white lie would be best. The owner would certainly be vexed. It seemed charitable to spare him the additional discomfort of wrath.

'Let's tell him,' I proposed, 'that a car came round the corner in the middle of the road, and you had to swerve to miss him.'

This plan, so sensible as I thought, was received with small enthusiasm. After a long silence he said: 'I've thought of a good excuse. Let's say that first the brakes wouldn't go off, and after-wards they suddenly wouldn't go on.'

An excuse, I suggested, ought at least to be plausible; my idea, for want of a better, was agreed to. When he heard our story the owner, I was told, said angrily: 'Why didn't you run into the other car?'

The casual visitor could hardly be aware that, in broader parts of the peninsula, there rises a system of mountains comparable to the Cairngorms. Behind Positano is Monte S. Angelo a Tre Pizzi, of about four thousand eight hundred feet, and thus higher than any mountain of Britain. M. Cerreto, north of Ravello, is also over four thousand feet. In this complication is much upland country above three thousand feet, and several peaks of but little under four.

The peninsula is crossed by road in three places. A mile or so to the west of Amalfi the road divides. The road from the right-hand fork coils and curves up the mountain side until it reaches, at about two thousand feet, the hill town of Agérola. This, with its neighbouring villages, stands on rolling uplands, gradually becoming built over; cool nights have made it a summer resort. Eastward, this gentle country ascends to above three thousand feet, among mountains less harsh, less broken and precipitous than the grander peaks. Beyond, above Ravello and Scala, are high woods and pastures, the lands about S. Maria dei Monti, which for a long time seemed legendary to me. Many things over the years conspired against my seeing that lofty Arcadian haunt of flocks and herds.

A short way north of Agérola the road passes through a kilometre-long tunnel, opening on to the folded and forested southern slopes. Whether it be luck or cunning I cannot say, but this tunnel was so constructed that it points like a telescope at Vesuvius; as you approach the southern end, the opening is half-filled by the form of the volcano. A friend, who was in these parts during the war, has told me how, after spending an evening on the coast, he came out of the tunnel to see against the night the tremendous beginnings of the 1944 eruption.

Westward again, the road beyond Positano climbs easily to a low col, at an altitude of not much more than a thousand feet; at one point are visible at the same time the bays of Naples and of Salerno. This road divides into several branches which lead to Sorrento and other towns on the northern coast.

One road crosses the peninsula east of Amalfi. This runs up the valley above Maiori, through the rural community of Tramonti, to the tower of Chiunzi, at about two thousand three hundred feet. The tower stands above the road and is visible from many parts of the valley beyond. Here is a small, crooked defile which, with a twist of the road, suddenly reveals Vesuvius and its plain, and Naples beyond. The road descends northward through wooded hills to the towns of Pagani and Nocera Inferiore which, like Cetara on the Amalfi coast, were occupied for many years by a colony of Saracens. Nocera Inferiore has sometimes been referred to as Nocera dei Pagani, thus confusing it with the neighbouring town.

Early during my first visit, I wrote to an Italian friend in Tuscany, the daughter of a Neapolitan. I had spent much hospitable time in her household, either near Florence or in the hills about Vallombrosa. I had concluded that no landscape could be more beautiful than in the noble regions of Tuscany and Umbria, whose wonderfully moulded hills had delighted such men as Fra Angelico, Baldovinetti and Pierco della Francesca. Those are humanistic landscapes entirely suitable to the great painters who, following Giotto, represented divinity and spiritual beings in human flesh, and who exalted man as a creature of his own natural kind, yet also as the inhabitant of a supernatural universe. That judgement I still hold; in hills of those regions are a depth of beauty, a spiritual splendour, an unfailing spring of sober delight, such as I can hardly suppose to be equalled anywhere else in the world.

The Amalfi coast has a loveliness which took me like strong drink. I wrote to my friend something like this: 'I was going to say it hasn't made me unfaithful to Tuscany. But that's just what it has done. However, I think it's only an affair: not a divorce and re-marriage.' Later, when we met, I said: 'It seems to me a beauty like fairy gold — something which may vanish away before it's been thoroughly enjoyed. The Tuscan landscape is eternal.'

'No,' she responded. 'You see, I spent a great deal of my childhood on that coast. It seems to me a very substantial and lasting beauty.'

With this permission, divorce and re-marriage went through. My heart moved south. However, as a man, passionately in love though he may be with a glamorous wife, can allow other women to be more beautiful, I still do not question the superiority in serious and spiritual beauty of those ranges to the north.

Dazzled as I was by my first vision of these natural beauties, I had eyes exuberantly alert for other felicities. It seemed altogether proper that street and pavement should be swept with besoms of myrtle. I observed the comeliness of the inhabitants. I rejoiced in the welcoming, as of an old friend, which I at once and un-failingly encountered.

Delights in such a mood cannot last. Exasperations I have known since the sunshine of that first visit: cold and rain and snow, and all the troubles of entering and mixing into a strange community. The force of my original passion has soberly endured. The landscapes remain for me unexcelled in their original nature. So strong is my unfailing love that the country and its people seem almost like the deserved reward of a cunning choice. To praise them too forwardly would become like an indecent praise of myself. Let me call on two eminent authorities.

'Opinion hath made it famous for a long time,' says Boccaccio, 'that the sea-coast of *Rheium* to *Gajeta* is the only delectable part of all *Italy*, wherein, somewhat near to *Salerne*, is a coast looking upon the Sea, which the Inhabitants there dwelling do call the coast of *Malfie*, full of Towns, Gardens, Springs and Wealthy men.'[1]

From our own day I call to my support this passage from Bernard Berenson, written at Salerno on June 11th, 1952:[2]

'The landscape between Sorrento and Salerno, the Amalfitano especially, one would not believe in a picture. Indeed, it recalls Mantegna to such a degree that one could almost believe that he had studied it in some of his pictures. The vast toppling crags, cliffs, rocks, promontories, full of vast orifices, niches, cavities, and human habitations filling most of them, clinging to the sides, every bit of cultivable ground shored up into terraces and pergola horticulture. Endless stairs leading everywhere, as paths do elsewhere. One wonders whether these habitations were not suggested by Byzantine Meteora, and like them to get away from danger of attack, and to be safe against gales and tidal waves sweeping over the dry land. You have to see it to believe it.'

[1] I have quoted from the seventeenth-century English translation of *The Decameron*, second day, fourth novel. This narrates adventures of one of the Rufolo family from Ravello.

[2] *Sunset and Twilight*, page 264 in the English edition.

CHAPTER II

Introduction to Antiquity

A n amateur wishing to discuss and record the works of art in territories of Amalfi is beset immediately with a large problem of vocabulary. Authorities have no general name for the style of architecture which prevailed over Christendom from about the year 400 until the final dominance of a new style from France. By the happiest of errors this last acquired the name 'Gothic'. (It has nothing to do with the Goths; so fixed has it become in our artistic vocabulary that we are almost startled when Gibbon refers to ancient churches in Ravenna as the oldest Gothic buildings — which historically they are.) A name is the incarnation of an idea. The word itself, 'Gothic', once we are practical in its use, makes it easy for us to understand how a late structure, such as King's College Chapel at Cambridge, has a blood relationship with Salisbury and Chartres, while it has little with the contemporary Renaissance buildings of Italy.

Once Constantine had established Christianity as the state religion, many churches were built openly, above ground. These are generally held to have been modelled on part of the Roman secular basilica, which was roughly the equivalent of an English town hall, magistrate's court and all. Influence is also attributed to the private house where, during times of persecution, services were secretly held. Many of the earliest surviving churches are circular, and these are often said to have been originally baptistries. The most famous is S. Costanza, in Rome, with contemporary mosaics surviving on the roof of the arcade.

The argument may be interrupted to praise another such church not far from Amalfitan territories. At Nocera Superiore, in the valley between Salerno and Pompeii, is the round church of S.

Maria Maggiore. It is usually dated from about the year 400 and is therefore, like S. Costanza, among the earliest of all churches built above ground for Christian worship. (Some authorities give it a later date.) A circular arcade of twin columns carries low, narrow, round arches, and forms a base for the cupola. In the centre is an octagonal tank, with a solid balustrade; on this there are still standing several columns which probably once supported some sort of baldachin. Baptism was by immersion. At the east is a small apsed chancel. Although lacking mosaics, this church is, in my opinion, more beautifully designed than S. Costanza, and is of a more imposing form. It is, of course, purely Roman; yet, with its contemporaries, it represents a pattern to be followed for centuries in baptistries round or polygonal. There is not always an encircling arcade; this is lacking, for instance, in the slightly less ancient baptistries at Ravenna. Were it straight, the arcade of S. Maria Maggiore would not have looked out of place in any Italian church built during the next eight centuries or more.

S. Maria Maggiore has been unfortunate. Not so many years ago a flood filled it with mud which destroyed some fourteenth-century frescoes; the faint remaining fragments prove that the loss was a sad one but not, like the destruction of Giotto's frescoes in Naples, a disaster. During the 1944 eruption of Vesuvius, the weight of fallen ash brought down the centre of the dome (this has since been tactfully repaired). More restoration is needed, and part of the church is still shored up with timber. Even in its present condition, it is one of the noblest buildings in Campania.

The form of a Christian Church was established very early. Most notable of the kind are two in Ravenna of the fifth century, S. Appollinare in Classe and S. Appollinare Nuovo: and, in Rome, S. Maria Maggiore which, in spite of later splendours in its decoration, preserves the ancient form. The design is called, architecturally, a basilica (an expression artistically confused by its use as an ecclesiastical status granted to certain churches). In such a building there is a nave divided from two aisles by columns holding up round arches;[1] nave and aisles end almost

[1] In Italy these columns are almost always spoils from classical remains. In corresponding churches in England and other northern countries the columns

3. Amalfi from the sea, showing on the skyline the Torre dello Zirro and, above the valley, the church of Minuto.

4. Amalfi: thirteenth-century belfry of the campanile (page 43)

invariably in apses (in Britain an apse is uncommon). The oldest surviving churches in this form date, as I have said, from about the fifth century and the style persisted for seven hundred years (to be revived in Renaissance and Baroque churches).

One important addition was made to the classical pattern. This was the dome. The Romans, of course, had built domes, which were founded on circular walls or colonnades; the greatest example of this form is the Pantheon in Rome. Some of the earliest Christian domes were built on a polygonal base as in the sixth-century S. Vitale at Ravenna; from the polygon, supported on arches, the transition to a round base was easy. The problem was to support the circle of a dome on a square base.

Two rather similar devices were adopted. The simpler was to build a tall arch, or arches, in the angle of the square. These are called squinches, and on them an octagon is constructed, from which a circular dome can be built.

The second device is more delicate in design. The segments of a dome are built in each corner, and all four, widening as they rise, meet in a circle. These segments are called pendentives. An excellent example has survived in the lands of Amalfi. The ancient Palazzo Rufolo, in Ravello, is entered through a towered gateway. The square entrance is covered by a dome. This rises from a drum supported on pendentives. The walls have inlaid decoration of interlaced arches, elaborated with Saracenic motifs; the drum is similarly embellished, but with simpler patterns; the dome is fluted. These adornments give great richness to the structure. Sicilian influence is revealed not only by the style of the decoration, but also by the arches between the pendentives being pointed and not round. A half-ruined tower in the grounds of the palace has a similar structure, but nothing remains above the drum.

A dome in early churches was often built over the choir, with an apse beyond it. Where there are transepts, the dome is usually over the crossing. Some churches, of which S. Sophia in Con-

are usually built up like small towers, and our Norman churches tend to be heavier, and sometimes in consequence more majestic, than the southern equivalent. Form has followed the material.

stantinople is the supreme example, are in the form of a Greek cross, with transepts, nave and choir equal in length. Here the dome is central. A very simple form of domed building can be seen in the late fifth-century baptistry of the cathedral in Naples; this is a square, with a dome on squinches. It is also notable for large fragments of mosaic, comparable in quality with the best at Ravenna. (It opens out of the old church of S. Restituta, which adjoins the north aisle of the cathedral; at present it is only accessible in the morning.)

The dome built on a square, as you may read in many handbooks, is looked on as the hall-mark of Byzantine architecture, and is generally considered the great innovation of Byzantine architects. There are, it is true, authorities who maintain this beautiful device to have been derived from farther east, from Armenia, or even from Persia. The amateur, more safely than the expert, may venture reckless conjectures. In a relic on the Amalfi coast there is an implication that we need not look so far as the mysterious east, or even to Byzantium, for the origin of the pendentive.

At Minori is a large and impressive Roman villa. Unlike those on the northern coast of the peninsula, it was not buried in ash, but silted over. Accordingly, many of the roofs and ceilings are intact, and we can see rooms unrestored, in their original form. (In the process, almost all of the frescoes decayed, and it lacks the brightness of decoration preserved in houses engulfed by the great eruption of Vesuvius in A.D. 79)

One of the rooms is rectangular, with a vaulted roof, and the roof is supported by concave vaulting built up from the corners. Had the room been square, we should have seen a round dome on rough pendentives. This room is probably not later than the early second century A.D. and is said to be unique among antique structures. Can it, however, be probable that it was unique at the time of its building? Of this we can be certain: at least one Roman builder had discovered the engineering principle by which a round dome can be raised on a square base.[1]

---

[1] Some time after I had written this, a friend showed me Professor Picard's little book on Roman architecture (*Living Architecture: Roman*, by Gilbert Picard,

My digression on the structure of early churches, although it began with a problem of nomenclature, will be of use when we examine the antiquities in Amalfitan domains. For my present purpose, it must be pointed out that no consistent name is in use to cover this style of building. Berenson, since the form derives directly from classical Rome, suggested 'Mediaeval Hellenistic', and he sometimes used the phrase 'late classical'. I, for myself, wish we could call it Byzantine, for the style was perfected in or under the influence of Constantinople which, like Paris in the Gothic world, was for many centuries the spring of visual art in Christendom.

There are, of course, noticeable local variations in this art as we get farther and farther from the source of inspiration. For all that, a rough Norman parish church in England is more closely related to the Greek-designed basilicas of Sicily and Ravenna than it is to a Gothic church built some one or two centuries later in a neighbouring parish. Byzantine motifs abound in England. My own parish church has fragments of thirteenth-century frescoes, and among them is a formalised vine-scroll which I have seen, like an old friend, carved and painted, in many old Italian churches. These happy recognitions add a new delight to my life by church-hunting in Italy. Over some eight centuries, the language of art was continental, and local schools are dialects of that language. To define the differences between provincial schools is interesting; the activity, indeed, may become historically important by revealing how great schools of art have evolved from the germ of parochial variation. But these researches are analogous rather to biology than to aesthetics. To feel and savour the art of

Oldbourne). I read that in Nero's *Domus Aurea* there had been a dome supported on eight pillars: and that another dome, derived from this scheme, had been built at Hadrian's villa near Tivoli. More significantly, Professor Picard writes in his concluding paragraph: 'Byzantine architects pursued their researches in fresh directions, devoting themselves especially to the problems of domes, but the Romans, despite their reliance on single stones and rubble fillings, had already outlined the two solutions which were to be required for this type of vault. Pendentives are to be found in some second-century mausolea and in the Baths of Caracalla, and squinches were used in the construction of the tatrapylon at Tebessa.' It is a droll reflection on some experts that the solution which they had pursued in long voyages of thought was to be found in Rome itself.

these centuries — to understand the insubstantial message — we must first comprehend it as the surge and sweep of all artistic Christendom. Afterwards we may get delight in discovering how the works of one community differ from another's. Never must we forget the breadth and consistency of the whole. From Asia Minor to Orkney there will be found a style of architecture which, for all its regional variations, is fundamentally the same: and that style is Byzantine.[1]

Unfortunately the word is ambiguously used by experts, sometimes in a stylistic and sometimes in a geographical sense. In his great book on Byzantine art, Dalton says of a certain ivory that we cannot be sure if it is Byzantine or a Rhenish copy. Professor Talbot-Rice gives to a book on Balkan wall-paintings the title *Byzantine Frescoes*. This ambiguity has emasculated a word which could so easily have covered the style of European architecture which prevailed from the liberation of Christianity by Constantine down to the emergence of Gothic architecture (which was never satisfactorily used by Italians). The Italians have a useful word '*Bizantineggiante*'; unfortunately we cannot use in our own language — generally so accommodating — the literal equivalent, 'Byzantining'.

Few experts are more parochial in their affairs than art experts. Thus, in Italian architecture of the sixteenth century and later, we are instructed to observe the difference between Renaissance, Mannerist and Baroque building, although each defined form merges imperceptibly into the other. Geoffrey Scott in his *Architecture of Humanism* wisely accepted all architecture of a classical style, from the fifteenth century until the Gothic revival, as being essentially of the same kind. Petty divisions are helpful in talk, but confuse the wider view of movements in art.

About the year 1000, times relatively more settled, together with increasing continental prosperity, made possible much building of churches over western Europe. Local inflections of

[1] When an amateur propounds heresy, it is good to have the support of a great expert. In 1931 Berenson said: 'In all the years that I have studied the question, I have always become ever the more convinced that Byzantium is at the root of all the art which developed in our western world, down to and including Lorenzo Monaco.' Umberto Morra, *Colloqui con Berenson*. Garzanti, Milan, 1963. Page 25.

style naturally followed, and modifications of detail largely due
to the elaboration of monastic systems (for instance extra chapels
were needed for the daily saying of Mass by many priests). There
followed an interaction of mutal influence. To the body of all
this development the name of Romanesque has been given.

No expert definition of the term has ever seemed to me as
anything but of the vaguest. Under the cathedral at Trani in
Apulia there is an eighth-century crypt opening into another of the
twelfth. Each speaks in the same language; yet the latter would be
called Romanesque, and the earlier — what? The temple of
Mithras, lately discovered in London (and immediately after so
infamously destroyed) differed little in plan from many a church
of the eleventh and twelfth centuries.

As any assiduous sight-seer can tell, classical influence was a
pure stream, ever flowing, never far below ground, and often
emerging. In many figures, carved and painted, over a vast period
of time, we can recognise, in pose or limb or drapery, a Hellenistic
nature. The same is true of countless formal decorations. Neither
the Carolingian nor the Ottonian school was a revolution such as
occurred in the French nineteenth century; they were plantations
in the north of classic art, each, of course, evolving its own local
individuality, but looking always to Rome and above all to
Constantinople. Rome itself, although preserving a certain sturdy
individuality, was artistically subordinate to Byzantium. The
whole world of Christian art, from the date of Constantine until
the triumph of Gothic architecture, is, in essence, late classical.
One term can cover the whole of it and that term, I suggest, since
unluckily we cannot say Byzantine, should be Romanesque.

With the effrontery of an amateur I shall, for my purposes,
free the word from its undefinable restrictions, and use it for all
buildings and all visual art dating from about the end of the
fourth century until the Gothic centuries. (Were I an expert,
dominant with unsurpassed authority, I would impose the word
'Romanistic'.)

CHAPTER III

Around Amalfi

I.

Except for the great villa at Minori, there are no significant Roman buildings apparent on the Amalfi coast. To enjoy such things you must cross the peninsula to where, about Sorrento, you may stumble romantically on classic ruins. And beyond, in ancient Stabiae, in Pompeii and Herculaneum, is a richness of ancient art unparalleled in any other region of the world. Most of the zone's masterpieces can be seen in the Museum at Naples — most, but not all. Nothing of the kind surpasses, in my opinion, the frescoes in the Villa dei Misteri at Pompeii; in two villas not long discovered at Castellammare there are frescoes of enchanting freshness, including tree-studies almost worthy of Gainsborough or Constable; many treasures from these villas are in the small Antiquarium at Castellammare.

On the Amalfi coast there is, although recognisable structures have been lost, much evidence of ancient habitation. Many are the Romanesque buildings in which have been incorporated classical columns (unfortunately a good many have been buried in plaster during Baroque conversions of churches during the seventeenth and eighteenth centuries). These are often said to have come from Paestum; if all such attributions were accurate, the ancient city must have been larger than Liverpool. In Salerno all the columns of a Roman temple from Paestum were re-erected as a hall of the Archbishop's palace; and during her great days of maritime prosperity, some spoils of the kind were very likely shipped to Amalfi. The quantity is too large for every column to have been an import. Here and there are columns built into the corners of alleyways or of houses. In the cathedral piazza at Amalfi such can be seen and in the arched way out is part of an old architrave and of a huge Corinthian capital.

The usual substance of houses is a coarse concrete; little or no stone is quarried on the coast except for burning into quick-lime. It is not at all unusual, when a house is demolished, to find in the walls fragments of columns and capitals, and even carvings. Some are truly antique, and others more probably date from the days of the Christian empire. In some, for example, I have noticed evidence of the drill, a method not used in carving before the fifth century. It is most unlikely that all such objects were imported, and their existence confirms old reports of rich villas on the coast and tourist settlements. Tourism has been from the first an important industry in the domains of Amalfi.

As on all Mediterranean coasts there is a profusion of picturesque watch-towers, on the Amalfi coasts. Some derive from republican times and these are all round in outline; their present form is probably of the thirteenth century. The latest towers were built in the seventeenth century. They were mainly to shelter sentinels who gave notice of hostile ships, sometimes by means of smoke-signals. Their latest use was to give warning against the approach of Barbary pirates. It is difficult to appreciate the immensity of this danger. When, during the reign of Charles I, Joseph Hall was Bishop of Exeter, one problem he had to deal with was how to receive back into the church redeemed slaves who, during their captivity, had, for their comfort and safety, become Mohammedans; they had been seized on the coasts of Devonshire. Ireland was not exempt, and even Iceland suffered. It may be imagined, then, how vulnerable were the Christian coasts of Spain and France and Italy.

2. AMALFI

For the exploration of antiquity, it is proper to begin with Amalfi. The city is built in the mouth of a deep valley. Its plan follows the natural steep slopes from the hills, and the configuration of the country has allowed only two large open spaces. Seaward is the large Piazza Flavio Gioia, into which descends, from east and west, the main coast road. Flavio Gioia is a legendary citizen of Amalfi and is credited with the invention of the compass.

The lack of evidence for his existence, has not prevented his fellow-citizens erecting, about sixty or seventy years ago, a statue in his honour. He is also claimed by Positano, where a plaque has been set up celebrating this great citizen of the town. Though he himself is no more than a myth, it is probable that the Amalfitans were, in fact, the first Europeans to use the compass for navigation. Its introduction appears to date from the early fourteenth century, ironically at the time when the country's eastern voyages and trade were finally diminishing.

I shall discuss elsewhere the living fecundity of myth in this neighbourhood. I once expressed to some young Amalfitans my reasonable doubts as to the existence of Flavio Gioia. There was, they assured me, proof, in the form of the ancient statue. This had been set up by the citizens of Positano and was captured by Amalfi after a brief war with that presumptuous community. They were referring to this statue, set up towards the end of the last century.

The Piazza Flavio Gioia, during the years in which I have known Amalfi, has been gradually extended into the sea. This, I understand, was partly to provide space for car-parking. Another, perhaps accidental advantage, is that the sea has been kept out of the town. Ten years ago, in winter storms, waves might rage over the piazza and into the shops and houses which stand on its inner fringe. This no longer happens.

Very strange are the high seas at Amalfi. Almost always they follow heavy rain. Then, with little or no wind, immense seas arise. I assume that this is the result of tremendous gales some fifty miles or so from the coast, which have driven the disturbed water against the land. I have seen, in winter, waves rush up cliffs below the eastwardly ascending road and fall heavily on to it; I have even seen waves rising high enough to fall on to the roofs of houses on that road. The only time I ever took a bus the short distance from Amalfi to neighbouring Atrani was when it would have been difficult to walk that way without being drenched by enormous waves. Once, in a deluge, I sheltered in a café on the piazza while rain fell out of the sky like rivers. I was there an hour or more, but the time was not tedious. I saw the sea rushing towards me over the paved space while, beside the ascending road, explosions of spray burst like white flames into the air and fell on to the road, or backward in intricate convolution over the sea. Sometimes, after such a storm, I have sat at night in the same café, looking out to darkness beyond the land; and all the time shoots of spray, lit by the lights of the town, rushed up like spirits out of the blackness. Winter in Amalfi has many beauties that summer visitors know nothing of. 'Men scarcely know how beautiful fire is,' said Shelley; has nobody remarked on the beauty of sea-foam in lamplight?

The Piazza Flavio Gioia has another trivial monument which, for my love of it, I cannot let pass uncelebrated. This is an absurd, endearing little fountain. Two children, huddled happily together, hold up a copper umbrella down which water trickles into a pool. In consequence the fountain shows something which was never the intention of the artist. The children become covered with moss. This is never allowed to rise beyond their necks. Sometimes, to my dismay, I have found the figures clean; but I can be sure of finding them, on my next visit, well wrapt in their dewy, green, unintended covering.

I would not advise a visit to Amalfi just to look at this little folly, however charming; still less to see the indifferent statue of Flavio Gioia, imaginary spoil of an imaginary war. The curious tourist must be warned that we are not here in such a region as Tuscany, or Umbria or Lazio, where it seems that every third parish church has a masterpiece in it. Rather must we adopt the state of mind of an enquirer in England, who is ready to be delighted by any fragment of an early fresco. Having given this warning, I can point out that the old paintings to be seen around Amalfi are, on the average, far finer than we would dare to look for in England. Many frescoes unrecorded in the regular guide-books would be objects of pilgrimage in England. Moreover, in Amalfi and its close neighbourhood there are masterpieces great by any standard. At one corner of the Piazza Flavio Gioia is an

alleyway, just broad enough for traffic, leading to the Piazza
Duomo, the cathedral square. To the south side is an eighteenth-
century statue of St. Andrew the apostle, protector of Amalfi.
He stands in front of his cross, with a bundle of metal fish hanging
from one arm; with his right hand behind it, he supports his
cross. Below him is a fountain, with water gushing into a basin
from a jar held by a triton, and two smaller ones held by putti,
from the breasts of a nymph, and from the beak of a bird. Though
not a masterpiece, this is one of the most enchanting statues that I
know. People drink or fill jars from the spraying water. There
are always one or two vases of flowers in honour of the saint.
I saw this statue at its strangest in January 1963 when un-
precedented cold had coated with thick ice the water in the
basin. No inhabitant, however old, could remember having seen
such a thing before.

To the east is the cathedral with, undetached to the north, the
Crocifisso, probably the original cathedral, and the oldest existing
building in Amalfi. The twin buildings are ledged on a steep
slope of the valley and are reached by a noble flight of steps built
in the early eighteenth century, and sometimes attributed to the
Neapolitan architect Domenico Antonio Vaccaro. They lead to an
open gallery or narthex. Underneath, and facing the piazza, are
quatrefoil windows with bars across them. Within was once the
local prison. I have been told how, through these windows,
prisoners would call to their friends for such comforts as wine, food
and tobacco. Above, the façade blazes with mosaic.

I often think that the front of Amalfi cathedral must be the
ugliest piece of serious architecture in Italy — except, of course,
the Vittoria Emmanuele monument in Rome, supreme in its
abominable class (with which may be included the façades of the
cathedral and of S. Croce in Florence). Before I knew its story,
I would gaze at the Amalfi front, seeking for some repose, some
evidence of antiquity and fineness of art. The guide-books told
me, it is true, that the structure had collapsed in the last century,
and implied that it had been reconstructed. Nothing of the kind
took place.

One or two paintings of the last century reveal the original

appearance. In the sacristy is a poor eighteenth-century painting of
St. Andrew at prayer with a view of the cathedral behind him —
a view which, however crude, confirms the rough truth of later
representation. It is curious and unfortunate that no old photographs have been discovered. The broad and dignified stairway
was crowned by a high portico, probably of the same date, and in
a restrained Baroque style; arches of the narthex would seem to
have had tracery of an Islamic form, such as is copied, complicated and vulgar, in the present structure. Some explanations
of the latter I have found, but little excuse. The three central
arches are evidently borrowed from the wonderful church of S.
Angelo in Formis not far from Capua, and famous for its
Romanesque frescoes; the animal figures in inlaid stone, where
mechanic precision has smothered all magic, are copied from
originals on the cupola at Casserta Vecchia, that wonderful
small town, high up in the hills above the great palace of the
Bourbons. The mosaics are from the design of Morelli whose
sketches for them, in the little municipal museum, confirm their
mediocrity.

Near by is a structure on which the gaze may wander and
rest with never-ending delight. The twelfth-century Romanesque
campanile (Pl. 4), which stands a little to the north, is built
of large blocks of stone; arched openings, with small columns,
lighten its massive dignity; tall columns fill the lower angles of the
tower. (It has been suggested that the massive lowest story may be
earlier than that immediately above it.) It is surmounted by a
Gothic cupola of the thirteenth century. The cupola is echoed at
each corner by smaller cupolas. All are of the same elongated
form, and decorated with interlacing arches of inlaid tiles (those
existing date from an eighteenth-century restoration). The scheme
is said to have been borrowed from the cathedral tower at Caserta
Vecchia which in turn, as Signor Schiavo points out, may have
been influenced by a beautiful Roman tomb, called La Connochia (the spindle) on the Appian Way between Capua and
Caserta. This has a round central tower, with a round pinnacle
at each corner; a slight graceful edifice, it seems almost frivolous
beside the nobility of the Amalfitan tower of which it may be

formally an ancestor. I doubt a little the need for tracing this particular influence; it is not at all uncommon in old English churches to find the transition from a square tower to a round or polygonal steeple, eased by four pinnacles at the corner of the tower; Edward the Confessor's Romanesque Westminster Abbey, as represented in the Bayeux Tapestry, reveals such a tower. Whatever the influence of its form, the campanile more than atones for the vulgarity of the neighbouring façade. More than once, in times of war and civil strife, it served as a fortified refuge.

It is dangerous to presume, for early works, artistic ancestors, of which probably less than one in a thousand has survived. We can see many Campanian towers as being of a single family; yet we cannot be sure that the forms we see are characteristic of only this region. The convention may have been more widespread. War, earthquake, neglect and, worst of all, modish reconstruction have been the ruin of innumerable ancient buildings.

There exist Byzantine manuscripts of the twelfth and thirteenth centuries which have as frontispiece the hieroglyphic representation of a church.[1] The first floor is decorated as though to signify a carpet; on the next floor, Mass is being celebrated; at the summit is a cupola between four smaller ones. The longitudinal plan of a church has been represented vertically. The consequent form is of a tower like the campanile at Amalfi. I am not suggesting that the architect had taken his plan from such a miniature; but is the hypothesis impossible that an eastern miniaturist had taken his design from a once existing tower?

The fallen portico was, it would seem, Gothic in form; the present structure probably gives a plausible if pathetic echo of the original, which was built in the thirteenth century by the Amalfitan Cardinal Capuana, of whom more will be heard. Three buildings stand behind the portico: first, the cathedral; next the already mentioned Crocifisso, which probably dates from the eighth century, and which once made up with the present cathedral a broad single building. North of the Crocifisso, and laid out at an angle to it, are cloisters of the late thirteenth century,

[1] I owe this knowledge to the catalogue of the Byzantine exhibition held at Athens in 1964. Two such designs are reproduced in plates 358 and 359.

built as a cemetery for notable people; in them are housed objects, all interesting and many of them beautiful, from the adjoining churches.

It is unfair to quiz uninstructed visitors; yet my sense of the ironic has been endlessly tickled by the spectacle of tourists arriving in Amalfi. First there is the photograph, taken from a careful view-point, of the hideous façade (acres and acres of film must every year be blemished with a record of this view); then, a laborious ascent of the steep approach, with a rest perhaps, excused as a look back at the picturesque piazza; a pause again in the less than mediocre portico, followed by a quick entry, passing, without a glance at it, a masterpiece of Byzantine art.

The entrance is framed by two tall Romanesque pillars, carved with foliage in which are entangled fantastic creatures, a common and always delightful motif; the architrave is a modern dull echo of old work. Framed in these is a pair of bronze doors made in Constantinople in 1062, to the order of an Amalfitan named Pantaleone; the artist, who signed his work, was called Simon of Syria. An old photograph shows the doors in less than the perfection which they now reveal. I do not know if the restoration involved the replacement of detached details, or whether copies were made so skilfully that they cannot be detected. However that may be, we now have the doors complete in their original form. There are twenty-four panels, on twenty of which are foliated crosses, with formal vine leaves curving up from the foot. Above the second course of panels are six masks of lions, each with a ring in its mouth — a common classical motif of which marble examples may be seen on a pagan sarcophagus in the cloisters. In the middle, two on each door, are four panels with inlaid figures: above, Christ, and the Madonna with her hands held out to Him in prayer; below, St. Andrew and St. Peter. The drawing of the figures was contrived by filling incisions with inlay. Lines of the garments are indicated by a substance like enamel in which faint traces of colour still remain; flesh is represented in silver, with incised features.[1] Figures of the same

[1] It has been suggested to me that all the incised lines were filled with silver and that the faint colouring to be seen is due to weathering of the metal. I am not

nature can be seen in icon or fresco or miniature, and in mosaic. Degrees of great beauty are hard to assess but, whenever I am looking at her, I feel there can be nothing in art lovelier than the figure, in all its magic solemnity, of the Virgin. A foolish conclusion perhaps, but, at the same time, irresistible (Pl. 5).

Apart from the degree of their beauty, these doors are historically of the greatest importance. They are the earliest bronze doors to have been put up in Italy after the fall of the western empire. They were the beginning of a series, all made in Constantinople, during the latter years of the eleventh century, and almost all to the order of the same Amalfitan family; strangely enough, only in Italy are examples of such work to be found.

The doors of Amalfi were seen and admired by that great patron of the arts, Abbot Desiderio of Montecassino. Desiring similar doors for his monastery, these were ordered for him in 1066 by Mauro, son of Pantaleone. They differ from all other doors of the series in having no figures on them. Across the bottom are four foliated crosses. In all the panels above are inscribed records of monasteries subsidiary to Montecassino. The lettering, inlaid with silver, is beautiful, and when the doors were new the effect must have been very gorgeous. Nevertheless, noble though they may be, they are artistically least of all the Byzantine doors in Italy. They were dreadfully broken, and much of them was destroyed during the abominable bombardment of the monastery. They can now be seen most admirably restored. Some panels are entire, and reveal the quality of the old lettering; those that were broken have been tactfully completed. Lost panels are replaced in a manner which suggests their original appearance, while not counterfeiting ancient work. The doors of Montecassino are a peculiar offshoot in the noble succession.

Next, the Roman Benedictines of S. Paolo fuori le Mura, emulating their brothers to the south, ordered doors on a far more

qualified to decide on this. I have noticed, in these and similar doors, traces of red and green in the lines, and I doubt if oxidization would give different colours to different strips of silver inlay. Artistically the figures are closely related to Byzantine enamels.

ambitious scale.[1] The Abbot Hildebrand, soon to become Pope Gregory VII, had them commissioned in 1070 by Mauro, son of Pantaleone (perhaps, it has been suggested, a different Mauro); the artist was called Stauracio da Scio. There are forty-eight panels and all, save a few with inscriptions, have scenes, figures, or decorative motifs in them. The incised work has become neater and freer, and assumes in several panels the quality of fine drawing. Early in the last century a catastrophic fire destroyed a large part of the church. The doors were warped and dis-coloured; much of the inlay was lost. They are now kept in the sacristy.

Although a notice outside lists theses doors among the major treasures of the basilica, they are curiously difficult of access. When I first made the attempt with friends we were told very churlishly by an unpleasant priest that we could not see them with-out permission. How could we get permission? we asked. He thought, and then, in the rudest of tones, blurted out: 'Write to the Vatican!' This did not seem a practical suggestion. Fortun-ately my friends knew an English lay-brother from another Roman monastery; Brother David, for so he is called, knew a canon of S. Paolo, who in the kindest manner showed us the doors. Only a wreckage of their original beauty remains, and they stand against the wall of a very dark room. Yet beauty enough remains in them; with a pictured memory of other such works, the fancy can restore something of their original magnificence. I cannot imagine why they are so resolutely hidden. They have not the occult quality and attraction of some works which are exposed only on great and sacred occasions. For centuries they were visible to all who were going into S. Paolo.

Similar doors to those of S. Paolo, though on a smaller scale, were made for St. Mark's in Venice. In these, too, every panel carries a figure. The date of this construction appears to be un-known. They are in a side door of the portico; in the centre are larger doors, an imitation of them made by an Italian in 1112.

In 1076 a new form appeared, in doors ordered by a younger

---

[1] There are those who maintain that these may have been second in the series, preceding the doors of Montecassino.

47

Pantaleone for the sanctuary of St. Michael at Monte S. Angelo in Apulia. Like the Roman and Venetian doors, each panel has figures in it; here are represented apparitions of angels. The freer delineation to be noticed at S. Paolo has been extended. Berenson has compared this work to the drawing of Pollaiulo. Little inlay has been lost, and the silver flesh is bright. The doors are in a grotto at the foot of stairs and they have never suffered seriously from weathering. The other doors bear figures in hierarchic solemnity. Here all is movement and a flutter of angels' wings. These doors lately occasioned an admirable display of local pride and patriotism.

In 1964 there was a large exhibition in Athens of Byzantine art. Among masterpieces chosen for this were the doors of Monte S. Angelo. The inhabitants of the little town were passionately unwilling that their chief treasure should be, even temporarily, carried away from them. No workman could be found to take them down; every inconvenience contrivable was practised; eventually the Byzantine treasures of Italy went to Greece — without the doors. In the same year I had found Byzantine works missing when I travelled to see them, at Pisa, at Bari and, in England, at Luton Hoo. I was gratified by the resistance, and heard about it from a workman engaged on restoration in the sanctuary.

'Nobody slept in the town that night!' he ended almost operatically, 'People crowded the steps, and it was impossible to take the doors away.' This resistance displayed to my mind all that is finest and wildest and most lovable in the Italian character.

Next in order come the doors in the church of S. Salvatore at Atrani, the little town adjoining Amalfi. These imitate, in a simple plan, the doors of Amalfi. They were ordered by Pantaleone, son of the other Pantaleone, and were made in 1087. Christ and the Virgin appear above; St. Sebastian and S. Pantaleone below. They have suffered from time, and much of the inlay has gone. They are simpler than most of the other doors and have no lion masks on them. The figure of Christ seems to me more beautiful than that at Amalfi; it has life and movement, and was

5. Amalfi: figure of St Andrew on the cathedral door. The silver face has been polished by the devout, touching it with a finger which they kiss (page 45)

probably copied from a representation of the anastasis, or descent into hell, when He is portrayed trampling the broken gates (Pl. 6).

Last in the series are the doors of Salerno cathedral. They date from 1099, and were not ordered by the beneficent family of Amalfitan traders. Though of great beauty, they seem to me the least beautiful of all; the proportions are less noble than at Amalfi; the decorative work is less finely carried out. Had they been the only thing of the kind, they would have been reckoned as a very notable work.

We have wandered far from Amalfi in considering these doors. The diversion is relevant. Amalfi had introduced into Italy a form of art which was to culminate in works of supreme beauty.

During the first half of the twelfth century, an Italian artist, Ruggero da Melfi, made doors for the tomb of the crusader Bohemond at Canosa, in Apulia. (This land, it must be remembered, had lately been a province of the Byzantine empire, Greek-speaking; a local form of Byzantine architecture evolved there, and Ruggero was artistically at least half-Greek.) This building is one of the most enchanting in Italy. No larger than an ordinary room, it is a toy Byzantine church, complete with dome and apse. The doors are of an irregular pattern. There are two inlaid panels, mysterious with crusaders standing together and kneeling in adoration of the Virgin. What are significant are reliefs on the other panels, purely decorative and Islamic in pattern. (Such motifs spread over western Europe, even to England where I have seen them in wooden bosses on the roof of Blythburgh church in Suffolk.) Work in relief went further in the west doors of Troia Cathedral, in Apulia; these, too, are the work of an Italian, Oderiso da Benevento, who made them in 1119 (the same reservations must be made about his artistic nationality). Although they have suffered damage, and have some curious and incongruous Renaissance panels from an early restoration, enough of old work has remained to demonstrate their originality. The foliated crosses, even, seem capable of movement. Eight lion heads in relief are intricately modelled. Two coiled dragons in high relief carry metal knockers. Oderiso also carried out inlaid panels in the older style; later he made smaller doors for the south entrance, decorated with inlaid figures of bishops who, eschewing Byzantine solemnity, mince and dance in their panels with a divine frivolity that is altogether enchanting. Oderiso was a beautiful artist, and in his reliefs he had opened a way which was to culminate in the unexcelled beauty of the golden doors on the baptistry in Florence.

Latest in the series of essentially Byzantine doors, whether executed in the east or in Italy, were those of the cathedral at Benevento. Lamentably, that building was almost entirely destroyed during the war, and the doors were dreadfully shattered. The fragments have been collected. Only a few panels were altogether lost, although many are incomplete, or warped by fire. Their quality shows them to have been the chief glory of a splendid succession. The modelling is masterly; the grouping of figures is magnificently contrived; the simpler panels reveal a perfection of design. Architectural backgrounds, although deriving from a Roman past, hint, as with so much Romanesque art, at work by great masters of the Renaissance. An earlier stage in this marvellous progress will be visited later at Ravello.

Benevento can be visited on a day's trip from Amalfi, although it may turn out to be impossible to see the doors. Troia can be reached on an even longer day's excursion. When I first went there, I left at half past four in the morning; so early a start is unnecessary; six would be soon enough. It is a journey worth making for its own sake, through the cleft Apennines by Avellino and Benevento, and then on to the strange down-like uplands of northern Apulia. Troia Cathedral, too, even without its doors, would be worth a journey far less enjoyable. It has carvings of superb quality — some probably copied or imitated from Byzantine ivories — and its form, like the doors of Benevento, foreshadows great designs of the early fifteenth century.

I had a curious encounter in Troia. In the cathedral, a boy of sixteen or seventeen showed me some hidden works I should otherwise very probably have missed. He then told me of a church earlier than the cathedral, and took me to see it: a tenth-century prototype of many Apulian churches, and built under Byzantine sovereignty. A most intelligent lad, I thought to myself. When I got back to my driver, who had been chatting with several young men, he told me that the boy had only been a few weeks out of the asylum. A year or two later I went back with two friends. The boy was there. We asked him to take us to that old church. On the way a cat crossed the road. 'A cat,' he said, pointing to it and added, seriously, 'cats eat mice.' Then he turned confidentially to me and said: 'The cat has four legs.'

I realised then that his memory was an indiscriminating rag-bag of diverse information. The date of the early church, and the number of a cat's legs, had equal value. His phrases about cats were, I surmise, relics of his time at school when he was learning to speak Italian — a process most necessary in Italy where in almost every region the natural speech is a dialect incomprehensible in other parts.

Among great works it is difficult to set a precedence. The doors of S. Paolo in Rome are so damaged that their beauty is little more than an indication of what it has been. Therefore, among the purely Byzantine doors, the present supremacy, in my opinion, is to be disputed only between Monte S. Angelo and Amalfi. In the former there is a freedom and variety of drawing in the design which give a most magical effect and curiously unify the whole assembly of panels. Yet the proportions of the Amalfi doors, with the rectangle of figures so admirably framed by foliated crosses, and the rather sombre plan enlightened by the splendidly modelled lion masks, establish them, I would judge, as now the most beautiful of all those Byzantine doors which were introduced into Italy within the space of forty years.

The doors open on to a vision of splendour which by contrast reveals the more the vulgarity of the unfortunate façade. The nave is defined by massive pillars patterned with an inlay of coloured marbles; crystal chandeliers glitter along each side of it. The transept extends no farther than the walls of the aisles. All this apparent work dates from the eighteenth century, during which period a beautiful altar-front of silver was made, representing scenes from the life of St. Andrew. This is brought out for all important festivals.

The building is splendidly roofed, with gilded patterns in relief, and large painted panels. An authority on baroque art has said, of the German eighteenth-century ceiling-painters, that there are so many that, for all their excellence, it is difficult to assess their merit. The same is true of the Neapolitan ceiling-painters. Were the paintings at Amalfi the only ones of this kind, they, with their painters, would have been famous. Those over the nave are by Andrea dell'Asta: those over the transept by Giuseppi Castellano, young Neapolitans, chosen as the most skilful disciples of Francesco Solimena. The Martyrdom of St. Andrew in the apse, with the three accompanying figures, is attributed to dell' Asta, the superior of the two.

Amalfi cathedral lacks the light air of holy frivolity which we would expect in a baroque design of the eighteenth century. And with good reason; the skeleton is, in the main, Romanesque. The nave and aisles were built in the tenth century, and have preserved the nobility of their original proportions. The eastern end — transept, choir and northern chapel, together with the crypt beneath them — dates from the thirteenth century. The construction was done to the order of Cardinal Pietro Capuana and his uncle of the same name, archbishop of Amalfi; the division of responsibility has never been certainly established. At that time the façade was decorated with arches and small columns, and a large mosaic of St. Andrew.

An archbishop of the early fourteenth century decorated the apse with mosaic and frescoes; the former represented St. Andrew between the four doctors of the church, no doubt Byzantine in manner. The high altar was enriched with marble, probably Cosmatesque work. In the late fifteenth century, another archbishop renewed the ceiling, and had it painted with scenes from the life of St. Andrew.

The transformation was begun in 1703 by Archbishop Michele Bologna. Till then, the cathedral had formed one building with the contiguous church, the Crocifisso. The combined buildings made in effect a church of five aisles. Archbishop Bologna divided them with a wall; the northern row of chapels probably represents the south aisle of the Crocifisso. His work did not please the citizens. The municipality complained to the Holy See, saying that, whereas all the cathedral needed was a new roof, the said archbishop, instead of leaving the church in its original admirable state, had spent unnecessary sums in building up a large part of the church, 'in knocking down almost all the columns that were there', and had left it half as wide as it formerly was. I have often been told that, inside the pillars, classical columns are hidden as they originally stood; if the accusation against the archbishop was justified, this may not be true. A column has been uncovered in a pillar of the south aisle; it is difficult to see how, in its present position, it could have supported anything.

Archbishop Bologna must not be too harshly blamed. There is no doubt that the structure was dangerous, and the form he gave to the cathedral was one entirely concordant with the taste of his time. For his architect he sent to Naples for Arcangelo Guglielmelli who had done important work there. The design and workmanship of the ceiling are splendid. It is undoubtedly a pity that the archbishop did not follow the wishes of the municipality. Since the work was to be done, it could hardly have been done better.

But still, how can we not regret the five-aisled Romanesque cathedral, with its forest of columns? At S. Maria Capua Vetere, between Caserta and Capua, the cathedral has a nave and four aisles. These are divided by four rows of classic columns with old capitals. In all there are fifty-one columns and, in such a collection, style and material naturally vary. Most of the building is smothered in bad plaster-work of a late period; some heavy pillars interrupt the procession of columns along the nave. For all that, wandering around, one can strip away in fancy the unfortunate additions, and conceive the church as it originally was. Amalfi cathedral was a nobler building and on a larger scale; yet from the columns of S. Maria, we can conjure up mistily a ghost of its original magnificence.

The curious enthusiast will find himself searching for traces of the old cathedral remaining in the present structure. The first chapel on the left is the baptistry, and contains a massive antique

vase of red porphyry which serves as a font, and was said by
Camera to have come from Paestum. In the same chapel is a
large stone eagle of Byzantine form — almost certainly from the
pulpit, or rather from one of the pulpits.[1] A few fragments of
these remain in the cathedral. On either side of the choir are two
small pulpits of 1647; fragments of old mosaic have been built
into them. On the altar of the south-east chapel are more fragments and, on the front of it, a large panel.

Once again a difficulty of nomenclature arises. This work is of
decorative patterns carried out in mosaic. Such designs are liable
to much variation; the commonest form, which appears on the
altar I have just mentioned, is a pattern of intertwined circles,
each often enclosing a piece of fine marble, the innermost circle
usually being the largest. This work, which appears on pulpits
and altars and floors, is often called Opus Alexandrianum, for
the artistic idiom is said to have originated in Egypt. This I
doubt, since the conventional decoration of interlaced circles can
be seen in the earliest art of the eastern Mediterranean. I have been
shown photographs of the typical form from Chios and from
Constantinople — but probably contemporary with much similar
work in Italy. The earliest example I have seen which corres-
ponds with that typical altar front at Amalfi is in a little church
in the hamlet of Casanarella, in southern Apulia. The mosaics
date from the fifth century, and are on the vault of the choir. The
pattern might have been carried out seven or eight centuries later;
it differs from the arrangement most commonly seen, in that the
circles do not enclose fine marble, but figures of animals.

[1] Ambiguity must be avoided. The structures I am speaking of were not used for
preaching, bur for reading the epistle and gospel, the former usually from the north
and the latter from the south side of the church. There are two such pulpits, as
will be told, at Ravello: and, on a sublime scale, at Salerno. These are often called
ambons; it is simpler, I think, though the warning must be given, to use the more
familiar word. The book-rest for the gospel is almost always in the form of an
eagle. The usual explanation of this is first, that, being the symbol of St. John, it is
appropriate since he saw further than any other, into the mysteries of God: second,
because the eagle was said to gaze at the sun with unclosing eyes, and so fittingly
symbolises the discerning of God's truth in the gospels. I sometimes think that this
use of the eagle, which also frequently appears over church doors, may have come
from the application to God of the imperial emblem.

The rounds of rare marble are an antique motif. There are floors at Ostia with coloured inlay encircling rounds of marble such as are typical of Cosmatesque work. It seems possible that the later craftsmen may, in some cases, have used marbles cut to their shape in classic times. However that may be, this particular theme of Cosmatesque decoration has ancient origins.

At the beginning of the second millennium, and for two or three centuries after, much work of the kind was done in Rome and in its neighbourhood. (Some was carried out even in England, at Canterbury and Westminster.) Many of the artists are known by name, and among them was a family called Cosmato; from them the term Cosmatesque has been applied to decoration of this kind. From the little I have said, it will be evident that this is a convention dating from long before the days of the Cosmati; however, the name is useful and has a clear meaning, although it is usually applied only to the Roman group. My plan is the more justified by the characteristic parochial weakness of experts in the field. An Italian has said that stars in the decoration are peculiar to Campania; I have seen stars in Cosmatesque work as far north as Pisa. An Englishman somehow distinguishes Roman from Campanian work and, among the latter, he classes the fragments at Amalfi; in the cloisters is a carved inscription of singular beauty, obviously from the pulpit, in which two artists, Cesare and Angelo, describe themselves as Roman masters.

At the entrance to the choir on either side are two huge columns of red porphyry, said to have been brought from Paestum. In the choir itself are two candlesticks — columns with spiral decorations in mosaic. These, I suspect, were two of four pillars which once supported a baldachin over the high altar. In the sanctuary of Monte Vergine, a holy mountain high above Avellino, there is a beautiful Cosmatesque baldachin whose columns have similar decoration. It is, of course, possible that those at Amalfi may have supported the pulpit, of which there are many fragments in the cloisters. Most engaging of these is a pillar, inlaid with mosaic and surmounted by the figures of David (or Samson) killing the lion. There are mosaicked arches which give the dimensions of one of the pulpits. One of these has a peacock on either side, pecking at grapes, and signifying the soul's eating of the True Vine; sometimes such formalised birds are represented as drinking the water of life. These spiritual birds — though not always to be related to birds of this world — are to be seen all over Europe. (They appear on Norman capitals in a church near my English home.) There is also in the cloister a cornice, perhaps from a pulpit, though it may be from a door, in which diminutive animals are running through carved foliage.

In the crypt are preserved the relics of St. Andrew the Apostle. The way down is from the south aisle. At the first turn of the stair is a beautiful and moving crucifix; I have found no authority to give it a certain date, but suspect the thirteenth or fourteenth century; at the second turn is a stone casket of the thirteenth century with an inscription indicating that it once held the body of St. Andrew. It is far too small for such a load, but, according to a lettered marble below, it once contained the head of the saint, which was lost for many years after its translation; the head was recovered in 1603, and the box only in 1846. The relics are kept within the altar of the crypt, which was designed by Domenico Fontana, an artist from the north who worked in Naples, where he designed the Palazzo Reale. There are three figures on the altar. In the centre is a large bronze effigy of St. Andrew, beautiful and lively, by Michelangelo Naccherino, a Florentine sculptor. (This statue is reproduced in the silver altar-front already mentioned.) There is work by him in Naples and in other places; if I have seen there the average of his accomplishment, this St. Andrew must be his masterpiece. On either side are marble figures by Pietro Bernini, father of the great sculptor and architect, Giovanni Lorenzo Bernini, who added so much to the beauty of Rome.

Pietro Bernini left some works in Naples, and Naccherino more. On several occasions they worked together in that city and, at least once, as at Amalfi, in association with Domenico Fontana. The Corso Umberto I, which runs from the station towards the Piazza Municipio, ends in the Piazza Giovanni Bovio. Here is the fountain of Neptune; it has marine monsters by Pietro, and

the figure of the god is by Naccherino. The fountain was designed
by Fontana, and once stood in a different place. It was later enlarged by Cosimo Fanzago and finally, towards the end of the last
century, moved to its present position. In a chapel of the Gesù
Nuovo is a statue of St. Matthew by Pietro Bernini, and of St.
Andrew by Naccherino, who carved another St. Andrew for a
monument in Naples cathedral (the last is almost a replica of his
bronze St. Andrew at Amalfi). Other work which they carried
out together will be familiar to innumerable tourists. At an angle
of the sea-front in Naples, close to the small port of S. Lucia, is
a fountain called the Immacolatella — the little Immaculate.
This is in the form of a triple arch. The fountain is in the centre;
in the outer arches are excellent figures by Pietro Bernini; at the
extremities are caryatids by Naccherino. It should be added that,
in the crypt of Salerno cathedral, where in the tenth century the
bones of St. Matthew were enshrined by a Lombard prince,
there are two statues of the apostle by Naccherino. The most
widely known work by Pietro Bernini is in Rome, where he
constructed the ship fountain at the foot of the Spanish steps.

The crypt of Amalfi cathedral was floridly decorated, at the
expense of Kings Philip II and III of Spain, with coloured
marbles, and with frescoes by the Neapolitan painter Ariello
Falcone (1600–1656). (It is strange somehow for an Englishman
to find, in Amalfi, work carried out for the king-matrimonial of
England, husband of Mary Tudor.) The work was well done
but, as with that in the cathedral above, it must be regretted that
it was ever done. An inscription proclaims that it replaces a
rude crypt; in fact it is a baroque form imposed on a mediaeval
structure; what old beauty of detail was lost we can never tell.
It was built in the early thirteenth century by Cardinal Pietro
Capuano (or possibly his uncle the archbishop), especially for
the reception of the relics of St. Andrew. The archbishop — or
the cardinal — is said to have built at the same time the transept
and eastern chapels, and the belfry of the campanile.

Among the frescoes in the crypt is one representing the procession which brought the relics into the cathedral. This is
interesting, since it shows the cathedral interior as it was before

the great alterations of the eighteenth century. An arcade of pointed arches is surmounted by a triforium with pairs of round arches. Above there must have been pointed arches, of which a few have now been revealed by the removal of plaster in the south transept. (These pointed arches derive, not from French Gothic, but from half-Saracenic Sicily.) It is recorded that during the procession a boy, leaning too far over, fell, and in the fresco he appears, head downward, in mid air.

Of fine Gothic work, little remains in the cathedral. There are two figures of Virtues, and two companions to them in the cloisters. It is suggested by Schiavo that these are part of a monument to Archbishop Augustariccio, whose sarcophagus is in the cloisters carved in panels with, in the centre on one side, Christ, on the other the Virgin and Child, each between six apostles. At one end is a severe effigy of the archbishop.

Little, too, is left of Renaissance work. The altar in the first chapel on the right is of the sixteenth century, though some of the figures on it are later. At the far end of the south aisle is the monument of an archbishop with his effigy, and above it are the Madonna and Child between saints carved under Florentine influence.

Of treasures known to be lost, it would be painful to speak. Of those which remain there are not facilities for showing all of them. In the sacristy are dismembered parts of a sixteenth-century altar-piece. There are two mediaeval coffers of ivory; one I have seen through the kindness of the parish priest. There is a splendid jewelled mitre of the fourteenth century; I have been given to understand that it is at present so frail that it cannot be safely shown until it has been restored.

There is a beautiful Pietà of the Renaissance. I knew of this, but could not find it anywhere in the cathedral. Eventually I asked for it. It had been taken, I was informed, to the archbishop's residence. 'He would let you see it,' I was encouragingly told. A messenger was sent and the invitation came back. I had often seen Archbishop Rossini in holy functions. At home he revealed a kindliness and a feeling of fine culture I would hardly have dared to look for.

The Pietà has generally been attributed to Antonio Solario, called Lo Zingaro, an artist of the Venetian renaissance who worked in the south; Berenson, however, lists the picture as by the Florentine, Raffaelino del garbo. The archbishop, who died in 1965, had saved many pictures from imminent danger in out-lying churches. There were paintings of the sixteenth, seventeenth and eighteenth centuries, and one or two late icons. Among his rescued treasures is the carved wooden effigy of a saint; I would judge it to be that of the late fourteenth or early fifteenth century. He fortunately visited, in time, a small country church where it had been thrown out to be burnt. He was planning that the Crocifisso might become a museum for the treasures of the cathedral. When I left, he smiled and said, with ironic intonation: 'Well, that's my picture gallery.'

The Crocifisso probably derives from the eighth century, and to this date is assigned the door opening on to the cathedral portico. From the cloisters the north wall of the church can be seen, with a row of double-arched openings, and a row of single openings above. All these are pointed arches of Saracen-Sicilian form and can hardly be earlier than the twelfth century. How much of the existing structure is more ancient it would be difficult to say. In the cloisters are two carved panels, plausibly assigned to the eighth century. One is pierced, and perhaps closed the *Confessio*, the opening in the altar to the chamber containing relics; the other is carved with interlacing circles and rectangles, and very likely formed part of the surround to the altar. The latter panel, during the sixteenth century, had its reverse crudely but engagingly carved with the Madonna and Child, between the Baptist and St. Andrew.

There are substantial fragments of fourteenth-century frescoes in the cloisters. The best are in a small chapel which links them to the Crocifisso. Most are very faded, but enough remain to show their quality; especially beautiful are an angel and the noble figure of a bearded saint. Both Giotto and Cavallini worked in Naples and no doubt they left behind them imitators and emulators (Pls. 7, 8).

The cloisters were built in the latter part of the thirteenth century by Archbishop Filippo Augustariccio and were intended, apparently, for an aristocratic cemetery. It has been said that Augustariccio was appointed archbishop at a time when his sovereign, the Emperor Frederick II, was excommunicated, with an interdict imposed on his kingdom. The death of the Emperor in 1250 did not ease matters for the archbishop, who was not installed until 1266. Amalfi had supported the Pope against Manfred who, whenever he was able, revenged himself on the city. His death made possible Augustariccio's accession. During many of these years the revenues of the archdiocese were administered by John of Procida, physician and loyal friend to Frederick, and a chief instigator of the Sicilian Vespers.

The arches of the cloister are narrow and pointed, and interlaced in relief on the walls above; they are supported on pairs of small columns. The style of the cloisters with four columns at each corner is Saracenic in origin. All authorities agree that the Crocifisso was originally a basilica, with a nave and two aisles. There is now only the nave. The south aisle, as I have said, was apparently incorporated into the present cathedral. In the present north wall old columns have been discovered, and it probably stands on the line which divided the nave from the north aisle. This wall, with its pointed openings, would seem to be older than the cloisters. It is possible that the north aisle was demolished when the main cathedral was first built, with its five aisles.

I have already mentioned notable relics there from the cathedral and from the Crocifisso. There is in the cloisters a panel of mosaic, probably from a floor; the foliate pattern is Byzantine, and this is very likely a fragment from the floor of the Crocifisso. There are two fine Roman sarcophaguses; these were used regularly for the tombs of eminent personages. In one side of the chapel is a vigorous, but far from first-rate, fourteenth-century fresco of the crucifixion. The courtyard is pleasantly planted with greenery. I have been there many, many times, always to discover at each visit some fresh, delightful detail. A most pleasant aspect of the cloisters is that from there one can see the great campanile and the wall of the Crocifisso unencumbered by later, disfiguring structures. There it is possible to conceive the cathedral as it originally appeared.

Several churches in Amalfi suggest antiquity, but they have been so altered and decorated that, as too often in Italy, we can now see them only as attractive and modest baroque structures. An alleyway runs north from the cathedral to a small piazza. Here is the little church of S. Maria Maggiore which dates from the tenth century, but is internally covered with sober baroque ornament; here is kept the image of the Addolorata, Our Lady of Sorrows, who is carried in procession, with the effigy of the dead Jesus, on Good Friday. The tower echoes in form the great campanile of the cathedral.

Notable are two monastic cloisters. At the east end of the town, above the road where it is highest, is a monastery founded by St. Francis. It is now the Hotel Luna. The cloisters, of the thirteenth century, are Romanesque in feeling, although the arches are pointed; for their support double and single columns are interspersed.

Across the city, at the same level, is the Hotel Cappuccini, a former monastery founded in the early thirteenth century by Cardinal Pietro Capuano. Frederick II gave generous assistance to the project. (I wonder how many satisfied clients know that they owe something of their comfort to a papal legate to the crusader kingdoms, and to the great Emperor, *Stupor Mundi*.) The cloisters have been partly destroyed by falls of rock. They have thin pointed interlacing arches similar to those in the cathedral cloisters. In the chapel, which is still in use, is a large *presepio*, or crib. These cribs are passionately tended in the neighbourhood of Naples and often comprise, not only the manger and Holy Family, but whole populated landscapes. The magi will be there, and the shepherds and, as well, country people working at their trade. About Christmas they are set up in private houses, and little figures for them are for sale in the shops. A friend of mine has told me how he used to earn pocket money by collecting moss for sale to people making their *presepio*; another earned cash by painting brown paper to be used for rocky backgrounds. I think the most extraordinary one I ever saw was in a Neapolitan

church. It was advertised outside as having *pastori mobili* —
mobile shepherds. It was worked mechanically. Horses trotted,
carpenters planed, women cooked. Best of all was the massacre
of the innocents; each soldier held a babe by the feet and jabbed
a spasmodic sword at it, while a woman in the background
shook a broom at them. One soldier had lost his innocent, and
stabbed his sword into the air.

Of secular monuments in Amalfi, most important is the ancient
arsenal, usually described as 'of the republic'. Since it is certainly
later than the time of Amalfitan independence, this attribution is
purely romantic. Built of concrete, rough with stone, it is probably
of the thirteenth century. The style is Gothic; there are two long
aisles separated by huge pillars from which rise broad, heavy
ribs supporting the roof. Devoid of any decoration, it is a most
imposing structure. It is only a fragment, however, large parts
having been destroyed in ancient storms.

Without its great treasures, Amalfi would remain a bewitching
city; beautifully disposed against the contours of a romantic
valley, it has all that could be asked for in the way of the picturesque. The main street is narrow and deep; arched horizontal
buttresses link many of the houses. On each side roofed ways,
like passages, run up to others. Doors open on to an arched and
vaulted warehouse. In one place at least, a pattern in dark stone of
interlaced arches decorates the wall of an ancient, lost palace or
church. Here and there a built-in column or capital carries my
thoughts back to imperial days. The city seems to be dreaming
still of its lost, prosperous freedom, and of its Roman heritage.

3. ATRANI

I have often thought that, if I had to live in one of the towns on
the coast, I would choose Atrani (though always I should prefer
a house by itself in the country). Like Amalfi, it is built in the
mouth of a valley, down which rushes the Dragone; the valley is
narrower than that of Amalfi and its flanks are steeper. On
either side houses climb up, often overlapping one another, until a
precipice makes further building impossible. A friend of mine,

whose house is among the highest, jokingly claimed to inhabit the tallest sky-scraper in the world. Since he is living about two hundred and fifty feet up, this was not quite true, but the joke had its point. Most of the houses are in the ancient tradition, dating back to Roman times; they are of rough concrete, the rooms being vaulted, and the roofs having flattened domes; as with timbered houses in England, it is impossible just from the appearance to guess even approximately at their date.

The road crosses the bay on tall handsome arches. Behind them are houses which form one side of the well-like piazza. This, when I first knew the place, could only be reached by foot. Now a road runs curving down, starting from the east end of the tunnel which is all that noticeably divides Atrani from Amalfi.

There is nothing of architectural importance in the piazza, though also nothing unpleasing to the eye. Some classic columns can be seen, built into houses. At the west end is an arcade on massive pillars, at the east a nondescript fountain. There are balconies with attractive iron-work. Overhead to the east looms an enormous cliff; westward the steep hill-side is piled with houses. To the north-west begins a road which eventually narrows into the path up to Ravello. Next to it, at the top of steps, is the little church of S. Salvatore, pleasant but now show-ing itself in a not very distinguished eighteenth-century guise. Yet all these together, with the depth and proportions of the place, make up as picturesque a little square as I know. On the south side a low, wide arch opens on to the sea glimmering and mur-muring beyond. Larger than a village, less than a town, Atrani is a community small enough to reveal its character, and over the years I have come, quite unillusioned as to its faults, to love it like a place of my own.

Two rough breakwaters now jut into the little bay of Atrani. They have been there only a few years. Before, for winter protec-tion, all the fishing boats were taken into the piazza — those lovely objects, of immemorial shape, pointed fore and aft, and often carrying a lateen sail such as we can see in antique paintings.

I have long been an addict of the country pub, where one can meet neighbours and gossip and chat. In Atrani there is a bar more like a pub than any other bar known to me in Italy. Hours have I sat there talking with local friends. One winter evening, when the sea was high, I was sitting in the bar and heard from outside a not unmusical clanking and the sound of laughter. I was told that a wave had come in and had nearly washed away some empty gas-cylinders. People ran out to help and I to watch. No sooner was I outside than a wave roared in through the arch-way. I had just time to jump on to a boat when water a foot deep or more spread over the piazza. At that time, in stormy weather, one had to wait for the interval between waves, before starting off up the new road.

Of the great antiquities there, I have already mentioned the Byzantine bronze doors of S. Salvatore. This church was, in the eighteenth century, so altered and done up that it seems no older than two hundred years. Yet the Romanesque pillars remain beside the marvellous doors, and inside there is a remarkable early treasure. This is a panel, Byzantine in style and age though possibly of Italian work, of two peacocks carved in high relief (Pl. 10); it was probably part of an altar surround. The birds have their tails spread and are standing, one on a hare, the other on a human head, a symbolism which I have never seen properly explained.[1] For the peacock itself, the flesh was thought to be incorruptible, and so signified immortality; the renewal of coloured feathers was taken as a sign of the resurrection of the body. In this church there is a pleasant sixteenth-century painting and, as a stand for the holy water stoop, a Roman marble, with the figure of a Cupid — an admirable piece of carving. One is shown with great pride a bell which is called the bell of the republic. Since it dates from the fourteenth to fifteenth centuries, this designation is obviously wrong, for the bell was cast at least two hundred years after the extinction of Amalfitan independence. However, though the political attributions of the bell may be false, this church is important in the old history of Amalfi. It is

[1] At Teggiano, near Padula, in south-eastern Campania, is a fine Romanesque pulpit. The eagle of the reading-desk stands on a hare, which is supported on the head of a man.

6. Atrani: figure of
Christ on the door of
S. Salvatore (page 48)

7, 8. Amalfi: fourteenth-
century frescoes in the
cloisters (page 59)

sometimes called S. Salvatore della Beretta. Here, and in the portico, now demolished, the elected doge was formally installed and received his cap — *beretta* — of office. During fascist times, the municipality of Atrani — independent again since the war — was united with that of Amalfi. There was a certain historical propriety in this overbearing act for, in the days of independence, Atrani was, as must be evident, very closely linked with the city of Amalfi.

It is told in the historical appendix to this book how, after having been twice sacked by Pisans, Atrani received a settlement of Africans: and how Manfred introduced a community of Saracens. This vindictive treatment is gravely admitted to have corrupted the language of the town. To this day, as in Apulia, one can see faces which seem almost purely Arab, and even the inhabitants of Atrani, and of almost equally corrupted Amalfi, will admit, if in honest mood, that their dialect may be the ugliest among all forms of Neapolitan.

Scenically, the most imposing church in Atrani is the parish church, dedicated to the Magdalen. (The view of it across the small bay from the new road has become not uncommon on travel posters.) It stands nobly above the town, facing the sea. The east end is swathed in ecc'esiastical apartments; these must be recent, for a lithograph from the first half of the last century shows three tall apses such as are found in many Romanesque churches of the neighbourhood. From here, on her feast day, is carried the large image of the Magdalen, patron of Atrani, which provides, to be described later, the finest spectacle I have seen on the coast. A large dome is flanked by two smaller ones, all adorned with patterns of coloured tiles. The tower is square for three stories which are surmounted by two polygonal stories, pierced by arched and round windows respectively. Windows and stories of this tower are emphasised by protruding dark stone, some of it decoratively carved. It closely resembles the tower of the Carmine in Naples which has, in addition, an onion cupola. Schiavo suggests that the tower of Atrani is copied from the Neapolitan. This may be so, but the form is not uncommon. The scheme of round arches in one story, surmounted by circles

E
G–H.A.

in the next, may be seen in many earlier towers. The tower of the Carmine in Naples, as it now appears, dates from the seventeenth century, although building was started in the fifteenth; it may be assumed that our tower is earlier than 1700. The delightful and tactfully restored façade of the church is the only example on the coast of work which may be called rococo. It is painted white, and faces north on to a space so narrow that the sun never shines on it; in bright weather it is alive with a light which seems intrinsic to the structure (Pl. 9).

Rococo work is to be seen in private houses near the road which leads from Vietri to Cava dei Tirreni. The finest of all, to my mind, is in Vietri itself, to the right of the road after you have crossed the valley on the way to Salerno. Difficulties of the site forced its builder to make the nearest corner at an acute angle, so that the house has the outline of a box squeezed out of shape; the main façade is slightly curved. Carvings and mouldings decorate the walls; not over florid, it is a delicious, high-spirited building.

A church on the site of the Magdalen was first built in 1274, against a fortress known as Castrum Leonis, from which Pansa derives, rather improbably, the name of the adjacent hamlet, now in the community of Ravello, Castiglione. Alterations were made in the sixteenth and seventeenth centuries; in the eighteenth it was enlarged. Its final alterations, entirely sympathetic, were carried out in the nineteenth century. It still contains old relics. The organ-loft is of the seventeenth century, with paintings illustrating the life of the saint. (Beautiful organ-lofts are common in the neighbourhood; a friend of mine suggested that someone should make a study of them.) The church is adorned, like Amalfi's, with inlaid marble, some of the work dating strangely from late in the last century. Over the altar are sixteenth-century panels, worth looking at, by an artist called Giovannangelo D'Amato from Maiori; the name is still known on the coast. The chief treasure of the church is a painting of the Incredulity of St. Thomas by Andrea Sabatini (1487–1530), generally known as Andrea da Salerno.

Andrea da Salerno is the finest of all the Renaissance painters who worked in the surrounding country. Born in Salerno in 1487, he died at Gaeta in 1530. Traditionally he is said to have been at first a pupil, and than an assistant, of Raphael; he is credited with having worked with his master in the Vatican, and in S. Maria della Pace. Some, however, affirm that he never left Naples, where he was much esteemed. Vasari, it is true, does not mention his name among the young associates of Raphael; and yet, so Raphaelesque are many of his Madonnas that I find it hard to disbelieve the common tradition. I do not know of any models for him in Naples; in Rome there were many.

The association with Raphael obscures his merits, for it is difficult not to make unhappy comparison; indeed there are pictures where we can see little save an insipid echo of the master — for instance in a Madonna and Child in S. Giorgio in Salerno, and in much of a large altarpiece at the ancient monastery of Corpo di Cava, in the mountains above Cava dei Terreni. Yet there was a true artist in him. In S. Giorgio there is a beautiful altarpiece by him of the martyrdom of the saint, though damaged and dreadfully obscured by dirt. (Once when I was in that church a priest, seeing me, popped out from the Confessional where a penitent had just knelt. We discussed the paintings and I commended the St. George, but he submitted that its authenticity was doubtful and asked me to admire the Madonna, an accepted work of Andrea. This has, to my eyes, the debility of a false Raphael. We discussed other works, and at last he went back to the patiently kneeling penitent.) The landscapes in his paintings have an almost Venetian poetry. The Incredulity of Thomas at Atrani is by any standard a fine painting, although the figures may lack the weight and substance which a great master would have given. In our strict area there are only two other paintings which have been confidently attributed to him, both in the sacristy of the old cathedral at Ravello. One is of a beautiful St. Sebastian in front of a rocky, mountainous landscape, and the other a rare subject, the Assumption of the Magdalen, who is being carried up to heaven by cherubs, and almost covered by her long hair.[1]

---

[1] In the Touring Club guide, *Napoli e Dintorni* (1960), these paintings are given disconcertingly, and against all the authorities I know, to Giovanni Filippo

This unusual theme is evidently alluded to by Vasari in his life of Garofalo, where he speaks of a sculptor in Milan who carved a 'St. Mary Magdalen carried up into the air by four cherubs'. There is a fine example by Lanfranco in the Naples picture gallery at Capo di Monte, and two examples in the church of the Magdalen at Atrani, one on the organ-loft, and one above the altar. The finest of all Andrea's paintings which I have seen is in a suburb of Pagani, a town on the road from Salerno to Pompeii. On the hill above, in the hamlet of S. Egidio di Monte Albino, is a church dedicated to the Magdalen. It has a huge polyptych by Andrea da Salerno, dominated in the centre by a large and splendid Assumption of the Magdalen, carried upward by a crowd of cherubs; in every panel Andrea's work appears at its finest. This church is worth visiting for other things. There are a rather flaccid St. Nicholas attributed to Francesco Solimena, and a Madonna of the Rosary by Luca Giordano. In the sacristy is a panel of the Madonna and Saints, described as Byzantine; though an enjoyable painting, I could not support this classification. There is a crypt, half filled with mud and full of uncollected human bones, which scrunch under-foot; here, very faint, are remains of tenth-century frescoes. There seems to be an Entry into Jerusalem; when fresh, the paintings must have looked like marginal decorations in an early manuscript. If any should find themselves moved by Andrea's paintings in Atrani and Ravello, they would be well rewarded by an excursion to S. Egidio. Beautiful as are his paintings at Ravello, I feel that the polyptich at S. Egidio must be his masterpiece. In any case, the landscape to be passed through on the excursion is sublime.

In the Magdalen at Atrani we come, according to my narrative, on the first of the baroque altars, so common in Italy (there are small, subsidiary ones at Amalfi). The convention is simple — a marble altar, backed by marble extending above and beyond it on either side. At each end of this extension there is almost

Criscuolo of Gaeta. I should be distressed were Andrea deprived of these lovely paintings. For several years the panels were away being cleaned and restored by the department of fine arts. So far as I know, they returned unquestioned as Andrea's. No reason is given for the altered attribution.

invariably a cherub; in the middle is a tabernacle for the Host. On this uncomplicated plan — in my opinion one of the great inventions of art — very gorgeous objects have been made. Usually the decoration is of coloured marble inlay, and often with the addition of sculpture. In poorer churches the structure will be of wood, painted like marble, with plaster cherubs. Of grander examples not far away is a fine one in the often-mentioned S. Giorgio in Salerno, but finest of all is that at S. Ágata.

This village, called S. Ágata sui due Golfi, stands on a low col on the road from Positano to Sorrento, looking down on to the bays of Naples and Salerno. It is not in Amalfitan territory. The altar is described as Florentine of the sixteenth century, both an origin and a date which I doubt. It is a magnificent object, marble inlaid with crystal, coloured marbles, mother of pearl and lapis lazuli; the patterns are chiefly of bunched flowers and wreaths and birds. It is said to have come from the church of the Gerolomini in Naples but I was told a better story at S. Ágata, which I would believe if only I could.

A parish priest of the village found a document describing how and where there had been buried, in fear of the Saracens, a very precious altar. (They cannot have been in any case Saracens; Barbary pirates would have been more convincing.) The land belonged to a monastery, from which he bought it, and disinterred the altar, upon which the monks claimed it as their property. The law was on his side. He took the altar, and set it up at S. Ágata where it fortunately remains.

One other church remains to be mentioned in Atrani. High on the western cliff stands the little church of S. Maria del Bando. The climb up there is laborious, and entry difficult, as keys must be found, and in Italy keys may be the most elusive of all objects. This is in origin a Romanesque church, and from below can be traced the remains of three apses as it stands, small yet most noble, on a huge pillar of precipice. Inside, it seems to be a small eighteenth-century room, but a panel has been left open on the eastern wall where there is a fresco, probably of the early fifteenth century. A delicious work, though of no very great merit, the Child sits embraced by its mother and with arms open in a proffered welcome to the world of men. The Virgin has been crowned. Such paintings are common in Italy, but there is a strange addition: at the Virgin's feet, to one side, is represented a man, standing below the gallows, with a rope round his neck, and evidently about to be hanged.

This I have been told, explains the name of the church. *In bando* can mean in banishment; *bando* can also mean proclamation. The story I was told was this: a man had been unjustly condemned to hanging, when the Virgin appeared. '*Grida il bando*,' she ordered — 'Shout out the proclamation', implying of course a proclamation, on her authority, that the man was innocent.

I have also been given a more mundane reason of the name: that, after a doge had been installed in S. Salvatore, he was proclaimed with a *bando*, from the little church on the cliff. I prefer the former explanation, which in any case is more consistent with the fascinatingly curious fresco.

Another tradition has strayed alongside the Madonna del Bando. In the cliff nearby is a huge grotto, called the Grotta di Massaniello. In 1647 Tommaso Aniello, known as Massaniello, led a revolt in Naples against the Spanish viceroys, and in effect ruled the city for some months, to be overthrown and executed in the spring of 1648. The local tradition is that he was born in Atrani and, after his failure, hid in the grotto. There seems to be little evidence that he was anything but Neapolitan, or that, after his overthrow, he was ever out of Naples.

4. RAVELLO

I have mentioned the footpath which, starting from the northwest corner of the piazza at Atrani, leads up between the mountains to Ravello. Many times have I walked down it. Very much less often, to arrive almost exhausted, have I walked up. It is a climb of some twelve hundred feet. Yet, whether up for the strong, or down for the lazy, it is a walk to be attempted. Few valleys in the world can be more beautiful than the valley of the Dragone, as the little but inexhaustible river is called.

Its waters used to be reckoned as of singular purity, and were sometimes, on the recommendation of doctors, taken as far as Salerno. No doctor or sanitary officer, however indolent in his duties, could make such a recommendation nowadays. Two small paper-mills regularly pollute the stream; other substances even less palatable dribble into it. I remember once in summer a sudden cloudburst. I was in Atrani. A short time after it was over, a vast gush of water burst into the little bay, as though a Cyclops had pulled the plug of his lavatory. Yellow currents polluted the Tyrrhenian sea, and a miscellany of filth was scattered over the shore. A slightly dotty boy ran about barefoot inspecting the unsalutary spoil, among which I noticed a sheep's head.

At Atrani, the valley is narrow. Above, it widens and deepens. To the west, at the southern end, the ridge rises above cliffs to what is called the Montagna di Pontone, vertical on almost all sides; this drops southward, in two great steps, to a prominence, where is a mediaeval tower, the Torre dello Ziro, of which full mention will be made with its proper municipality, Scala. Inland of the mountain, on a saddle of hill, spreads out the village of Pontone. Woods and cliffs, interspersed with terraces of vine and lemon, diversify the hills. Often the bare rock is rendered smooth or festooned with stalactites. Pillars and walls of rock soar into the air. Eastward the land is perhaps more intensively cultivated, and above the cliffs may be seen buildings of Ravello.

The community of this town covers a large area of land, including two bays, that of Castiglione and, to the east, the deep water bay of Marmorata. The former, with its village above, was once a part of Atrani.

Where the foot-path passes out of Atrani, there is a narrow archway near the little church of the Carmine (whose name is often given to men in these parts). I have been told how, less than a hundred years ago, this, together with another gateway above, was closed at night to keep brigands out of the town.

Upwards the valley closes in again, though never so much as to become a gorge. Here there are the small paper-factories and an oil-mill. The effect is not that of an industrial area. The river rushes round water-sculpted rocks and, passing under a small bridge, drops in a deep waterfall, the southern image of a Scotch burn. Since water is channelled off for industrial use, very rarely does it come down here in full glory.

About this point, on the east side, looking on to the deep immense concavity, stands the house that I stay in. From here I have watched the valley sparkling with fire-flies. Sometimes, in certain seasons, I have heard shepherd boys singing as they drive their sheep and goats down to the sea. There the flock is washed before shearing. I remember the extraordinary sight of sheep going down the steep, long steps to the bay of Castiglione, where each in turn was very reluctantly dipped in the sea.

The shepherd songs have sad, drooping cadence, often — or so it sounds — with half-tones in them. A local musician has told me that, in the hills, songs are still sung with Arabic elements in them, as a Spanish gypsy sings. In this matter I have a tentative heretical theory. I have heard, in the country about Rome, songs with the same dying fall sung spontaneously. Before they came to Roman Sicily and Spain, the Saracens occupied African country which had been entirely Roman. May it be that the Arabic element in some western music is not Arabic at all, but an ancient Roman manner picked up by Arabs traversing Roman countries?[1]

Let this valley be a type of Amalfitan territory over the year. In summer the vines are of a rich green, while lemons hang, lamps of pale gold, under the trees. Both lemon and vine are trained on pergolas, a little less than six feet high. In warm days the lemon flowers, far sweeter than orange blossom, make a heavy incense of the air. When autumn comes, they are covered with evergreen branches, usually of ilex, as a protection against hail and rain. The green of these cut boughs fades and, before they are token off in late spring, the terraces seem to be covered with

[1] I have heard lately that, near where I heard the strange singing in Lazio, there had been a colony of Spaniards, and this might well have been a translated music. Yet, even though this be true, my hypothesis is not thereby invalidated. Arabic music from Spain and Africa might still owe something to indigenous music of the Roman empire.

a net of moveless grey mist. One year this protection was of no avail.

Rarely can the valley, or indeed the whole of the coast, have looked so strange as it did in January of 1963. I had been there for about a week during which there was continuous rain. An enthusiast had asked me to get him some plants of *Crocus imperati*. I had noticed flowers and resolved to collect them as soon as the weather changed. Then, one morning, I woke to bright sunshine. When I opened the door, there was a clinking crash as of glass falling. What could I have done? I wondered; and then I found that I had shaken down a plate of ice. Where rock had been running, icicles as big as myself were hanging; ice glittered over the drenched road. For about a week a clear, bright, freezing wind blew southward over the land. In Amalfi the fountain of St. Andrew had ice an inch thick over it; icicles hung from the tunnel between Amalfi and Atrani. One day I cut a lemon to make myself a drink — and found chips of ice inside it.

The consequences were disastrous. In south Italy some nine-tenths of the lemon crop was lost, the main resource of many country people. They showed a stoic fatalism: '*È le vita*,' some said to me, when I showed my sympathy — 'It's life'. I happened to visit an elderly man up the valley who said that his lemons were destroyed. I looked at them.

'They're shooting,' I said.

'That,' he responded, 'is the smile on the face of a dying man.'

Few of the trees died, but they had to be pruned back to the trunk. In 1963 there was no crop; little in 1964; only in 1965 was the old richness returning. The government gave help to the afflicted and, for all their bravery, many, I was told, wept as they officially recorded their losses. Our English winter then was the worst in a century or more. No one alive had ever seen such things in south Italy. We should pray that it may never happen again in any existing lifetime.

As you walk up the narrower valley, there are woods on either hand, woods of chestnut and elder and ash, but the last two not of a kind that we often see in England. Cyclamen of two species, and crocus, flourish in their season among the trees; pimpernels and lithospermum wink blue in the undergrowth. Then the valley becomes more open, thought not cavernously deep as below. Mountains are ahead with, to the left, the romantic little town of Scala, origin of the state of Amalfi, and to the right, the long hill-top stretch of Ravello.

I sometimes think that the best season to arrive would be in the autumn, with the woods all russet and gold, and with a brighter gold on terraces of vine. Dignity and antiquity seem implicit in the florid landscape: moreover, there is not the crowd of hustling strangers making a short, obligatory visit. But of one thing I am sure: the wisest approach would be to go first up to Scala and gaze across the valley to Ravello. It is not one of the great sights of the world as that of San Gimigniano from below, or from above, looking eastward, of Orvieto. Yet there are lucidity and simplicity in the spectacle, almost as though the little city were a natural growth, like lovely vegetation, and not the resolute triumph of a great spirit, as in those towns to the north. Apsed churches rest on the hill-side like gulls. Towers interrupt the sky-line. Walls of elegant and small palaces dignify the mountain.

The history of Ravello is bound up, as part of the republic, with the history of Amalfi. Yet there is a story that in early days Ravello rebelled against Amalfi and attempted to form a republic of her own. Hence, it is said, the origin of the name, deriving Ravello from *ribelle* (B and V have easily interchangeable sounds, as the most elementary student of Spanish can tell). It is tradition-ally said to have been founded during the fifth century, when the Goths were conquering Italy. It is not unlikely that, in those dangerous times, when the ancestors of Amalfi took refuge in Scala, other Romans settled across the valley, in Ravello. The two communities became part of the same state, yet a tradition of separation may well have lingered on. There was always some sense of differences and detachment in Ravello. The bishop was never subject to the archbishopric of Amalfi, but derived his authority directly from Rome.

In 1150 an event took place in Ravello which must be of concern to Englishmen. Its origin is complicated. Robert

Guiscard had united under his rule most of the Norman territories of south Italy. When his grandson Roger, having succeeded to all that was to become the kingdom of Naples, or of the
two Sicilies, wished to be king, he unwisely had his rank confirmed by the Antipope Anacletus, an arrangement which
gravely displeased Pope Innocent II. Although Innocent was
eventually appeased, and confirmed Roger as king, dislike remained. When, in 1149, Roger was succeeded by his son
William, the Pope, Hadrian IV, refused to confirm his kingship,
upon which William invaded and occupied considerable parts
of the papal territory. Eventually, a reconciliation was made and,
in Ravello, Hadrian IV confirmed William as king and said
Mass in the Cathedral. Hadrian IV was Nicholas Breakspear,
the only Englishman ever to be made Pope.

I have expressed my private devotion to Atrani. Norman
Douglas once said to a friend of mine that, if ever he had to
settle in a town, he would choose, above all, Ravello. This I
think would not have been because in art Ravello is by far the
richest town in Amalfitan territory. His writings reveal him as
having been in many things a philistine. Natural beauties and the
beauties of writing he could perceive and feel; to the visual arts
he was blind. Friends of his have told me that on his travels he
took it badly if a companion went sightseeing. No: he had
surely found in Ravello a quality which it has always had.
History has not died here. Amalfi still has the air of a rich and busy
metropolis, pious it is true, as well, and proudly artistic; Ravello,
for all the terrible interludes of its past, is a paradisical resort of
great people, a Greenwich to Amalfi's London. Kings of Naples,
in the late middle ages, would spend the summer there, and today
the town is not unvisited by royalty. The great quantity of
ancient columns in the town has been taken as evidence that it
was always so, and that many eminent Romans came here for
their ease and pleasure.

You go into the cathedral square through an opening in old
fortifications. These, naturally, have been altered many times; something can be seen of the old form, with pointed arches outlined in
dark stone, and now filled in. The arches over the road are modern.

The cathedral stands on the east side of its piazza. It was founded in 1086 towards the end of Amalfitan independence. The façade has undergone vicissitudes. There was once a raised narthex or portico, borne on four great columns of marble, and many smaller columns and arches; the whole was faced with marble. All that remains of this is an open terrace, with the four large columns. To the right, standing free, is the Romanesque campanile, with patterns of dark lava inlaid in lighter coloured stone; similar decorations are on the cathedral. These patterns are Islamic in origin, and the finest examples in the neighbourhood are around the great courtyard of Salerno cathedral.

Very soon a masterpiece will be seen. The central entrance is closed, as at Amalfi, by bronze doors. These were made in 1179, and the artist was Barisano da Trani. There are forty-one panels with figures in relief, and thirty-eight with formal decorations, the latter designed under Saracenic influence. One panel is inscribed with the date, and the name of the donor. (Pls. 11, 12.)

Barisano made three pairs of doors like these, using always the same moulds for the figures, but varying the frames and decorations. His earliest he made in 1175, in Apulia, for the cathedral of Trani, from which he takes his name. These fit into a round arch, and traces of that plan can be deduced at Ravello, in panels with raised lines which converge towards the top of each door.

Another set he made for the cathedral at Monreale, in the hills above Palermo. Trani and Monreale have each a unique panel; those to be seen at Ravello appear in the other doors. At Trani, St. Nicholas the Pilgrim is represented with an adorer — alleged by some to be Barisano himself — prostrate at his feet. Trani presumably hoped, with their lesser St. Nicholas, to rival in riches of pilgrimage the great St. Nicholas whose relics are cherished not far away at Bari. Since St. Nicholas of Bari is also represented on the doors with a prostrate adorer, Barisano had evidently copied an existing design for a special commission.

At Ravello there are some panels low down which represent men fighting with shield and club, or with bow and arrow. These are accepted as typifying the struggles of a virtuous soul. At Monreale, to the right of one door at its inner side, is a panel representing a Cupid, with that foretaste of the Renaissance so often apparent in Romanesque work. When the doors are closed, this Cupid is next to an archer, aiming at him from the corresponding panel on the other door — the virtuous soul fighting here against bodily lust.

Many of the panels at Ravello are duplicated, and some are echoed by similar designs: St. John the Baptist by Elijah; the knightly St. George by St. Eustace (these last two appear twice each in the same row). Each panel is a masterpiece of modelling, and the idiom is entirely Byzantine. How far the designs are Barisano's own, and how far copies, it would be impossible to say. Three panels, at least, must have been derived from Greek originals, perhaps in ivory. Most of the panels have Latin lettering; three — the Descent into Hell or Anastasis, the Deposition, and the Madonna and Child — have Greek lettering.

As in the case of the Byzantine doors, whose succession began at Amalfi, the assessing of artistic superiority is irresistible. The problem is, in this case, a little different. Apart from the two unique panels, these three doors are variants of the same theme. I think that, in beauty of arrangement and design, the first place must be given to the doors at Trani, although they have suffered from blown salt of the sea, on which the great cathedral so magnificently stands; the bronze is green, and the reliefs have been eaten into.

The doors at Monreale, however beautiful, are altogether a lesser affair, with fewer panels. Those at Ravello, larger than at Monreale, have always been well protected, originally by the portico, and in later years by wooden doors which are closed whenever the weather is bad. If we consider at the same time design and condition, the doors of Ravello are now the finest, although originally, in their pristine state, those of Trani must have been the most beautiful of all.

It is strange that such an artist as Barisano has left no other trace of his existence. At Trani the doors are surrounded by carving of exceptional quality. I have sometimes wondered whether Barisano himself may not have been the sculptor.

On entering the old cathedral (it has been since 1818 a parish church), it will be seen that the floor rises gently towards the choir, a feature common in many Romanesque churches. The nave is divided from the aisles by rows of ancient columns with capitals that are probably later; a large part of the church has been covered in baroque plaster-work of a simple character. The ancient proportions are still perceptible. Pansa's description brings a melancholy sense of loss (he was writing before 1724): 'The cathedral is supported by sixteen huge columns, eighteen palms high, two of which are *verde antico*.'[1]

Inside the cathedral at Ravello are works of art worthy of the doors. A fresh visitor will notice the pulpits or ambons. To the left is one with steps leading up from each side to a reading desk, which protrudes forward; this is a form often to be seen in Rome and its neighbourhood. In the front of the steps are representations in mosaic of Jonah being swallowed by the whale, and escaping from it. Underneath each whale are two big interlacing circles. This pulpit dates from the twelfth century. Jonah's three-days sojourn in the whale was taken as foreshadowing Christ's three-days sojourn in hell, between the crucifixion and the resurrection. This is a common symbol in Campania. You can see carved versions of it in the Museo Correale in Sorrento, in Mintorno, under the great tower of Gaeta, and perhaps best of all in the cathedral at Sessa Aurunca, where Jonah, a spritely figure, already has one foot on the shore. This motif, though evidently popular there, is not confined to Campania. I have seen photographs of it on Armenian churches in Turkey; on the door-pillars of a church at Malagno in Lazio it is crudely represented. No doubt there are many others. In early devotional books, Jonah emerging from the whale often appears next to the Resurrection. In Ravello, it is worth while going behind the pulpit to see an inscription of great beauty.

Opposite is a large pulpit of the following century; it is supported by six columns, which stand, as is often the case, on

---

[1] These were stolen, or bought, in the eighteenth century, by King Charles of Naples, for his new palace at Portici. A pleasant story is told about the enterprise. Some courtiers hinted that it might be unwise to build so near Vesuvius. The king replied: 'God, the Immaculate Virgin, and St. Januarius, will take care of that.'

lions — in fact six lions and lionesses (Pl. 13). It has become an obsession with me to look for these sculptured holy lions. There are vast numbers to be seen in Italy, supporting structures, or guarding doorways. Sometimes they sit benignly quiet; sometimes they are scrunching horribly men or animals. Even in England they may occasionally be seen, as in the sedilia at Exeter; and at Ely are sadly weathered vestiges on the splendid Romanesque south door. Nowhere else have I seen such delightful and lively examples as these at Ravello. Vigorously and excellently carved in the act of walking, they seem to be carrying the pulpit northward. Once, during an Easter service, I saw a child riding barebacked on one of them. I have discovered only one lion as a fit comrade for those at Ravello. This is part of the pulpit already mentioned, at Teggiano in the south-east of Campania; the arrangement of the reading desk is unusual, in that, though attached to the pulpit, it is supported by a spiral column which rests on a lion, a fine lively one, looking half up, with its head turned a little to one side.

The larger pulpit at Ravello was made in 1272 by Niccolo di Bartolomea da Foggia, at the expense of Nicola Rufolo and his wife, Sigilgaita della Marra. The substance of the mosaic — coloured ceramics, gold under glass, and coloured stones — is, although the work of an Apulian, much the same as that on the fragments at Amalfi, which as I have said, were made by Romans. At the west side, in the central largest circle, are depicted the Madonna and Child. It is interesting to notice that the cheeks have round patches of red. This feature appears in many paintings of the tenth, eleventh and twelfth centuries. They, together with representations of Jonah, and with another Jonah in the Ravello church of S. Giovanni del Toro, are the only figure mosaics to be seen on the coast.[1]

The nearest surviving wall mosaics are in Salerno cathedral

---

[1] Pansa, in his old history, has many tantalising references to mosaic. The loss of art on the coast has been dreadful. In the great days of the republic many churches there must have glittered with Byzantine splendour. However, Pansa — his expressions can be ambiguous — may have been alluding to Cosmatesque work which has vanished, and not to mosaic on the walls of churches.

and they are only just surviving. The apse of the south-eastern chapel is complete with mosaics given by John of Procida, already mentioned as a collector of diocesan revenue in Amalfi; but they were too enthusiastically and indiscriminately mended in the last century, and have now that sad air of lost antiquity which we can discern with grief in many over-restored churches. Looking at these mosaics with half-closed eyes or, if you are short-sighted like me, by taking off your spectacles, it is possible to guess and feel what they ought to look like. In the main apse is a huge, post-war mosaic of the Madonna, of which the less said the better. (The Italian guide-book does no more than evasively and politely describe it as modern.) The north-eastern chapel has fine work, a Baptism, incomplete and strangely finished in fresco — I should guess of round about 1400, though a romantic watery landscape below might be of any date. The mosaics have the strength of authenticity and any restoration can only have been in detail. On the walls above are fragmentary symbols of the evangelists; one can only dream of what is lost, though I would surmise a Christ in Majesty. Over the west door is a fine mosaic image of St. Matthew, whose relics are preserved in the crypt.

In the Ravello pulpit, the walls of the steps have panels with animals and birds, and one beautifully inscribed stone. Coats of arms appear on the pulpit and, a rather unusual feature, the coils enclose, not circles of fine marble, but flowers and birds. On each side of the entrance are profiles in relief of the donors, curiously uncouth considering the splendour of the lions and the fineness of other sculptured work on the pulpit. The white marble cornices are freshly, deeply and intricately carved with formal vegetation, as are five capitals of the columns — fantastic variants of the Corinthian convention. One carries the fantasy ingeniously further; birds are arranged in the manner of traditional acanthus leaves.

After I had fallen in love — and that was at first sight — with the larger pulpit at Ravello, I assiduously sought out others of the same kind. (Two are in the immediate neighbourhood, which we will come to in their turn.) Not far away, though

9. Atrani: campanile of the Maddalena (page 65)

10. Atrani: peacock panel in S. Salvatore (page 64)

strictly out of Amalfitan territory, is one in the church of the
abbey at Corpo di Cava, which I have already mentioned as
owning an altar-piece by Andrea da Salerno. It is a beautiful
thing, put together again during the last century from dispersed
fragments. Beside it is a fine paschal candlestick. The colouring is
low, without the golds and reds of the Amalfitan pulpits. A
charming feature is to be seen in one of the lions, which so often
support the columns of such pulpits; this one, as if overpowered
by the weight, is sitting back on its hind legs. Most magnificent
of all are the two pulpits at Salerno. By the larger one towers a
paschal candlestick, with spiral mosaics. For splendours of
mosaic and quality of carving, these must be unexcelled. Yet
somehow they are too massive, too heavy, and a sense of life-
lessness is ever so faintly threatened.

A number are to be seen in the north of Campania, and just
over the boundary in Lazio: at Caserta Vecchia, Mintorno,
Fondi, Sessa Aurunca, Terracina, Teano (a strange one this,
with a later, Gothic top, and half of it buried in concrete which
supports the war-shaken edifice), and at Calvi Vecchia.

Not all of these have the coiled patterns; some have decorations
which seem to derive from textiles. It is the radiant, spiralling
motifs which are the most fascinating. I have never seen these in
purely secular structures; centuries of association have endowed
them with an air of piety, but of gaiety too, as in much sacred
music of Mozart. Like some religious paintings which, through
the intensity of devotion paid to them, acquired, it was said,
prodigious and miraculous powers, these patterns have become
intrinsically sacred. They seem like the lesser decorations contrived for heaven.[1]

I have by implication criticised experts who, falsely in my
opinion, have tried to separate, too rigidly, local variants of

---

[1] A friend of mine, the excellent young painter Timothy Behrens, wrote to me
about the coiled mosaic of Ravello: 'It interests me in one way as a magic sign
(although I've no idea if it was intended as one) of the same kind as the wrought
iron S signs on English houses to ward off bad luck, but much more as an approach
to decoration. That these interlocking bonds are so *thick* seems to make them organic
like intestines, and so architectural, and yet they are at the same time, purely
decoration.'

widespread schools of art. I must retract a little. Only once outside
the mainland south of Rome have I seen a pulpit of quadrangular
plan and fully decorated in mosaic. But that was in the Capella
Palatina at Palermo, and still, therefore, in the same old kingdom
where most of these others are to be seen.

I doubt if any of them are exactly in their original form.
Ravello lost some panels when part of the pulpit was covered by
eighteenth-century plaster. At Sessa Aurunca, one of the supporting lions has been turned round, and the reading desk mis-
placed. All retain their beauty. It is not, I think, an acquired
local patriotism which has led me to set Ravello above all the rest.
Terracina and Sessa Aurunca are close rivals. But at Ravello, the
sculpture of the striding lions, the colour and variety of the
mosaics, the liveliness of the carved marble, and, with all this
exuberance, the disciplined proportions of the whole, make it, I
think, one of the loveliest things I have ever seen.

Standing on the architrave of the upper entrance to the pulpit
is an object which, although it has long stood there, is no part
of the structure. This is the marble bust of a woman, dating
from the thirteenth century. She wears an elaborate crown, and huge
Byzantine ear-rings hang down over her shoulders. There is
enough of her dress to show that it was a rich jewelled garment,
as we see in Byzantine coins and paintings. Her nose is classical,
her mouth wide with well-shaped lips; her hair curls loosely
back and falls in plaits over her shoulders. The whole, in spite of
some idealisation, gives the feeling of a portrait.

Much has been conjectured about this work, but nothing is
certainly known. For a long time it was called a portrait of
Sigilgaita, one donor of the pulpit; a comparison with the profile
just below should always have made this theory ridiculous. It
has been suggested that she is the personification of a town, an
idea which one instinctively rejects. Nothing is known of the
sculptor. It has even been put forward that this may be an early
work of Nicola Pisano, who probably came from Apulia. The
attribution does not seem a likely one, but it gives a fair measure
of the bust's artistic worth.

There is an altar under the pulpit, which thus constitutes

a tiny chapel. A painted altar-piece of the thirteenth century represents the Madonna and Child, between St. John the Baptist, and St. Nicholas of Bari. On the floor of the chapel are circles of dark marble; these must have once filled in the coils of a Cosmatesque floor, of which a good example may be seen in Salerno cathedral.

Eastward, to the north side, is a throne with many beautiful panels of mosaic. Glad of their survival, we must bewail, nevertheless, the sad story implicit in them. Pansa writes that there was a baldachin, raised on four columns, standing on the eagle, the bull, the lion and the angel, symbols of the evangelists. Above these four columns was a kind of cupola on twenty-four small columns, and on that a smaller cupola on sixteen little columns, above which, in a circle, was the Lamb of God. The front of the baldachin was all of mosaic.

The fragments of mosaic on the throne are mostly from this splendid demolished object. Over the font, in the north-west chapel, is the Lamb of God in a ring of mosaic, and close by, on the west wall, are three little columns which must be of the same origin. Two symbols of the evangelists, the lion and the bull, now stand on a fountain, well to the north of the cathedral, in the Piazza della Fontana.

On the east side of the throne is a panel, famous for its beauty (it has been exhibited abroad). It is said to have come originally from the high altar of S. Giovanni del Toro, soon to be visited. The pattern is of superimposed semicircles, a scheme not uncommon in Roman and Romanesque decoration, but here it is much glorified. Each semicircle contains a conventionalised flower against a gold background. There is a narrow border of mosaic on either side; coiled vine-scrolls grow out of urns, these, too, with a background of mosaic.

In the north-east chapel of S. Pantaleone, where the saint's blood is preserved, there is a cupboard for reliquaries. Among these is a cross, with a figure in relief at the end of each arm; it cannot be later than the fifteenth century. There is also a silver arm, which probably dates from the times of Norman domination. A miracle, to be described later, takes place annually in this chapel.

To the right of the choir, in a glass case, is a figure of S. Barbara; the noble, silver head must have been a reliquary, probably of the tenth or eleventh century; the bust is later. To the north of this a door leads to the sacristy, which is the second of two rooms. Its entrance is framed by two columns. That on the left has figures on its capital, including an archer and a man carrying a bundle or a bucket on a stick. (These might be two signs of the Zodiac, Sagittarius and Aquarius.)

At the far end are three pictures. On either side are the S. Sebastian and the Assumption of the Magdalen by Andrea da Salerno, which I have already mentioned. Between them is a Madonna and Child, with two angels and a donor. Some guidebooks describe this as Byzantine, though I believe that Sienese would be a truer adjective. Its artist must surely have looked at work by Simone Martini, two of whose pictures survive in Naples. Having adored her, you will, as you leave, pass again all the treasures of the cathedral. Yet this Madonna is a fitting end for an examination of this church, which is among the most lovable of all the churches I know.

There are many ancient churches in Ravello. Next in value to the cathedral is the church of S. Giovanni del Toro. (It stands just opposite the Hotel Caruso.) The origin of its name is obscure. There was once, it is said, a large fortified palace called *Il Tuoro*, a word which suggests the corruption of *torre*, a tower; it was then, I would surmise, corrupted to *toro*, which means a bull. It is in this neighbourhood that the church was built, later than the cathedral, in the twelfth century. Its chief glory is a Cosmatesque pulpit, said to have been constructed a century earlier than that in the cathedral. It is smaller, and stands on four columns; its lions are very small, and they are climbing over the bases like mice. A peculiar and perhaps unique feature is that the circles enclose, not marble or mosaic, but rounds of Islamic pottery. It has been much, though well, restored and lacks some of the original decoration. On the western face of the pulpit are two bulls, chosen evidently because of the name, *del toro,* though whether historically justified must remain doubtful. On the entrance is a whale in mosaic, with Jonah emerging from it. On the other side there must once have been a panel of his swallowing. The mosaic adornment was left incomplete and, in the fourteenth century, the decoration was finished in fresco, the finest part of the additions being a *Noli me tangere* at the entrance.

One of the capitals is remarkable, in that it has wind-blown acanthus, with the leaves turned over to one side. This is a widespread motif; the earliest example I know of (I have not seen it) is in the ruined basilica of St. Simon Stylites, in Syria. There are two on the larger pulpit at Salerno; others are to be seen at St. Mark's in Venice. I have even found examples in English Gothic churches. In the Ravello specimen, animals and men, including an archer with drawn bow, clamber delightfully about the deflected formal leaves.

Antique capitals, with human figures on them, are to be seen at the Terme Museum, in Rome. I have been told by a professional archaeologist that such figured capitals, even during the widest expanse of the empire, were made in Italy alone. Plentiful fine examples of Romanesque times are to be seen on the pulpits in Salerno. The carvers have given themselves up to every form of high-spirited fantasy. It is improbable, I think, that there may be deduced from these works any particular symbolism; they are most probably no more than light-hearted creations, to be matched in England on many misereres.[1]

S. Giovanni possesses a second great treasure. In a thoroughly restored chapel to the north is a fourteenth-century figure in stucco of St. Catherine of Alexandria, with some original colour still visible on it. Iconographically it is peculiar; she has two wheels instead of one. If you go north from the cathedral, through the Piazza della Fontana, and follow the way up the hill, you will pass, after about a hundred and fifty yards, a house with an arched entrance. At the back of this is an old copy, in wood, of this St. Catherine, with two wheels. A third version, in stone,

[1] At Glastonbury, in the abbey ruins, is an ornate Norman arch, much weathered. In one series of its decorations can be detected three signs of the Zodiac — and no more. Thus, they are meaningless. It seems clear that the carver had seen originals somewhere else, had liked them, and then, without troubling about their significance, had put them on to his arch. Their purpose was purely decorative; the same is almost certainly true of the fantastically treated Italian capitals.

is in the little church in Scala, called S. Pietro in Campoleone, which will be mentioned with that community.

In the crypt of S. Giovanni are fourteenth-century frescoes of Christ in Majesty, with symbols of the evangelists above Him. They are fine, but have been drastically restored.

The church is built with massive antique columns surmounted by Romanesque capitals. The arches are pointed. There is a turret-like cupola over the choir; this is a recent restoration. In shape, the church is very like another in the town, S. Maria in Gradillo, which stands by the road, just before you pass through the gates into the piazza. It was for long half ruined. It, too, had, over the choir, a cupola which collapsed a good many years ago; this, too, has been restored. Photographs exist of the undamaged church, now restored to its original form. (A workman engaged there told me that they had found under the floor vast quantities of human bones.) Each of these churches has external decorations of Islamic style in dark lava, those of S. Maria being more elaborate. A third church in Ravello, unrestored and much smaller, has a similar cupola, matched by its bell-tower. This is the Annunziata, which sits very picturesquely, a little way down the hill, on the east side of the town.

Externally the design of these churches must have been influenced by the early churches in Palermo, which have similar tall, thin cupolas, internally supported on narrow arches, or squinches. I expected to find the same, as I did in the ancient church of S. Costanzo in Capri, to be mentioned in my chapter on that island. Assuming that the two cupolas have been correctly restored, this is not the case; they stand on rough quarter-domes, or pendentives. However, a modern reconstruction cannot be certain evidence. To make an adequate conjecture as to their original form, I knew that I must visit the Annunziata (Pl. 14).

In all the years I have been visiting the Amalfi coast, I have never been able, though I have asked for help from many competent people, to get the key to that little church. Nobody seems to know anything about it. It is in a state of very lethargic restoration. Once, I got into part of it. There is a later aisle, probably of the seventeenth or eighteenth century, built at right-

angles to the main church. Here there is a charming altar-
piece, of painted wood and stucco, of the Annunciation — now
lacking many figures — with a background of painted landscape;
it is more or less peasant art, and the figure of the Virgin is
missing. Lately I tried once again to get in; neither the head of
the local tourist office, nor the parish priest, nor any friend in the
town could help me. I went down to the church. There was no
question of getting in, but the door, closed with a chain and
padlock, has a very large key-hole. I had burglarious day-
dreams, but lacked the skill to carry them out. I looked through the
key-hole. I could make out that the cupola stands on rough
pendentives, rising from between bluntly pointed arches. In their
method of construction, these three early churches are not copied
exactly from Sicilian prototypes. (I think we may assume that
two of them were modelled on the earliest of the three.) Had I been
a professional local specialist, I would, absurdly, have postulated a
local school of architecture. But it is interesting to know that
provincial architects, although modelling their churches on
earlier designs, were able to adapt the buildings according to
their own taste.

I have not visited all the churches in Ravello, any more than I
have in Amalfi. The few I have seen suggest what riches may be
in store for the curious enquirer. Between S. Maria in Gradillo
and the Piazza della Fontana is the little chapel of the Madonna
dell'Ospedale — just a smallish room with an apse. An old guide-
book says that the church was an imposing structure until the
cupola collapsed. All we have left is the choir; the cupola, we
may plausibly suppose, was a turret, as in the other early churches
of Ravello. In the apse is a charming Madonna and Child,
probably late forteenth century. The belfry is above, detached on
the battlements. When I first found it up there, I did not realise
that it had any connection with a church. The bell is beautiful;
there are reliefs of the Madonna and Child, and of St. George,
together with an arabesque decoration, imitated from Barisano's
on the cathedral doors.

If you go north beyond the Piazza della Fontana, where stand
the two evangelistic beasts, you get to a narrow street which

climbs the hill. (It is up this way that you may find the old wooden replica of the St. Catherine in S. Giovanni del Toro.) Some way up on the left is the church of S. Martino. This has, in effect, been turned round. Like most early churches in these parts, it has three apses. You go in by the eastern end, where the central apse now houses the sacristy. The altar, at the flat west end, is a Roman sarcophagus; a small Roman cinerary urn is the holy-water stoop, a feature by no means uncommon on the coast. There is a crude, but moving, fresco of the Madonna and Child, probably of the fifteenth century.

The nomenclature of these churches is unstable. At the top of the little street is the cemetery. Its church has also at one time been called S. Martino. The building itself is not interesting, but the ancient tower, which is pierced at the base by an arch, has merit. A square tower of three stories carries a polygonal summit with arched and round openings, and a conical turret above. This form is said to derive from an eighth-century Lombard church in Salerno. I have sometimes wondered whether the broad principle of design, a square tower, with a narrower summit, round or polygonal, a plan to be seen in many parts of south Italy — may not derive originally from the Pharos of Alexandria, one among the seven wonders of the world.

If you go southward from the cathedral, you will get to the church of S. Francesco, attached to a monastery founded by St. Francis of Assisi. The church is not architecturally very interesting, except for its antique columns. Visible under the altar is the undecayed body of the beatified Buonaventura of Potenza. Once when I was there the sacristan said to me, in loyal excitement: 'He has only two miracles to do, and he will be canonised'. He was taken not long ago to Rome and back again in a motor car but the hoped for canonisation has not been realised.

The best feature of S. Francesco is the portico, supported on fine columns; the pathway goes through it. It is notable for its rather small Romanesque cloister; spaces above the arches are pierced by baroque openings.

Traversable porticoes are to be seen in other small churches. Eastward, below the Annunziata is the tiny Romanesque church of S. Maria Maggiore, with a portico covering the path. Each of these little churches has classical columns, indicating the antique prosperity of Ravello. The path which goes by them, leading eventually to Minori — a pleasant walk — passes lower down under the portico of an even smaller church.

Equal in importance to Ravello's finest ecclesiastical buildings is a private palace, the Palazzo Rufolo, a famous resort of tourists. It is a curious fact that it once belonged to the only Italian I was ever connected with. During the troubles of the Risorgimento, a certain Lacaita fled to England where, becoming almost completely Anglicised, he was knighted as Sir James Lacaita. His son Carlo married my grandmother's first cousin, both of them being grandchildren of Sir Francis Doyle, Lady Byron's adviser and friend, who, after the long and famous discussion at John Murray's, put, with his own hands, Byron's memoirs into the fire. (This taint in the records of my family has for ever been a warning to me in dealing with private papers.)

Carlo bought the Palazzo Rufolo from the estate of a Scotsman, Neville Reid, a benefactor of Ravello, who is commemorated there with a marble plaque. Reid left notes about the town and its neighbourhood which my Italian relative put together into a useful, but not always reliable, guide to Ravello. I regret that I never met him.

The palace is among the oldest which are still inhabited in Italy. It was built during the thirteenth century. The gateway has inside it the Byzantine cupola which I mentioned in my preliminary discussion of Romanesque art. There is also a small chamber of similar structure, with a ribbed dome; this is described as a bath — a sign of luxury imported from half-Arab Sicily. Perhaps the most remarkable feature of the palace is a well-like courtyard, adorned with arches and complicated interlacings of dark stone in Saracenic conventions.

The beautiful garden of the Palazzo Rufolo is famous, curiously, for having allegedly inspired Wagner to write the music of Klingsor's Magic Garden in *Parsifal*. Phrases of the flower-maiden's song, reproduced from manuscript, are printed on post cards of the palace.

Around Amalfi

Early in this century, the second Lord Grimthorpe was staying in a small hotel near Naples, where he was recommended by a Ravellese waiter, Nicola Mansi, to buy a property on the southern precipitous edge of Ravello, a house, orchard and pasture belonging to a near-by monastery. Having bought the property, he asked the waiter where he could find an architect to redesign the house. Mansi replied that he knew something about architecture, and could easily learn more. The result was the Villa Cimbrone, a triumphant pastiche, built in large part out of old fragments. Whatever original genius Mansi may have been born with, I find it difficult to believe that Lord Grimthorpe himself had no hand in the project. There is an open crypt, Gothic in style, with ribs rising from massive columns without capitals. It recalls the great refectory at Fountains Abbey and the abbot's cellar at Abingdon. Mansi might have got the idea from the arsenal at Amalfi; it is easier to see English influence. If this be true, the second Lord Grimthorpe was at heart a better architect than the first, who left some unfortunate work at St. Albans. In the garden is a large collection of old sculpture, some of it, however, of rather doubtful authenticity. The climax of this garden is the belvedere, where there are a round temple and a row of eighteenth-century statues, on the edge of a stupendous precipice. The view up and down the coast is magnificent beyond description, but a little disturbing for those with a bad head for heights.

The two principal hotels, the Caruso and the Palumbo, are housed in old palaces. The latter, though now on a different site, was once the chief habitable hotel of the town, and was much used by English visitors; many of them, now famous, stayed there in their days of obscurity. Ottoline and Philip Morrell on their honeymoon met there the excellent poet Robert Trevelyn. Ottoline has recorded how he disturbed the other guests by emptying the whole dish of spaghetti which was meant for everyone at the table. E. M. Forster stayed there and, then or later, wrote about Ravello, *The Story of a Panic*. Another hotel claims to have entertained D. H. Lawrence when he was writing *Lady Chatterley's Lover*. The Caruso is in the Palazzo d'Afflitto — the home of a very old family from Ravello and Scala, and of which there are still members on the coast. They were closely connected with Scala, and more will be said of them when we pass to that community.

5. SCALA

Scala, as I have told in my historical appendix, is traditionally the birth-place of the Amalfitan state. The area of the *Commune* is large, stretching along the ridge between Amalfi and Atrani, as far as the ancient watch tower which still lords it over the precipitous mountains. Above are the hamlets of Campidoglio and S. Catarina; seaward are Minuto and Pontone.

As with Ravello, it will be wise, before going there, to look across the valley at Scala. Ravello is a gentle, lovely assembly of temples and palaces; sombre and serious is the face of Scala. It has something of the aspect of a ruin, with an air of diminished grandeur, and indeed this feeling is historically justified. It has probably suffered more than any other city of the old republic. It fell out sometimes that Scala and Ravello took different sides in the internal wars of the kingdom to which they became subject. Battles were fought at the bridge between them. This bridge was once the scene of a pacification between Ravello and Scala.

The scene is more fitting for peace than for hatred. Enmity between neighbouring towns lasted well into the present century, nor has it yet altogether faded. Amalfi, I have been told, cannot put up with Atrani, nor Atrani with Minori; Amalfi and Minori, on the other hand, are good friends, as are Atrani and Maiori. Not so very long ago, if a young man from Ravello courted a girl from Scala, he could not safely pass the bridge without a large escort of friends who kept guard while the lovers talked and planned. Well within living memory it could be dangerous to walk up the footpath from Amalfi to Pogérola; you might have stones thrown at you.

Just above the bridge is a thin waterfall, a white skein, some thirty feet or so in height, its fall being echoed to one side in still-ness by many stalactites from an overhanging rock.

Even in the last century Scala suffered, after the union of Italy, from occupation by bandits who, at that time in many parts of south Italy, uniting with Bourbon resisters, seized villages, and ravaged the country around. Chief evidence now of Scala's lost glory are the works of art still to be seen there.

The view of Scala is dominated by the imposing church of S. Lorenzo, once a cathedral. Huge and severe, it stands on the steep mountain-side, secure, it would seem to all eternity. Its three tower-like apses, rising massively from the slope, recall the tower-like buttresses of Albi. Nor is this plain magnificence belied by nearer views, or by the spectacle of the interior (Pl. 16).

The building was originally Romanesque; mention of a church here was made in 1169. As will be seen later, this may not refer to the original church. Although the plain façade has evidently been much altered, the original Romanesque decoration of the principal door remains. A griffin stands on either side, each supporting a pillar carved with foliage. Above the architrave is a Gothic relief, a little crude, of the Virgin between two saints. A curious feature of the cathedral is a vaulted alleyway which runs from side to side beneath it. At the south-west is the austere monumental bell-tower, probably of the fifteenth century.

The interior, with a nave and two aisles, is like the hall of a great palace. Its original appearance has been masked with baroque work. On the ceiling is the Martyrdom of S. Sebastian, by an eighteenth-century painter called F. Cacciapuoti; I can find out nothing about him, although another artist of the same name, but with different initials, was working in Naples about 1770. This ceiling seems to me better than dell'Asta's in Amalfi. There is a very simple Cosmatesque pulpit, removed here in the sixteenth century from an abandoned church of All Saints. It has been restored — perhaps on that occasion — and probably its form was altered. Fragments of mosaic work can be seen on the steps. A pleasant sixteenth-century painting of four saints with the Virgin above, probably by a local painter, has an excellent predella plausibly attributed to Andrea da Salerno. An Ecce Homo attributed to a pupil of his, is not interesting.

On my first visit, in the company of a friend, an English-speaking inhabitant was sent for. He was a returned emigrant, proficient in two languages — dialect and cockney. He expatiated on the excellence of ancient work: 'Look at these toils,' he said, tapping one foot on the pavement: 'bin 'ere fowsands and fowsands of years, and good as new.' There is indeed beautiful ceramic work on the floor, with, in the centre, a large wreath, supported by putti and enclosing the arms of Scala, a crowned lion mounting a ladder (*Scala* in Italian). It dates, as an inscription records, from the 1850s. Our new acquaintance soon betrayed an unbalanced piety, and it appeared that he had conceived a desire to convert my friend. 'Oi'll pry naow,' he said at one moment: 'You can too. But downt if you downt wan' to.' At the end, perhaps in desperate expectation of a miracle, he splashed my friend with holy water.

To the north is a staircase, leading down to the fourteenth-century crypt; on the wall, at the first turning, in a fine Romanesque relief of the Madonna and Child. The crypt is Gothic and the vaulting, now decorated with stucco reliefs, rises from antique columns; beautiful in itself, the crypt is of interest as showing what the interior of the original portico at Amalfi cathedral must have looked like. Above the altar is a most superb wooden crucifix, to which miraculous powers are attributed; on occasions of especial danger or distress it is carried in procession. (A photograph of such a ceremony — I should guess some sixty or seventy years ago — is to be seen in many houses.) It is a strange work. The Virgin and St. John, carved separately, stand on either side. The right foot of Christ, with a nail in it, and the right hand are detached. When the group is complete, the Virgin is holding the right hand of Jesus. This is, in fact, the beginning of a Descent from the Cross. Various dates have been suggested for this work. The most likely seems to be about 1250. It is thought by some to be French work, or at least to reveal French influence; some have professed to find affinities between it and the sculpture at Rheims.

The scheme is unusual. In most Descents from the Cross, the Virgin appears to one side, swooning with grief among many attendants. The ancient theme of Christ crucified between only the Virgin and St. John is not a representation, but an allegory, in which Mary signifies the church and St. John, strangely enough, the synagogue; these are sometimes referred to as the church of the Gentiles, and of the Circumcision (two such personifications appear in a fifth-century mosaic in the Roman church of S. Sabina). This group is known as the deesis. To blend the deesis with the descent from the cross is unusual, but not unique. Sometimes a figure is added lowering the body, and sometimes another still, drawing nails from the feet. I have seen reproductions of this scheme from Byzantine and early mediaeval works, and once in ancient French glass. Always the Virgin holds the right hand of Christ, and always St. John is stylised as in the most formalised presentations.

At the north end of the crypt is a large Gothic tomb, a fine florid construction, with many figures carved in stucco on it, and some of the original colours still remaining. It is attributed to a follower of Tino di Camaino, the Sienese sculptor who worked in Naples. The tomb was commissioned during the fourteenth century by Antonio Coppola for his wife Marinella Rufolo. The most conspicuous figure is a recumbent woman, and for a long time I took this for Marinella. One day I discovered my mistake. There is represented here the Dormition, Assumption and Coronation of the Virgin. The body is the Virgin's; behind, according to the lovely tradition, stands Christ, holding her soul in the form of a swaddled baby. The Assumption is represented inconspicuously towards the right, near the top: above, in the centre, is the Coronation. In front of the recumbent Virgin can be seen one figure wielding a sword, and another falling back with handless arms. This records a strange legend.

When the apostles were carrying the Virgin to her tomb, they were accompanied by singing angels. This so exasperated the high priest of the Jews that he attempted to overturn the bier, upon which his hands became fixed to it. St. Michael then appeared with a sword and cut his hands off. A more merciful version says that St. Peter proclaimed that if he would believe and testify that the Virgin was the Mother of God, he would be released, and so it fell out.

With the steepness of the hill, the crypt is still above ground. There has been opened halfway down what seems at first sight another crypt, with its roof supported by a few short, ponderous columns. This is almost certainly an earlier church, and may date from the eighth or ninth century. Part was once used, so the parish priest told me, as a repository for the dead, who were thrown down, head-first. When this section was opened up it was found to be full of bones; these have been decently interred in the wall. There were, he went on, several aisles to this church, and one of them is now the alleyway under the cathedral.

The greatest treasures of Scala cathedral have yet to be mentioned. First is a chalice with its paten; the two are rarely found together. On the foot are enamelled figures of great beauty. The neck has a ring of bosses carrying figures in translucent enamel. In the centre of the paten is an enamel of the Resurrection. The chalice is dated 1337.

I used to be told that it was French: or at least when I said 'It is French?' whoever was showing it to me agreed. The proposition was not improbable, for Limoges work is to be seen in many Italian church treasuries; and the figures on the base seem to be French Gothic. Not long ago, I found the chalice described as Sienese, and this is certainly correct; I owe this conviction to an article on Sienese chalices by Mr. Charles Oman, published in *Apollo* for April, 1965.

As I have said, the enamel on the bosses is translucent, and this medium is found on all similar chalices from Siena. The manufacture and management of such enamel were perfected in Siena. The method allowed a new freedom in the manipulation of colour, and an image was contrived much nearer to painting than was possible with earlier methods, which had, artistically, more in common with mosaic. The highest achievement in the use of translucent enamel appeared in the great reliquary at Orvieto, constructed to hold the blood-stained cloth of the miracle of Bolsena. (A priest, unconvinced of the real presence, was celebrating Mass, when blood flowed from the consecrated Host in his hands. Stains are shown on the original altar; the cloth was taken to Orvieto, where the great cathedral was raised as its shrine. A similar miracle was said to have taken place in Amalfi cathedral during the eleventh century; since it left neither shrine nor anniversary, it was evidently unconfirmed.) The reliquary, with magnificent enamels by Ugolino di Vieri,[1] was commissioned in 1337 and finished by 1339; it is therefore contemporary with the chalice at Scala.

Lovely though the chalice may be, it is far surpassed by the other treasure, a mitre of the thirteenth century, which would be conspicuous even in the Vatican. It is elaborately embroidered with pearls and precious stones. Larger gems, uncut, are mounted separately; along the top are acorns in gold filigree. Finally there are enamels with figures, and many rounds of decorative enamel. On each side are eleven figures in quatrefoils, seven arranged vertically and four horizontally. In the space between are two larger enamels, lozenge-shaped, representing six-winged seraphim; above each of these is an angel. Whenever I look at the mitre as I have done many times, it seems to me impossible that there could be in the world a piece of jewellery more beautiful than this.

The style of the enamels is purely Byzantine. It has been suggested by some that they may have been made in south Italy. I do not believe it. In this world of art, all experts regard high quality as evidence of metropolitan workmanship. These must certainly be from Constantinople. Amalfi was at that time an emporium of splendid objects imported from the eastern capital; nowhere else in Italy, except Venice, could such things have been so easily come by.

This obvious attribution is supported by two figures of un-doubtedly western work, one representing St. Francis, and the other St. Louis, King of France and brother of Charles, first Angevin king of Sicily. These although beautiful, are markedly less rich and less fine than the rest. It is work one would have expected from a good provincial artist.

[1] Unfortunately, for the ordinary man, it is impossible to see these enamels, except when the reliquary is being carried in the Corpus Christi procession. Coloured reproductions have been published in the *Forma e Colore* series, by Sadea of Milan. There is a bishop's crozier with translucent Sienese enamels at New College, Oxford.

12. Ravello: cathedral door: Madonna
and Child (page 77)

11. Ravello: cathedral door: St George
(page 77)

The mitre is clearly not in its original condition, and has been remade at some time. The jewelled embroidery represents formal flowers in a manner said to be characteristic of the seventeenth century. So dazzling an object demands a monograph; it is to be hoped that some day one will appear, authoritatively disposing of any problems which it may present.

The tradition told of it is this. In 1270, on the feast of St. Lawrence, Charles of Anjou, in the company of his brother St. Louis, was engaged off Tunis with a larger fleet of Saracens. During the battle he vowed that if they escaped he would make a rich offering to the saint. On his return he redeemed his vow with the gift to the saint's church of the mitre.

An expert might confidently date the enamels. The amateur has one clue. The figure of St. Louis, like that of St. Francis, is clearly an afterthought. St. Louis was canonised in 1297. It is safe to conclude that the main work was carried out before that year.

Within the town of Scala itself there is one little excursion worth making. From that bridge of battles and reconciliations may be seen, above the steep confines of Scala, the three apses of a small Romanesque church. This is called S. Pietro in Campoleone. It had — sad word — only a few years ago, a curiously crude portico, a massive wall pierced by two round-topped windows with the bluntly pointed entrance between them; above, in a small opening, was the belfry. On my first visit a number of boys were playing football outside. I asked one of them if he knew where I could get the key. He said he would let me in, which he did by climbing in through one of the glassless windows and opening the door from inside. (Tipping afterwards was rather awkward, for of course the whole juvenile crowd followed me; I had managed to fix in my mind the faces of the obliging boy and of the friend who went with him. I tipped only them.) The second visit was almost odder. I took two friends to the church and, climbing up towards it, we happened on a man of Scala who was interested in the antiquities of his town. The church was locked, of course, when we got there and, to my dismay, the interesting portico was gone, or rather lying, a heap of rubble, on the little piazza.[1] The door had a piece of wood nailed across it. Our new friend sent for a workman, who knocked this off with a hammer.

'This is the first time,' said one of my companions, 'that I've had a church opened for me with a hammer.'

The church is a basilica, the nave being divided from the aisles by three columns on each side. The chief thing to see is a lively, fourteenth-century, carved figure of St. Michael, trampling and transfixing the dragon. There is also the excellent, rather small St. Catherine with two wheels, imitating in stone the stucco carving in Ravello. For these the church is worth visiting. Historically it is of great importance. The St. Michael is the memorial to Pauli de Sasso, and is dated 1358.

Before the first crusade, when Jerusalem was still in the hands of the Saracens, some Amalfitans established there in 1070 a hostel for pilgrims. It was dedicated to St. John the Almsgiver, a seventh-century saint of Alexandria. At the time of the first crusade the hostel was in charge of a Brother Gerard, who was a member of the Sasso family of Scala; this was their family church.

There is a legend that, during the siege of Jerusalem, the crusaders were in want of food, and Gerard threw bread to them over the walls. This was seen, and denounced to the Governor. He, having a great respect for Gerard, said he would not believe it unless he saw it with his own eyes. Gerard was caught again and, with loaves under his cloak, was taken before the Governor. He was searched and — lo and behold! — each loaf had turned into a stone.

Unfortunately for this pretty story, the Governor of Jerusalem had, on the approach of the invaders, expelled all Christians from the city.[2]

---

[1] In the spring of 1966 I passed the church. The restoration was finished. Stones of the old, all but unique portico were piled up round the little piazza, like the dry-stone wall of a terrace. The Italians are usually more excellent than others in the restoration of dilapidated old buildings. This destruction is a shocking affair, and quite unworthy of the nation.

[2] That Gerard was a Sasso, though long believed and very probable, is not entirely certain. Sir Stephen Runciman, in his *History of the Crusades*, from which my historical information is derived, says: 'The hostel was staffed mainly by

Under Frankish government many pilgrims joined the staff of the hostel; Gerard obtained large emoluments. Finally, a new order, the Hospitallers, was established owing obedience, not to the Benedictines, but directly to the Pope. Gerard died in 1118, and his successor, Raymond of Le Puy, enlarged the order to admit knights whose duty it was to fight against the heathen. About the same time St. John the Almsgiver was almost imperceptibly replaced as protector by St. John the Evangelist. The badge of the Knights Hospitallers was a white cross in the form which we call, from their use of it, a Maltese cross. This cross appears in the arms of Amalfi. On the final subjection of the Frankish kingdom in Palestine, the Knights moved to Rhodes and eventually, being driven thence, to Malta, where they ruled until the last century. They now have sovereign headquarters in Rome. In England their name is perpetuated in the first-aid organisation known as St. John's.

The thirteenth-century Sasso palace (built later than Gerard's days) is close by; here worse may have happened than to their church. When I first went there, I saw a most picturesque ruin — classical columns supporting round arches, and open, ruined chambers above, like something in an etching by Piranesi. On my last visit, not a single column was standing. We were with our friend of the church, and he took us through derelict apartments, with traces of painted decoration still faintly showing. Alas for human glory! Of Gerard Sasso, his family church has been grievously mutilated; the palace of his kinsmen is perishing.

I happen to know two authentic Knights of Malta — I mean members of the sovereign order. I told each of them about the decay of the church and palace of their founder's family. With their huge resources the Knights of Malta could easily have restored both, and made the care of them a sinecure for some recipient of their immense charities. They did nothing.

Amalfitans, who took the usual monastic vows and were under the direction of a Master, who in his turn was under the Benedictine authorities established in Palestine. At the time of the Crusaders' capture of Jerusalem the Master was a certain Gerard, probably an Amalfitan. With his co-religionists he had been banished from Jerusalem by the Moslem Governor before the siege began; and his knowledge of local conditions had been of value to the Crusaders.'

Another, far later saint, is associated with Scala, S. Alphonso de' Liguori, founder of the Order of the Redemptorists. Exhausted by work in Lecce, he had come to recuperate on the Amalfitan coast, and he lived for a time at S. Maria dei Monti, a hermitage on the heights of the peninsula. He became a director of a nunnery in Scala. It is said that, in November 1732, he saw in the Host the figure of Christ; this vision was confirmed by all who were there, including the bishops of Scala and Castellammare. In the same month, the Order of the Redemptorists was confirmed in the cathedral of Scala.

On the hill above Scala, but within its jurisdiction, is the village of Campidoglio (the name is sometimes taken as evidence that there was once a Roman city here). I had read in a guide-book of a church there with antique columns, almost always a promise of Romanesque architecture. To get to Campidoglio, you have to climb a steep flight of steps which begins opposite the cathedral. On may way up it began to drizzle. A small poor boy passed me and asked for ten lire, as usually befalls foreigners in such places. I did not answer, and then, considering the matter, I said I would give him a hundred if he found me the key to the church of the Annunziata. He agreed, and left me outside the church, where a number of children inevitably accumulated. I noticed classical columns lying on the ground and hoped that they presaged a fine interior.

After some time in the damp air, I asked what the boy was doing. He had gone to find his grandfather, I was told. At last he came back, without either grandfather or key, and asked me to follow him. All the time a small boy had been sitting, crouched from the light rain under the shelter of an olive-tree on the terrace opposite, eating nuts and watching. He did not come with us. The crowd of us set off and, after a little time, turned into a narrow, covered alley. I thought they must be taking me to the key. We came to a stall, with a calf in it. I tried to pat the beast, but it was out of reach and would not stand up. At last I said we must go on and, to my surprise, they turned back to the larger path. They'd just thought I would like to have a look at the calf.

They took me into a house where an elderly woman offered

me cold roast chestnuts. Knowing that these would be as hard as bone, I refused as politely as I could. Conversation was difficult, for in small hill villages like this both young and old speak little Italian. The children have not yet learnt it properly at school, while the old have probably never talked it among themselves. For myself, I still understand very little of the dialect. At last the grandfather arrived, with the key.

The church was not a fitting reward for the climb and the rain. It has two naves, at right-angles to one another (probably implying a later addition to an ancient plan, as in the Annunziata at Ravello). The interior is now baroque, decorated with stucco. The columns outside hint at what was once there. A dilapidated Romanesque church must have been almost completely rebuilt and added to in the eighteenth century. However, I was not to go altogether unrewarded. The sacristan — grandfather — asked if I would like to see the church of St. John the Baptist, at the other end of the village.

When we got there, I recognised the little mediaeval tower which I had often noticed from across the valley. This has two square stories, surmounted by a round turret, a common, always delightful, form, abounding in the country. The first story and the turret are pierced by pointed openings. This tower probably dates from the thirteenth century.

The main body of the church appears to be the late replacement of an early Romanesque church, whose original existence is implied by a capital built into the wall. This has a carved basket-work pattern, Byzantine in style, and not later, I should guess, than the ninth century, and maybe earlier. There is a large, very realistic Caravaggiesque painting of the execution of the Baptist. Organs of the severed neck have been rendered with ghoulish care — spine and gullet, and arteries bubbling with blood. I was shown the chief treasure of the church, a reliquary containing, I was assured, a finger-bone of the Baptist.

I had decided that day to go down to Amalfi from Pontone. The path takes you close to the tragic corpse of a church, whose majestic ruin is visible from the Ravello road. This is the church of S. Eustachio, which was barbarously dismantled in the eighteenth century. Parts of the walls and of the campanile remain, and of the three apses only the southern is incomplete. The eastern exterior is richly decorated with differently coloured stone; the work has been described as the clearest example on the coast of Sicilian architectural influence. Complete, it must have looked like a smaller version of the cathedral at Monreale, near Palermo. The church was built, probably during the twelfth century, by the d'Afflitto family of Ravello.

Some of its treasures have been tantalizingly recorded. It had a portico with three arches and three doors, the central one being flanked by pillars supported on lions. Inside were two monuments on columns, decorated with marble and mosaic, probably Cosmatesque work such as may be seen in many Roman churches. There was a mosaic pulpit. Beside it was a paschal candlestick with a capital, on three sides of which were the d'Afflitto arms.

Parts of these works have almost certainly survived. The entrance to the Palazzo d'Afflitto in Ravello (now the hotel Caruso) is flanked by a collection of old fragments. There are two Romanesque pillars with, respectively, a lion and a lioness at the base, the latter suckling a cub; these may well have been copied from similar, larger lions at the entrance to the atrium of Salerno cathedral. Above are two saints, almost certainly from a pulpit. In the palace are other old fragments, very probably from S. Eustachio; it is likely that other unattributable Romanesque objects in the neighbourhood may have the same origin. (In considering this, the dismantled baldachin of Ravello must not be forgotten.)

S. Eustachio, just above Pontone, lies beyond the village of Minuto, with its Romanesque church of the Annunziata. This has a massive portico, still too fresh on the surface after restoration; there are three arches to it, with three doors behind them. The central door is enclosed by classical fragments, one having the remains of an inscription. Over the door is a faded fifteenth-century fresco of the Madonna and Child, and a stone eagle. The nave and aisles end in apses, and are divided by arches on classical columns. The church owns a sixteenth-century Annunciation, attributed to a local painter of the fifteenth century, Giacomo de Pansco, from Praiano. It is certainly of a later date. The predella of Christ and the twelve Apostles has been attributed, as at Scala, to Andrea da Salerno. A predella superior to the chief painting is an unusual association. May it be that the two churches, desiring a work by the master and lacking the resources, contented themselves each with a modest authentic adjunct?

There was once a pulpit of the fourteenth century. It was constructed of stucco and terracotta, and was said to have been of excellent workmanship and delicate colour. There exists a water-colour of it, painted in 1852. I have been told the story of its fate, but was never able to verify it. Sometime during the second half of the last century the parish priest needed fine sand for building. To save transport from the sea-shore, he smashed the pulpit and ground it up. All that remains of it is the eagle over the door.

The climb to Campidoglio is laborious. (S. Eustachio can be comfortably reached by the path from Scala.) Had Minuto been three times as high as Campidoglio, it would be worth any fatigue or breathlessness to get there. Camera quite often mentions, exasperatingly, paintings 'in the Greek style', which ought to mean Byzantine.[1] Today, so far as I know, there are only two series remaining on the Amalfi coast. In the crypt at Minuto there are frescoes dating from about 1100 (Pl. 15). Probably the whole crypt was once painted, but now the only frescoes are in the eastern bay. On the central vault is Christ the Pantocrator, with St. John the Baptist and St. John the Evangelist on the adjoining vaults; Daniel and David are on the walls beneath them. On the east wall are scenes from the life of the Virgin, and from the legend of St. Nicholas. Even incompetent paintings from that world are magical; these, though not masterpieces, are far from incompetent. For some time I have been uneasy about their condition. Over several years a hole in the roof of the

---

[1] At Furore, west of Amalfi, is a masterpiece of the quattrocento, to be mentioned later. Camera speaks of it as being in the Greek style. Much Romanesque painting has certainly been lost in these parts; but some references by Camera may have been to later work.

church was getting bigger and bigger; I have been there and seen large puddles on the floor. The painted Annunciation was removed, but the frescoes had to stay. These had been restored some years ago, when a bad crack was filled with plaster. Water did not run into the crypt, but at times the air must have been very damp. On my last visit I saw that the wall round the crack had bulged alarmingly. I suggested to the sacristan that he should put old cushions or a mattress on the floor underneath, so that if any part fell it would not be hopelessly smashed. The whole roof is being replaced, and those in charge must surely be keeping an eye on the frescoes.

The path descends south from Minuto to Pontone. This is a village to be enjoyed for its ambience of lost splendour, rather than for any individual monuments. The three churches are worth visiting if you are in the village, but they would not demand the expense of limited time.

The first is S. Filippo Neri. This was an early church, probably of the twelfth century, which was largely rebuilt in the eighteenth. The path goes through the original, half-ruined portico, as in several mentioned churches of Ravello; beside it stands the old campanile. Inside antique columns and capitals, supporting a baroque structure, testify to their former use in a Romanesque building. In the little piazza is the church of St. John the Baptist. The exterior is Romanesque, and the three apses remain. The very beautiful campanile is original, and has small classical columns; a path goes under an arch through its lowest story. The interior was altered in the sixteenth and eighteenth centuries; several features, on altar and carved door, date back to the earlier changes. On the floor near the entrance is a carved tombstone dated 1346. The last church is the Carmine. The building probably dates from the seventeenth or eighteenth century. I once climbed, in some fear, the rickety steps of the campanile. It has four double openings, with round arches supported by old columns and plain Romanesque capitals. It must be the relic of an older church of the twelfth or thirteenth century.

Wandering about Pontone you will come on relics of old palaces, their walls and arches patterned with differently coloured stone. Once when I was eating with some friends there, I was taken to wash my hands at a tap in the yard; the soap was kept on an antique Corinthian capital. The old priest's house, the *Casa parocchiale*, now derelict and rapidly decaying, is a beautiful building, with suites of vaulted chambers, still showing traces of painted decoration. There is a thin, deep, well-like square courtyard with antique columns in it. Its grandeur testifies to the old prosperity of the village. When I first saw this house, I had day-dreams of a fortune coming to me, and of restoring it for comfortable habitation. This would involve, I reflected, keeping a team of mild horses or donkeys on which my less active guests might be transported up to the village. I think I should have whimsically chosen the sturdy dwarf donkeys which you may see in use at Castellammare and in its neighbourhood; they are sometimes little higher than a large St. Bernard dog.

Whatever the pleasantness of its buildings, Pontone is to be visited for the magnificence of its position. Northward the hills rise steeply towards the heights of the peninsula. Seaward is a precipice defining the north end of the Montagna di Pontone. On either side are the Valle del Dragone above Atrani, and the Valle dei Mulini above Amalfi. (The latter is named from the paper-mills in it; the manufacture of paper has been for centuries an industry of Amalfi.) A friend, a cultivator of vines and lemons, has a house in Pontone at the upper end of the village, and facing south; from it you look out across the village to the precipice of the mountain, and down on either side to the sea beyond the end of each valley. In all the years during which I have been visiting the coast, there has been talk of building a road to Pontone. If it ever is built,[1] this house will become a property of immense value. The easiest way into Pontone is by a path up through the woods from the Ravello road; the way from Scala involves, it is true, no climbing, but is long; the path from Amalfi has over a thousand steps to it. (I have quite often gone down it, but never up.)

The mountain was once entirely fortified, and bristles with

[1] In 1966, work on the road began.

masonry from an immense demolished castle. Seaward it descends in two cliffs, with a natural broad terrace between them, to a level space where stands the Torre dello Ziro. The walls of this round tower slope inward to a protruding ring of stone, above which it rises vertically. Particles of broken battlements stick up like broken teeth on the rim. This is, I feel, the most splendid of the guardian towers scattered along the coast. The Torre dello Ziro was enlarged by one of the Angevin kings, and it was probably adapted not only for seaward defence, but also to awe the Amalfitans, ever restive over their ravished autonomy.

It dates mainly from the thirteenth century, although these round towers probably originated under the republic; a similar tower, of about the same date, stands on the promontory at Praiano. There was much tower-building during the sixteenth century, and to this period belong most of the towers on a rectangular plan. By then the enemies principally to be feared were Mahommedan raiders. It was probably in the Torre dello Ziro — or so I have been told by educated Italians — that Webster's Duchess of Malfi was murdered at the instigation of her brothers.

There is a linguistic and historical interest in the name. You will not find in an Italian dictionary the word *ziro* or *zirro* (as it is sometimes written). An Italian told me that in north Africa he had heard an Arab using a similar word for petrol-can. I asked a man from the coast if he knew of the word in dialect; he answered that it was sometimes applied to flower-pots and vessels of a similar shape. *La Torro dello Ziro* means, roughly, the Tower of the Bucket. I suspect this to be a word of local dialect, and deriving from the Saracens imposed on Atrani.

If you turn west from the tower and walk against the cliff, you will come on a cave of small depth with its inner rock wall plastered over and showing traces of fresco. Heads of saints can be seen with incised aureoles, and a group which appears to be the Adoration of the Magi. The last seems to have a Romanesque air, while the former are probably of the fourteenth century. No remains of wall are visible, but the plastered and painted cliffs must have been the choir of a castle chapel.

This tower is a fitting end for a trip through the heart of the republic. On his way the wanderer will have passed among scenes of transcendent natural beauty. Across the valley to the left can be seen the churches and palaces of Ravello. At this point the valley of the Dragone widens and deepens, and the abyss is filled with woods and cultivated terraces with here and there the indication of a water-fall. Beyond can be seen Atrani with, sovereign over it, the lovely bell-tower of the Magdalen. To the right, cliffs and steep slopes rise to the summit of the mountain with all its ruins. During propitious seasons the whole place is radiant with wild flowers in delectable variety.

One warning must be given to the intending explorer. The land to the east drops down steeply to alarming cliffs. Those who, like myself, have bad heads for heights will find themselves taking impulsively every inward turn away from the huge depths. I myself erred once thus while taking a friend on his first visit to the tower; as a result we found ourselves on the edge of the cliff above it. The path to the left must always be taken if you want to get there from Pontone.

At the tower we are at the extreme end of the *commune* of Scala. Westward, below is Amalfi; eastward is Atrani and, above it, the mountainous extremity of Ravello. This is not, as I have pointed out, Tuscany, or Umbria, or Lazio; but in the small area there are many fine and many delightful works of art and three or four masterpieces.

CHAPTER IV

The Babe and the Death

———————

Having been advised to see the celebrations of Epiphany at Amalfi and Atrani, I went out one year at the beginning of January. In Amalfi I noticed, to the right of the cathedral steps and against the portico, a wooden platform. On this platform was the skeleton of a star, like a formalised comet, about ten feet long, or like the star of Bethlehem as it is often represented. From the platform, a strong cable ran up over the houses to the westward mountain. It ended not far below the village of Pogérola on a structure which from the piazza looks like a low tower, but is in fact a rounded protuberance of terrace. These were the physical preparations for a ceremony which I had long wanted to see. 'Have you seen the star at Epiphany?' friends used to ask me, both from Amalfi and Atrani. Each town at Epiphany has the ceremony of the star and each, of course, declares its own to be the more beautiful. The citizens of Atrani assert that the original star was theirs; the silence of Amalfi on this point may allow a little weight to the claim.

The ceremony at Amalfi, I was told, would take place an hour earlier than that at Atrani, and I would be able to see both; so to Amalfi I went.

In the cathedral I saw the splendid crib where, on the Virgin's lap, sat the Babe with arms outspread in benediction. Being anxious to miss nothing of the exterior spectacle, I did not attend the service, but stood outside in the portico. After a little while, the dark star was hauled jerkily up to the mountain. There was another wait and then, in a moment, its outline burst into a constellation of white, spurting flames. Slowly and waveringly the blazing star began to descend, down, down, down, until it came in the end to rest, trembling above the piazza, flaming and smoking and dropping fire. A few fireworks exploded in perfunctory salutation.

I went to Atrani, and found the ceremony over. The stars had descended simultaneously. Neither community, it would seem, wished its citizens to partake of the other's glory.

Ready to judge between the two stars I stood at last, a year or two later, in expectation above the piazza at Atrani. At the proper moment the flaming star sailed slowly down from precipices to the west. This star, to be sure, was smaller than the Amalfi star. The accompanying display was far more sumptuous. Rockets, flashing from all sides in celebration of the star which had guided the Magi, filled the black and cliff-enclosed air with rushing lights. The star hung over the piazza, steep like a well, and dropped brilliant sparks into it. And all the while fireworks were exploding and blazing around, making windows dazzle, and the whole valley roar with reverberating thunders. This was certainly a much better show. One thing, however — and a most touching thing — was lacking at Atrani. While I was watching the dwindled flames of the star as it hung motionless in front of Amalfi cathedral, I smelt incense. I looked round, and the ancient bronze doors were opening. The archbishop emerged, and then stood, holding the effigy of the Babe so that his face was covered by it. He turned left and then right, pausing each time; we were being blessed, not by the archbishop but by the infant Jesus Himself. Then the Babe was carried in again, but not back to the crib. It is the general, though not the universal, practice to remove Him at Epiphany as a sign of the flight into Egypt.

A pretty little ceremony followed two or three days later in Amalfi. I had seen preparations for it in other parts and, for all I know, it may be customary throughout Italy. It was a simple playing of the Adoration of the Magi. In Amalfi the Madonna was represented by a small girl dressed in white, with a full skirt like a ballet-skirt. To one side, facing her, stood an obsequious donkey with a boy on its back for Joseph, while behind him sat a boy of four or five as Jesus. Children came up and made offerings as, in their adoration, the Magi had made richer gifts.

The Babe and the Death

We have in the National Gallery a large altar-piece by Francia. The enthroned Virgin, attended on either side by saints, holds the Child upright on her knees. In a lunette above is a Pietà; there, old in her grief, she bears the insupportable burden of her dead Son. All of Christian mystery is contained in that picture, from the Incarnation to the Atonement.

It was strange for me to reflect, while I watched those pretty acts of homage at Epiphany, that the other image of Christ would, within three or four months, be dolorously displayed before the people of Amalfi.

The Good Friday procession of the dead Jesus is held in many parts of the Roman Catholic world. Civic pride is involved, as well as piety. Not long ago the Communist mayor of a town in the south was indignantly aggrieved when the bishop forbade him, as a professed enemy of the church, to have any part in the holy ceremony.

Neighbouring Atrani has its own sepulchral procession, referred to as the *Battenti* — the beaters, a name indicating that this was once a procession of flagellants. The participants are robed in white, some with long, eye-holed masks over their faces. (I have more than once been startled by a gay greeting from a friend unrecognisably masked.) All wear spiny wreaths, representing the crown of thorns. Crucifixes are carried, and lanterns with candles in them. The procession has its song:[1]

> *Perdono, mio dio*
> *Mio dio, perdono*
> *Perdono, mio dio*
> *Perdono, pietà.*

A single voice sings the moving, melancholy, minor-scaled air; then all in the procession; last the accompanying crowd.

[1] I have told in Chapter XII, *Amalfi Outremer*, how I got the music of another Amalfitan processional hymn, the hymn to St. Andrew. For the music of this hymn I am indebted to the parish priest of Atrani. For publication they were both written out, with expected kindness, by my old friend Mr. Lennox Berkeley. He commented that the rhythm is peculiar in each case, indicating that they probably derive from tunes composed at a time when, as with plainsong, music was written down without bars. It was gratifying to have my conviction of their antiquity confirmed by so fine a composer and musician.

White robes luminous in the dark, the wreaths, the flicker of candles, the deep-searching monotony of the repeated air, stifle all scruples of incredulity, until the holy enchantment of the ceremony seems to have become an unquestionable theme of natural life (Pls. 17, 18).

It is said to be the custom of the *Battenti* to visit all the churches of their community. Close to the confines of Amalfi and Atrani is that old monastery founded by St. Francis. The people of Atrani used to lay almost war-like claims to the chapel, claims as violently rejected by those of Amalfi. The aggressive policy of Atrani was manifest in fierce attempts to bring their procession into this chapel.

Processionals from Amalfi resisted with force, and the meeting of the two bodies, assembled in piety both warm and deep, turned into a sort of tribal warfare. Heads were broken; lanterns, crucifixes and other sacred objects flew in all directions — some of them very likely into the sea. To prevent such unseemly occurrences, the procession of the *Battenti* was put forward to Holy Thursday. I have seen it proceed, with the unreluctant compliance of all, into the very heart of ecclesiastical Amalfi, the cathedral itself. And there, on the next day, was to be ready, and thence was to issue, the procession of the dead Jesus.

I had been in early to watch the preparations. The atmosphere was entirely practical, like getting a hall ready for a party. A florid, gilded bier was put in place, and poles were adjusted for carrying it; a mourning cherub was fixed at each corner.

In a side chapel, and covered over with a transparent plastic sheet, was the dead Jesus, an accomplished work with a terrible and most moving realism (its date I cannot guess). The image was uncovered, and a plump woman dusted it busily with a feathered mop. To me, brought up in another land of the spirit, the operation appeared, for the place and occasion, indecorous. There was an air as of work going on in a church which had not yet been consecrated. This view, if rigorously held, would have betrayed an obstinate fanaticism. George Herbert would never have fallen so near to error:

> *Who sweeps a room, as for thy laws,*
> *Makes that and th' action fine.*

The writhen body was laid on the bier, and at once all was reverence and solemnity. To one side, clothed in black, with a white handkerchief, and a sword in her heart, stood the Madonna Addolorata, Our Lady of Sorrows. To the sound of the service, and in the light of candles, the *bondieuserie* of the Madonna, and the shocking realism of the Jesus, became transfigured. They were a dead man and his mourning mother. They were God and the Virgin.

The bier was lifted on to the shoulders of several men and carried through the doorway where, at Epiphany, the holy doll had blessed us. Police kept the way clear across the portico and, as the body of Jesus passed by him, their leader gave a smart salute.

Down the broad stone stairway gradually moved the bier; behind followed the mother, the quintessence of bereavement. A band in the piazza struck up a funeral march, and the slow procession went south out of the piazza and turned east up the crowded street. Just above the heads of the people moved the body; higher, behind, followed the mother. As the dead Jesus passed, cafés put out their lights and shops drew down their shutters — tokens of respect accorded to any dead body on its way to burial. This was no longer a symbolic re-enactment of the past; it had become the funeral of an eminent and much loved person. 'It makes you want to cry,' a local friend had said to me.

The body was carried to the church of a nunnery. A crowd came up to see it lying in state. Some worthies of the town were allowed in first, and a line of police held back the pushing people, pushing like would-be purchasers outside a bargain sale. In the church they went submissively in single file, each pausing at the body and kissing the feet and leaving a piece of money.

The Babe and the Death

The procession turned back to the cathedral, and now the Virgin went in front of the empty bier. After a short service, she was carried out again, and back along a narrow way to her own church, S. Maria Maggiore; in places the vaulted way was so low that her bearers had to stoop in their progress.

The effigy of the dead Jesus would remain in that church, watched by nuns, until Easter morning, when it would be brought back, early and unobserved, to the Cathedral. All would then have been accomplished, death and entombment and resurrection.

CHAPTER V

Plant Hunting

A passion for botany, as anybody knows who is touched with that divine infection, can enliven the dullest of country walks. Whatever the motive in walking and travelling, there is always an alert hope to see something rare or beautiful, and in the mind will usually be some knowledge of what is most to be hoped for. It is thus, not on the search, but walking or travelling with an eager, curious eye, that I have done most of my flower-hunting around Amalfi. My finds have almost all been accidental. Flowers discovered in this way are like acquaintances casually picked up. Life-long friendships may follow; often enough the encounter is something to be many times pleasantly renewed, but it is not the consequence of a definable passion.

There is another sort of flower-hunting which is analogous to a planned courtship. To hear of a rare, especial plant, to find out the locality it grows in and the quality of its likely habitat, and then, after long dreams of discovery, to make the planned expedition in a fearful ecstasy of anticipation, to wander over the given terrain with ever-diminishing hope, searching in space and time until, at the moment of ultimate despair, appears undeniably, the quarry. Failure is frequent but, with success, a joy is experienced such as few of life's lesser joys can equal. One such pilgrimage I have made in the territories of old Amalfi. That adventure — for an adventure it was indeed, and one not altogether without danger — is told in my chapter on Amalfi over sea.

To write a flora of Amalfitan territories would require a lifetime's work; it is not my intention to supply even a meagre summary of such a presumed compilation, nor indeed would I ever be competent to do so. Yet, with my botanical obsession,

I have enjoyed many ecstasies over the years about Amalfi; moreover, visitors to the coast have often asked me the names of conspicuous flowers. An account of those which have pleased me most may provide a tapestry, sometimes most gorgeous, behind the people and legends and habits and history of the place. These flowers must be pictured among cliffs diversified with a gigantic filigree of pinnacles, or punctured by grottoes, and often smooth or festooned with stalactites; or bright above the far-off dazzle of the sea, with a watch-tower solemn near the edge of it; or, on northern slopes, with always in sight the dramatic sentinel of the Neapolitan plain, the never-satiating Vesuvius.

Winter is generally a poor season for English gardens and fields. In south Italy, during the same season, a fortunate spell of weather may unfold flowers more naturally associated with later months. The sweet alyssum, *A. maritimum*, seems to be always in blossom somewhere, as it will be in most western Mediterranean coasts. In the hot, clean sun of a bright winter's day, in December and January, the honeyed scent may float into the air. A graceful, yellow-flowered shrub of the pea family, *Coronilla emerus*, seems to be always blooming. (A local friend told me that this is called the plant of Corpus Domini, for it is often strewn over roads at the Corpus Christi procession.)

Rosemary, like gorse in England, is always flowering somewhere during winter. The typical form of the coast is unusual, for it hangs down the rocks and, when growing on the flat, brings its little branches down so that they creep along the ground. Market gardeners may call this form *Rosmarinus officinalis var. prostratus*, though proper botanists do not, I believe, allow a named variation. It is abundant along the Amalfi coast, and in Capri. Occasionally a plant appears which tries to grow upwards: sometimes it shoots out and then curves downwards; over innumerable steep rocks it appears at its characteristic best, rippling down the stone face in a thin cascade of fragrance. In the little town of Cetara, beside the road where it turns upwards towards Salerno, I have seen a plant with white flowers. Such creeping forms turn up occasionally on the French Riviera, but never have I seen it there in such perfection as it generally assumes near Amalfi. Eastward, in the mountainous promontory of the Gargano — the spur of Italy — creeping rosemary becomes again a dominant plant, growing as beautifully and elegantly as it does on the Amalfitan coast. Nearer, in the delectable mountains of the Cilento, to the south of the Gulf of Salerno, rosemary accords with its regular form, and in many places is planted and trimmed into neat hedges beside the road.

Teucrium fruticans, a popular hedging plant in gardens of the French Riviera, will often, though properly a spring flowerer, show unseasonable blossoms; the leaves are grey and the flowers, like little long-tailed moths, usually of pale, dusty blue, though forms may occasionally be found of a finer, cleaner tint.

These and other pretty things may well be come on here and there with untimely flowers during the colder months. One flower, however, is the certain pride of the winter. Even during the terrible January of 1963, when dykes froze in the plains of Paestum and monstrous icicles hung terrifyingly from Amalfitan cliffs, I found, in the woods below Ravello, *Crocus imperati*, bravely pushing its filmy flower up through a crust of frozen earth. This is, to my mind, among the most beautiful of all crocus species. The flowers are large, and inwardly of lilac, varying in depth; the three outer segments (the 'petals') are stone-grey, and usually feathered with an intricate tracery of purplish-black lines. Although essentially a flower of the winter, I have seen it blossoming in March at something over two thousand feet, near the Torre di Chiunzi, where the road from Maiori to the Noceras crosses the col. It is common on the peninsula, and in Capri.

Crocus imperati is certainly the king of feathered crocuses. Best known in this group is *C. versicolor*, for this is common in spring on the French Riviera. Like jealous birds, each of the group keeps to its own territory; I have never heard of hybrids on the borders. Further south comes *C. etruscus* of the Tuscan Maremma; I have never seen this, and believe it to be local. Then, in Lazio, comes *C. suaveolens*, which looks, but for slight differences, like a lesser *imperati*. I have seen it in the north of the region, not far from both Umbria and Tuscany, into each of which it may well stray. *C. corsicus*, having ventured over sea, is to be found in Corsica and Sardinia.

Unfortunately crocuses from western Europe have always failed with me in England. I have collected and lost *versicolor*, *corsicus* and, of course, *imperati*. The last, after trying sunny places, I put, remembering its original home, in woodland. One plant, it is true, flowered after two years, but I have no hope of its long survival; certainly I never expect to see at home such splendid masses as decorate in winter so much Amalfitan turf.

With spring the spectacular plants — none of them particularly uncommon — begin to flower. The regular anemone of the western Mediterranean appears with black-centered suns of pale mauve; I, for years, have called it *Anemone stellata*, but we are now instructed to say *A. hortensis*. It is more frequent on the damper, shadier slopes to the north of the peninsula, where primroses abound. It can be seen here and there on the southern coast, and is common on the Montagna di Pontone, between Amalfi and Atrani. This can be grown in England, but success seems to depend on the individuality of a plant; in about 1937 I collected a good many specimens near Hyères, in the south of France. In the end, they all died except one, although their situations were much the same. The survivor, though it has not spread, can still be relied on for one or two flowers every year. In higher places grows the beautiful *Anemone apennina*, like a larger and more tattered form of our own wood anemone, but generally of a fine blue. This of course grows easily at home, and has got into the English flora as an often naturalised flower. On mountains of the peninsula it may be found associated with the lovely, blue-starred *Scilla bifolia*.

Orchids begin to be seen in March. The earliest, in my experience, has always been *Ophrys fusca*, that quiet-coloured relation of our own purple-winged bee orchid. Shortly afterwards follows *Ophrys lutea*, whose lip is bordered in yellow. These may frequently be seen growing in terrace walls beside the road; they are beautiful, though unspectacular, with their wings coloured a brownish-green. Finer, and roughly contemporary is *Ophrys scolopax* with wings of a pale pink. I once found on the peninsula what I believe to be a hybrid between this and *O. lutea*.

These orchids are not uncommon on the French Riviera. Proper to the south is *Orchis italica*, which extends from the centre to the south of Italy, and beyond into eastern Europe. The leaves are crinkled, and the large purple head bristles like a conical bottle brush. It is closely related to *O. simia*, the monkey orchid. *O. simia* — so rare in our own country — has the peculiarity of first opening its flowers from the tip, and then progressively downwards, so that the head has an oblong appearance. *O. italica* opens its flowers from the bottom upwards, in the proper manner generally characteristic of the genus, and the inflorescence is a shapely spike. The lip is elaborately formed into a shape which has earned it the Italian name of *Uomo nudo*, naked man; the reason for this becomes obvious on the briefest examination. The legs of the man give a tufted look to the large, beautiful flower-head, which usually appears in April.

Another fine large orchid to be found is the lady orchid, *Orchis purpurea*, with its speckled, turkey-feather lip; this, in England, is almost entirely confined to Kent where, although sometimes making abundant colonies, it is rare. I confess to lubricious joy at having once found a naked man coming up alongside a lady orchid.

At the turn of March and April, one of the loveliest flowers of the peninsula begins to flower. First, here and there, flicker singly, like amethysts, occasional flowers of *Cyclamen repandum*, with thin, sharp, twisted petals. Within a week or so of the first revelation, more and more may appear until, by about the second week in April, great sparkling colonies of it will be seen. It does not, I must admit, grow here in such vast profusion as I have seen in Corsica, where woods were crowded with it as some rich English woods may be with primroses. Yet, the effect is perhaps more bewitching when a large, unlooked-for colony over a space of several square yards, lights up suddenly like a large fragment of fine mosaic pavement.

This plant is not, of course, confined to Italy and adjacent territories, for it spreads to the Grecian islands and Asia Minor.

For all its wonder, I find drawbacks in it. In the first place, the small globular corm is very difficult to get at, and usually hides among long and difficult roots, or stones compactly crowded; how many times have I perforce abandoned the attempt to dig it up! In the second place, it is not floriferous like the other, soon-to-be-mentioned cyclamen; seldom does a plant open more than two or three flowers at a time. Lastly, it does not do well with me in England. I have never found it tender, as some authorities maintain; leaves always come up from the twenty to thirty plants I possess at home. The trouble is that I have never had flowers from more than six of them in a single season, and often fewer than that.

Cyclamen repandum is certainly the jewel of the spring, but there are other flowers which then make beautiful the wide countryside. There is the small wild onion, *Allium pendulinum*, with a triangular stem and an umbel of starry white, dark-centered flowers. (It must not be confused with another triangular-stemmed onion, *Allium triquetrum*, with white, hanging, bell-shaped flowers. This, which is naturalised in Cornwall, grows abundantly around Amalfi.) It turns up everywhere in May, but never have I seen it more dazzlingly effective than on the mountain of Pontone, near to the great tower, perhaps the death-scene, as I have said, of the Duchess of Malfi. When I saw it in the fullest glory, a steeply sloping patch of grass was luminous with innumerable flowers of the onion. The day was bright and blazing. Across the valley was Ravello, stretching out over great cliffs, like an enormous vessel putting out to sea; below was Atrani, with its tower of the Magdalen; farther off, fading into nebulous amethyst, were cliffs and peaks and promontories of the coast; faint as thin smoke, beyond the gulf of Salerno, could be traced the mountains of the Cilento. Discreetly scattered over the filigree of the allium were flowers of a pink gladiolus. This I have never troubled to identify. The European type of gladiolus extends from North Africa to England. (I have seen wild specimens in Teneriffe, Spain, Italy, France and the New Forest.) It has been pedantically divided, on the justification of very small differences, into many species, to me all but indistinguishable.

Sub-divisions of this order are baffling and boring to the amateur botanist and, as such, I have never bothered to distinguish them. All are beautiful, with delicately-poised delicate flowers in different shades of purple. Most forms — or species — will flower well enough at home in a dry, warm, well-drained spot.

Allium pendulinum, from the mountains of Pontone, has begun to spread in my little English wood. I am hoping it will not reveal the common defects of its kind. Apart from having, almost all of them, a fearful stench, they usually die quickly in England, or else turn into overbearing weeds. The beautiful, white, odourless *Allium neapolitanum*, a common Mediterranean plant, has never survived long with me. The pearly-pink *Allium roseum* as widely distributed, and also to be found on the coast, has on the other hand become a dreadful weed in parts of my garden. *A. pendulinum* seems delicate enough to give no trouble, however prolifically it may spread.

Beginning earlier in the spring, and persisting throughout May, blue light blinks in the woods from the lesser periwinkle, *Vinca minor*, and from the creeping gromwell, *Lithospermum purpureo-caeruleum*, the last a rare native in England, and the other just possibly wild there. Below Ravello a fine, fat form of the periwinkle is to be found; this has done well with me in England, keeping its proper quality. The gromwell is less satisfactory; I have never tried to collect it near Amalfi, for French plants have survived for many years with me in England without ever showing a flower. The periwinkle and gromwell are noble plants, and yet it could be held that the most beautiful flower of Amalfitan spring is one of vulgar origin, from a family whose members are usually dull and undistinguished — the hemlock family. The giant fennel, *Ferula communis* (Pl. 19), is of a different genus from the culinary fennel, *Foeniculum vulgare* (which is looked on as wild in parts of England). In form, except for their difference in size, the two are very much alike, with golden flowers and finely cut, dark-green leaves, fitting for the hair of a siren. The *Ferula* grows perfect in form and marvellous in colour, a green fountain topped with golden fire, up to the height of a man; indeed I have seen it over-topping eight feet. This is the plant in whose stem Prometheus brought from heaven to earth the stolen fire.

Towards the end of spring a most beautiful plant comes into flower, *Convolvulus cneorum*, a small, stiff shrub with silvery entire leaves, and blossoming at the branch ends into large white cups. It seems to be rare on the peninsula, and for a long time I was unrewardedly on the lookout for it. Several times I deceived myself with dull plants seen from a distance. And then one day, while being driven westward from Amalfi, and about three or four miles from the town, I saw silvery leaves and large white flowers. We were passing a colony of the convolvulus, the only one certainly known to me, although I believe it may be growing on the mountains of Pontone, so rich in ruins and flowers. It is commoner, I believe, on Capri than on the peninsula. It is sold in England as a rock-garden plant, but a bad winter will always kill it.

A friend has told me of seeing, on Capri, *C. cneorum* growing and flowering with *Lithospermum rosmarinifolium*. This, among the loveliest of its genus, I have never seen wild on the peninsula, and I suspect that, like the convolvulus, it is commoner on Capri. The narrow leaves are dark green, and the flowers of a deep resplendent blue.

June on the coast I have never seen, this being a month when unbreakable obligations have kept me in England. (And so I have never seen the great summer festival of St. Andrew, on the anniversary of the date when he summoned a storm which scattered an invincible Saracan fleet; St. Matthew had, at the same time, done as much for Salerno. Fortunate the town, sometimes, when protected by an apostle.)

In June, I have no doubt, begins the great glory of the coast. *Campanula fragilis* is not confined to the peninsula or to Capri, in both of which it is abundant. I have seen it on M. Bulgheria near the southern confines of Campania, and no doubt it grows on limestone in other parts of the region. But, from all that I can discover, its headquarters are in Amalfitan territory.

I have already, more than once, publicly celebrated it; so praiseworthy an act cannot be too often repeated. *Campanula fragilis* may be found usually in vast quantities up to two thousand feet or higher. The neat, round leaves make green blotches on the stone; sometimes they are greyish with hairs, but this distinction seems to have no relation to the colour of the flowers (with its close relation, *C. isophylla*, endemic at Noli in Liguria, hairy leaves usually indicate white flowers). Then, in its season, which comes to a climax in July, these leaves become covered with open, shallow, starry cups of varying blue. Everywhere you will see the flash of this wonderful colouring on rocks and walls, like fine ceramic work inserted into the stone.

Not far to the east of Positano the road curves in and out of a deep, steep little gorge, which it crosses on a beautifully arched bridge. The face of this bridge has become over-run by the campanula which, in high summer, splashes the stone-work with luminous blue, diversified by one rich variant of pure white. Many times I have seen the campanula at its most luxuriant; always, like a great work of art which cannot be seen too often, it has transported me as bewitchingly as the first time that I saw it. Unseasonable flowers may sometimes be seen as late as December, or even January; they make me think of postcards from a long-absent friend, confirming his existence, and the continuance of affectionate thoughts.

Some gardening authorities describe the campanula as hardy in England. I doubt this. My mother has tried it in her Suffolk garden, and has never kept it for long. I have always grown it potted indoors. Yet it may be less tender than I suppose. During the disastrous winter of early 1963, a slab of ice and snow, falling off the roof of my house, broke a pane of glass in my greenhouse, and the terrible frost killed many treasures, some of which I had preserved for twenty-five years and more. *Campanula fragilis* survived. As I have told in another chapter, the same winter tormented southern Italy with equivalent ferocity. The devouring, destructive wind shrivelled many wild flowers; *Campanula fragilis* was untouched.

The disaster of that English frost killed a plant whose tenderness is especially deplorable. This is a heather, *Erica multicaulis*, with large pink bells, bigger, I think, than in any English species. It is given as May-flowering, though I have seen flowers on it in July and August. It is said to grow about Naples, and in Corsica and Sardinia. As every gardener knows, few heaths will put up with lime in the soil. This one, with its dark leaves and large rosy bells, grows in limestone. I first saw it on the road up to Ravello, and the gardener within me leapt at the spectacle of a beautiful, lime-loving heath. English botanists have been collecting continental plants for the last four hundred years and more. It is unusual to come on a fine flower within fifteen hundred miles of England, and unknown in gardens there; it would probably have been collected and established long ago were it satisfactory at home. Alas, my sad frosty mishap showed why *Erica multicaulis* is not a popular garden plant in England.

Flowers fade in the fiery heats of August. *Campanula fragilis* goes over, although there are always a few flowers to be seen on it. In this season one plant may be flowering magnificently. The Sea Squill, *Urginea maritima* (it has been called *Scilla maritima*), is of a genus which links asphodel with eremurus. The bulbs are as big as a turnip and the leaves, which appear in autumn and last into the spring, suggest a very large colchicum. I have more than once been deceived by their similarity, until, digging, I came on the colossal bulb. In August or September, usually after the first heavy rains of summer, it sends up a slender spike to at least three feet. As with many of its kin, only a few flowers open at a time, in a little florescent band round the spike. This characteristic deprives eremurus and asphodel of the full glory which each appears to promise. However, with urginea, the closed buds are of the same yellowish green as the open flowers, so that the effect is given of a fully blossoming spike. A group of the sea squill in flower is a fine spectacle.

If, under terrible compulsion, I were forced to name my favourite plant for the garden, I would probably have to respond, 'Cyclamen neapolitanum'. There are lilies I love dearly, and narcissus, and campanulas, and orchids for all their awkwardness; but for beauty and ease of cultivation, I know nothing to surpass this cyclamen. The tint of the flowers is more variable than with *C. repandum*; the petals are broader, and rounded at the end; the leaves are usually shaped like ivy leaves, and beautifully marked. Leaves and flowers can be seen together, while *C. repandum* shows its earlier blossoms before the leaves have come up. When, some forty years ago, I bought my English home in a small Berkshire valley, I put some corms of *C. neapolitanum* in a miniature copse at the bottom of my garden. Over the years they have seeded and multiplied until, from autumn into spring, the ground is entirely covered with their leaves; seedlings have appeared and blossomed in the adjacent turf. Luckily for the conscience of plant-collectors, this plant is exceedingly common in Italy. I have plants from Tuscany, from the countryside neighbouring on Rome, and in large quantities from the hills about Amalfi. I have a special group taken from abundance in the Grecian walls of Paestum. From every visit to Amalfi, when plants are visible, I have taken home about thirty. In a small wood which I planted rather over thirty years ago, I am slowly filling the bare ground with Amalfitan cyclamen.

Most rewarding of all plants, many-yeared, readily flowering, and long in flower, it is as hardy as the English oak. An old corm will sometimes blossom so profusely that you may count on it thirty flowers at a time. In frost the leaves will shrink and the flowers droop; warmer days bring open leaves again and up-standing flowers.

It is either easy to collect, or impossible. You may find in road-side walls corms which you can pull out with your fingers. Often a beautifully flowering plant will have exasperatingly hidden its corm among stones, or the roots of a tree. I have learnt at last not to vex myself with vain striving for an evasive cyclamen: in fact, now, as soon as I find a corm to be well hidden, I stop probing for it. I have not yet, in spite of passionate searching, found the beautiful albino form and, if I eventually do, I have a horrid fear that its corm will be quite out of reach. Some very pale collected variants grow in my English wood, and I have hopes, perhaps too confident, of them one day giving me among their offspring the perfection I have failed to come on wild in the woods of Amalfi. In leaf, this cyclamen is almost as beautiful as in flower. There is great variation in shade, patterning, and shape. At home, when the cyclamen are flowering, I can usually be confident that a well-coloured form was collected in bloom, while those with leaves of peculiar beauty were taken at other seasons.

Cyclamen neapolitanum has curiously enough a longer flowering season in alien England than in its native haunts. At times my transported plants have given me flowers from July into November or even December; about Amalfi they usually begin towards the end of September and will probably be finished within a month. Moisture, or the lack of it, may account for this. The summer months in the south are sometimes utterly without rain. A sudden, heavy storm may bring on some flowers. One such plant I saw years ago, in July, at Paestum, flowering in the antique walls after a drenched day of unseasonable rain.

Have I said too much in praise of a flower which can never be praised too much? Hints for cultivation are hardly needed; it is very easy to grow. For propagation, it is wise to watch the plants. Most of its offspring will be found on top of the corm, for the stem turns into a spiral, like a spring which eventually forces the seed into earth above the plant. The consequent seedlings must be removed when they are big enough — that is, about the size of a large pea — and poked into the ground. However, the seed is covered with a sticky substance, looked on as a dainty by ants, which gluttonously carry the seeds away; consequently, without human assistance, the colony can spread of its own accord.

A later autumn flower of these parts is interesting, and has not been seriously classified botanically. At one time I corresponded with the late expert on European Narcissus and Orchids, W. H. Pugsley, to whom I often sent specimens. He published small monographs on the trumpet narcissus (the proper daffodils), and on the poet's narcissus. I once asked him to give us a monograph on the tazetta or polyanthus narcissus. He replied that the subject was too vast, since species of this group extend from the Canary Islands (where I have seen it wild), into Eastern Asia (where I have not). The material available for study was, he added, too meagre.

On the Amalfi coast a large form of this narcissus comes

into flower during November. It is particularly abundant on the cliffs above Castiglione, the bay just east of Atrani; it grows in crowds, too, on slopes beside the little church of S. Maria del Bando, high on the steep hill to the west of Atrani. (It is identical, I am convinced, with the false *Narcissus aschersonii* discussed in another part of the book.) Spring visitors to the French Riviera will have seen meadows covered with a small, elegant *Narcissus tazetta*, almost like an English field of cowslips when these are most abundant. The Amalfitan flower of autumn is probably three times as large as the French, in height, in breadth of leaf, in size of flower; moreover, the broad, long leaves are of a dark green, whereas the commoner type is of a greyish glaucous tint.

A spring-flowering form also occurs, but rather rarely, in Amalfitan territories. I have seen it blossoming in March above the road west of Positano. Plants collected from Paestum are growing in my English garden. They are much smaller than the autumnal form, but somewhat larger than the French.

The autumn form has done all right with me in pots at home. Out of doors it puts up buds towards the end of December. A mild winter will allow it seasonable flowers; plants from Capri survived for a long time in my mother's Suffolk garden; with me two winters, cutting the fresh shoots, killed it. The spring form flowers regularly in a well-drained warm spot against a south-facing wall.

It is not seemly, perhaps, for an amateur to instruct professionals. However, I believe that these two varieties, so distinct, should at least be classed as sub-species. The temporal separation of blossoming time — like distance in space — will prevent cross-breeding; in consequence, any difference between the forms will, through long inbreeding, eventually become conspicuous. There are many groups of flowers, the marsh orchids for instance, and the small yellow, starry tulips, where variants blend almost insensibly into one another. Absolute separation of such variants by time or space, will eventually lead to a variant so distinct that a new specific name may be called for. This I believe to be happening in the case of the Amalfitan tazetta.

Most visitors will notice little more than the lowland flowers, those which are to be found up to about twelve hundred feet. There is one fine denizen of greater heights. Colchicums, like the tazetta narcissus, are afflicted with a doubtful nomenclature. The plant in question should probably be called *Colchicum neapoli-tanium*. It is a dwarf, with short leaves in spring, and a flower in autumn no bigger than a crocus. (A plant, larger in all its parts, is given the same name on the French Riviera.) I first found it in woods of Tramonti, a little below the tower of Chiunzi. I have later seen it in other places, not only on the peninsula, and always of the same size. At home, it throws up leaves with me, but has not yet flowered. In appearance it is much like *Colchicum alpinum*, which will rarely or never flourish in England. A third dwarf has done well and increased with me, *Colchicum corsicum*. This is strange, for it is described as not being in cultivation, and it is not offered by nurserymen.

Thus is ended the tale of fine plants easily to be seen in the territories of Amalfi. What of the common things? There is the stock, beautifully fragrant and with flowers of imperial purple to be seen at almost any time of the year on the seaward cliffs. And the great shrubby spurge, *Euphorbia dendroides*, which grows to fine rounded bushes, a yard or more in height. During winter it decorates the cliffs with spheres of green: in early spring these are covered with inflorescences of greenish gold. In summer the parched shrubs reveal only spikes of green on an intricacy of bare branches. The tree spurge is not, of course, by any means a speciality of the Amalfi coast; it reaches its northernmost point in the neighbourhood of Nice. From there it extends southward and eastward over a vast distance.

I have many times tried to contrive effects with flowers in the garden, not from cultivated devices, but from associations I have come on in the wild. One that I have enjoyed about Amalfi could not be copied in colder England, but something of the kind might be carried out in any Mediterranean garden. Often I have seen the large coronilla flowering beside the spurge, the green-gold of the spurge harmonising most excellently with the yellow-gold of the coronilla. This harmony I had delightedly observed about Amalfi — a quiet vision which it seemed to me that nothing could excel, until I saw it on a far grander scale, a night's voyage to the south.

In the rich volcanic soil of Stromboli, familiar plants grow to a prodigious size. The tree spurge can be seen up to eight feet in height, and with thick trunks. Associated with it is the silvery, filigree-leafed southern artemisia, *A. camphorata*; this, a common plant, is to be seen in many parts, and occurs in Amalfitan soil growing in foamy bushes up to three or four feet. In Stromboli it equals the spurge and, everywhere among the two, I saw large flowering plants of the Spanish broom, filling the air with the scent which inspired Leopardi on Vesuvius. In that strange and lovely island the lyric beauty of the two golds takes on an epic splendour.

The woods of the coast have an especial beauty for a northern visitor. A dominant tree is the splendid alder, *Alnus cordata*. The younger branches are greyish, and form a luminous, ligneous mist during the leafless period; the form of the tree is graceful, and well served by the heart-shaped leaves; in late winter the branches are adorned with catkins at least two inches long. It is not widely distributed, and is recorded chiefly from places within a forty-mile radius of Naples. It is abundant in the Valle del Dragone, between Ravello and Atrani. It will grow in England, and I have two or three saplings of it in my little wood. Over much of the peninsula, its richness of dangling catkins is adequately replaced, in early spring, by blossoming hornbeams.

For good company it has the manna ash, or flowering ash, *Fraxinus ornus*. This has a far wider distribution than the alder; I have a plant at home which I collected, in its youth, in the Gorge du Loup, which runs magnificently up into the Alps from between Nice and Cannes. My own plant, although healthy and now over eight feet high, has not yet blossomed. The inflorescence is a fluffy white cone, perhaps six inches long, in appearance, although not botanically, like the flowers of a large spiraea.

Everybody knows the sweet chestnut, which grows abundantly in the Lattari mountains; I could never make up my mind whether they are lovelier when so sumptuously leaved in summer, or in the cold season, when its tangles of leafless grey twigs glimmer like a substantial mist over the steep mountain slopes.

13. Ravello: cathedral:
the larger pulpit
(page 78)

14. Ravello: church of
the Annunziata
(page 86)

And among them, scattered oaks, still with the tints of autumn in them, keep their dead leaves well into the new year.

In his *Gerusalemme Liberata*, Tasso describes how the crusaders fetched timber for siege-engines to be used against the holy city — a task not accomplished without much preliminary trouble from malicious enchantments. 'One exhorts another to fell the trees, and to inflict upon the grove an unexperienced outrage. Severed by the keen axe fall the sacred palm, the wild ash, funereal cypress and Turkey oak, leafy ilex, lofty fir, and beech and the wedded elm, to which sometimes the vine leans and, with twisted feet, climbs towards heaven. Some smite the yew, others the high oaks which a thousand times have renewed their leafiness, and a thousand times, unshaken at every assault, have tamed and triumphed over the fury of the wind. Others load on to strident wheels the perfumed burden of cedar and manna ash.'

Save for the picturesque introduction of palm and cedar, Tasso has transplanted to Palestine an Italian wood, such as might grow near his native Sorrento. Elsewhere he mentions the manna ash as furnishing the shafts of spears.[1]

---

[1] The Jacobean poet Edward Fairfax published a translation of *Gerusalemme Liberata* under the title of *Godfrey of Bulloigne*. This is how he rendered into English the relevant passage:

> *Downe fell the shady tops of shaking treene,*
> *Downe came the sacred palmes, the ashes wilde,*
> *The funerall Cipresse, Holly ever greene,*
> > *The weeping Firre, thicke Beech, and failing Pine,*
> > *The married Elme fell with his fruitfull Vine.*
>
> *The shewter Eugh, the broad-leev'd Sicamore,*
> *The barren Platane, and the Wall-nut sownd,*
> *The Myrrhe, that her fole sinne doth still deplore,*
> *The Alder, owner of all watrish ground,*
> *Sweet Juniper, whose shadow hurteth sore,*
> > *Proud Cedar, Oake, the king of forrests crowned,*
> > *Thus fell the trees, with noise the desarts rore,*
> > *The beasts, their caves; the birds, their nests forlore.*

I am not challenging the beauty of Fairfax's version. I will only say that mine is literal, and botanically more accurate. Literary historians point to Fairfax as an originator of the polished style which, perfected by Denham, Waller, Dryden and Pope, was to dominate English poetry for some hundred and fifty years — to dwindle into the vapid elegance of Erasmus Darwin.

And lastly Sweet Alyssum, *A. maritimum*, so common about all southern coasts, and which I have already mentioned. I was brought up to the pursuit of botany, and I will always remember seeing, for the first time, at eight years old, in the south of France, wild, flowering plants of sweet alyssum. I think this was the first plant of our gardens which I had ever observed growing wild. In England we treat the alyssum as an annual. It is, in fact, perennial, and old plants have a woody base, so that they look like miniature shrubs. All round the year you may see flowers on them. In summer, when arrives the proper bloom, its chief delight is of scent; how many times, from a source invisible behind wall or rock, have I felt overpoweringly, like something more palpable than its element, the weight and sweetness of honey-scented air!

CHAPTER VI

The Miracle of the Blood

It was the twenty-seventh of July, the second and most important day of the festa at Ravello; we arrived in time to see the end of the procession. In pomp of banner and canopy, archbishop and clerics gorgeously enrobed: as gorgeous the young men who supported the burden of the silver image of the city's patron and protector, S. Pantaleone, who had been carried around Ravello, visiting the lesser churches and saints about his old cathedral (since 1818 reduced to the status of a parish church). As we arrived, he was being borne up on to the terrace outside the cathedral. He was set down, facing outward across the piazza, beyond which the land fell steeply into the black night of a deep valley, a valley of vines and lemons and woods. I was close to him when a woman pushed me aside, rudely as I at first thought, until I saw that she was sticking a bank-note on to the image, which was plentifully covered with such offerings. And then, for the especial benefit of the saint, or so it seemed, there started up a long display of fireworks — coloured flames, a succession, uninterrupted, of soaring rockets, until all the valley and all the mountains roared, and the thick black air became full of incandescent clouds, bediamonded and illumined with innumerable, slowly falling stars. When the last explosion was over, and the last aerial flames had faded away, S. Pantaleone was carried, facing dark skies and the bright, noisy piazza, back into his cathedral.

One of my friends, long domiciled in England, although born and bred in a neighbouring town, had never witnessed the miracle, so I made him come into the cathedral with me. We went to the north-east chapel. Above the altar is a good painting of Pantaleone by the seventeenth-century Genoese, Girolamo Imperiale. The saint, with an expression of great calm is bound to a tree in readiness for martyrdom. Watching from below, with dismay in his face, is an obscure saint called Ermolao. A dark passage runs up and round, behind the curve of the apse, and down again. Below the painting is a tabernacle, which can be opened front and back. From behind, in the passage, could be seen a reliquary, holding a glass globe, flattened vertically, and with light beyond it. A slow crowd pushed forward; children elbowed in front of us to see the wonder. 'Let the foreigners see,' said an elderly man (we had been speaking English, and my friend was in English clothes).

The globe contained a dark substance like very dirty gelatine, through which usually no light can pass; as we saw it now, a thin upper layer was translucent, clear as glass, and the light shone throught it, red as a ruby. 'There,' said the man reverently, 'is the blood of our saint. See it,' he added, stooping towards the children, who had politely given way to us, 'the blood of our saint.'

I was trained in my boyhood as a scientist; at the university, I took my degree in law. For seven years I served on the bench as a magistrate. I should be able to claim, therefore, an experience of observation and deduction at least a little above the average and, in the same degree, a capacity for analysing evidence. The first time I witnessed the miracle I failed in all this, failed humiliatingly.

When I first looked at the blood in the re'iquary, I supposed that the miracle had just started, and that all the substance in the glass ampulla would soon become translucent. After leaving the chapel of the saint I attended a service in the south-eastern chapel. A vessel was brought in, beneath a ceremonial umbrella, and placed on the altar; it was in form like the reliquary, and such I imagined it to be. Amid prayers it was censed by priests in ascending order of importance. In the end the archbishop of Amalfi took his part and then, while the congregation knelt, he held the vessel aloft. The contents were translucent and, although I could perceive no trace of ruby light, I supposed them to be the finally liquefied blood.

The Miracle of the Blood

I was then altogether unfamiliar with the ritual of the Roman Catholic church. What I had been witnessing was the service of Benediction. What the archbishop had raised was not the reliquary, but a monstrance; it contained, not blood of a saint, but the consecrated wafer.

Fairly early a doubt had crept into my mind and at last, a year or two later, I decided to sit in the church where I could see the reliquary. Very soon the enormity of my error became apparent. The reliquary remained in the tabernacle. It was clear to me how hopelessly awry I had been in my original observation.

Three times I have seen that translucent sliver of red on top of the presumed blood. One year the process had been incomplete and there was discernible from the light beyond only little sparks of red. Whether the people of Ravello had not behaved themselves well that year, I cannot say; certainly the visibly effective activities of the saint were not up to justified expectation.

Guide-books claim that the blood also liquefies on May 19, the anniversary of the translation of the relic to its present place. This is not so. The blood is exposed then, but has been recorded to have liquefied at that date only once. This was shortly after electric light had been introduced into the church, and it was taken as indicating the saint's approval of the innovation. I have seen the blood exposed at that anniversary, at Easter, and at the celebration of the Assumption. Three times I have seen it thus in company with a friend; after my original confusion, I did not like to trust entirely to my own observation. At Easter and in May, the blood was entirely opaque; not a twinkle of light showed through it. On each occasion my observation was confirmed by that of a companion. At the celebration of the Assumption in August, about a month after the miracle, a faint translucency was perceptible, a vestige of the recent transformation; but the red tinge had gone.

The reliquary contains a substance which at certain times allows no light to pass through it. This is certain. At the feast of the saint a change usually takes place, producing the condition I have described. That the material becomes liquid, I cannot testify; to be sure of this, one would have to see the vessel moved and the reliquary, as I have learned, is not taken out of the tabernacle. That the substance becomes translucent in parts, I am, from my own disciplined observation, entirely satisfied.

The story of S. Pantaleone, with many of his miracles, may be read in a pamphlet on sale in the old cathedral of Ravello. The author was the scholarly but credulous Archdeacon Luigi Mansi, parish priest of Ravello. He was an excellent antiquary, and published the guide to Amalfi and its neighbourhood which I have found most valuable. I am acquainted with kinsmen of his. A discriminating judge of antiquities, he had a vast infusion of credulity; if it had a Christian flavour, he could believe almost any story of the supernatural.

Pantaleone, according to Archdeacon Mansi, was martyred during the reign of one of the last pagan emperors — which one, he admits, is uncertain (the passionate eloquence of the narrator makes his story sometimes a little obscure): it was probably Maximian, who was eventually put to death by Constantine.

Pantaleone was born in Nicomedia. His father was pagan and his mother Christian. He was trained to be a doctor. A priest, who had somehow evaded a massacre in the temple of Nicomedia, saw the youth and perceived that his was a spirit naturally Christian. Pantaleone respected the old man and listened attentively to his teaching. One day, returning from his lessons in medicine and from the instructions of his priestly mentor, he saw in the road a child dead from the bite of a viper, and the snake much swollen from the fruits of its attack. He said inwardly: 'The teachings of my master should not fail and, in the name of Jesus Christ, I desire that the viper may die, and the child live again.' And so it fell out. Pantaleone returned at once to the priest and, after seven days of passionate preparation, was baptized. An immediate effect was that all his patients were cured, not by medical skill, but miraculously. A blind man was given his sight, after all other doctors had failed. Many came to him and were cured in the same manner. He became a favourite doctor of the emperor.

His methods of cure, admittedly unorthodox according to strict medical usage, aroused the jealousy of his colleagues. They

The Miracle of the Blood

The yearly punctual liquefaction of his blood is not the only latter-day miracle attributed to Pantaleone.

I have been told by a lady, English but of a Ravello family, how, during the last century, a protestant, no-popery, English gentleman attempted to smash with the handle of his umbrella this object of idolatry, and that consequent cracks remain in the ancient glass. How he did this through bars of the tabernacle is not to be explained.

Cracks there certainly are, but traditionally of a different origin. This unsuccessfully attempted atrocity — if it ever took place — brings vividly to mind the iconoclastic horrors at several times perpetrated in English churches against coloured glass and stone carving. It also makes it easier for me to feel the religious fallacy implicit in these orgies of pious blasphemy. Even those who in thought and feeling most vehemently oppose the Roman Church (and I am not a member of it) must grant that the breath of its faith is not confined within material buildings, but blows and breathes in a wider ambience. To see a boy, before swimming, touch a finger in the water and cross himself, against what forgotten and fabulous dangers he probably could not tell — this is to me, though all incredulous, a moving spectacle. So it was to feel, as one could not but feel, in the noise and profane gaiety and huckstering at the festa, another tone, all but imperceptible to the senses, a mysterious and numinal whispering. 'A nation without superstition,' said a wise man of my acquaintance, 'is like a forest without undergrowth.' Here indeed was a rich and flourishing undergrowth, while soaring aloft, sturdy and rich, were the ash and ilex groves of a felt religion. It is not surprising that there is more to record in later days than the ancient and recurring liquefaction of this blood.

This is how Mansi accounts for the cracks in the ampulla. In the year 1769, a canon of Ravello, holding a taper too close to the vessel, heard it crack. The blood at that moment was beginning to liquefy, and he was afraid lest it would be spilt. On the instant he made a vow, if the blood were preserved, to donate to the cathedral a silver statue of the saint. The cracks became sealed, and the blood was not spilt. In his passion for miracles,

Mansi adds another. The cracks are closed up with a clotted substance — the solid blood. When the miracle takes place these clots, by a secondary miracle, keep their solidity, containing thus the transformed substance within.

Not only with his blood did Pantaleone work wonders. Other relics of his are preserved in the cathedral, and from one of these, according to his own account, Mansi himself enjoyed a full benefit.

'In my childhood,' he writes, 'being ill, and given up by the doctor, I was suddenly relieved of the sickness and the fever by the presence of the little relic which was brought to me in my bedroom. I, who was senseless, recall nothing: one thing alone I remember, which is to have seen the relic, and desiring to have it laid upon my breast. So was it done, and, being aware of nothing else, and amid the lamentations of my entire family, I fell asleep. I was woken up by a doctor from Maiori, who had been called for a consultation and who, finding me quite out of danger, asked me if I would like a nice dish of spaghetti. I at once replied "yes". But on account of my extreme weakness, both of the stomach and of the bowels, I had to make myself content with some soup, and light at that, and slowly I recovered my strength.'

From all the information I can collect, the miraculous liquefaction of blood takes place only within the neighbourhood of Naples. If it succeeds some antique rite, I have not been able to discover anything about it. The most famous case is of course the blood of S. Januarius, in the cathedral of Naples. According to Gibbon, before this blood was brought to Naples, blood of the now dispossessed protomartyr, St. Stephen, used regularly to liquefy in Naples. I have been told there is a saint's blood which liquefies in Capri.

A related miracle is claimed at Pozzuoli, where the stone on which S. Januarius was martyred is kept in a church on the slopes of the half-extinct Solfatara with its cauldrons of boiling mud. On the stone is the dark stain of his blood and, while the blood is liquefying[1] in Naples, the stain is believed to turn red.

---

[1] 'A similar phenomenon is attributed to blood relics of other martyrs in other places; these are nearly all in southern Italy and some of the relics are manifestly

The Miracle of the Blood

Some years ago two friends of mine wanted to visit in Naples a church which adjoins a convent. They arrived too late and the church was shut. They knocked at the door and were told that, although they could not go into the church, they might see it from the gallery. A nun took them round and afterwards said to them: 'Would you like to see the blood of our saint?' They naturally agreed, and she brought out a vessel with an opaque material inside it, no doubt much the same as may be seen in the reliquary at Ravello. 'If you have faith enough,' she said, 'it may liquefy'; and she began shaking the reliquary.

She seemed to pass into a stupefaction of ecstasy, shaking the vessel, and crying out to my friends: 'Aid me with your faith! Aid me with your faith!' They, doubters both of them, courteously bowed their heads: and lo and behold, the matter became liquid. I must point out that she shook the reliquary. In Naples, I understand, the blood of S. Januarius is held in the hands of the priest. From all I can discover, it seems certain that, at Ravello, the reliquary of S. Pantaleone remains unmoved and untouched.

In the crypt of the cathedral of Nola, between Naples and Avellino, are bones of the early saint, Felice. They are enclosed in a wall. A tube runs out of the wall into what, though old, looks rather like a small Victorian-Gothic letter-box. Down this tube flows a miraculous liquid given forth by the bones. Five times a year, according to a guide-book, the wonder takes place; the sacristan who showed me the crypt was less precise, but claimed that it happened quite often. The crypt is worth visiting, apart from its miracle; it contains two Renaissance panels of marble, carved in low relief. Finer, far finer than those, is a long Romanesque carving of Christ between the twelve apostles. Other liquefactions take place in the neighbourhood of Naples. According to Norman Douglas, a church at the foot of Vesuvius boasts a small quantity of the Virgin's milk, which liquefies at

spurious, e.g. those of *St. John the Baptist* and *St. Stephen*. On the other hand, from time to time the phenomenon was observed in authentic blood relics of *St. Bernadine Realino*. He was a Jesuit, the whole of whose long ministry was passed in Naples and at Lecce in Apulia.' Attwater: *The Penguin Dictionary of Saints*. I do not know the present whereabout of St. Stephen's or the Baptist's blood.

fixed intervals; but this story might be a fruit of his mischievous fancy. At Amalfi, from the bones of St. Andrew, on the twenty-ninth of November, a miraculous liquid issues.

Two exceptions to a Neapolitan vicinity must be mentioned. In Bari, the relics of S. Nicholas lie at the bottom of a well in the crypt of his church. They are in fresh water, said to issue miraculously from his bones. The claim is confirmed, I have been told, by the relics lying below the level of the sea, where sweet water could not be expected, a proposition geologically unsound. Moreover, the water is always there, and does not materialise on special occasions.

Another liquefacting saint lies farther afield — the English St. Walburga who, ending her life in Germany, is honoured at Eichstätt, where her body was finally buried. A medicinal oil is said to flow from her tomb. In an appendix to the *Apologia*, Newman discusses this miracle, of which he had at first been without evidence; he ends: 'The oil still flows; I have some of it in my possession; it is medicinal; some think it is so by a natural quality, others by a divine gift. Perhaps it is on the confines of both.' The date of the saint's translation to Eichstätt was May 1; grotesquely, she has thus given her name to the night of witches, the Walpurgis night.

In his *Grammar of Assent*, Newman alludes to the liquefaction of Pantaleone's blood as a type of miracle 'in which the absence of certitude is professed from the first.' He goes on: 'I may believe in the liquefaction of St. Pantaleon's blood, and believe it to the best of my judgement to be a miracle, yet, supposing a chemist offered to produce exactly the same phenomena under exactly similar circumstances... I should watch with some suspense of mind and misgiving the course of his experiment, as having no Divine Word to fall back upon as a ground of certainty that the liquefaction was miraculous.'

There may well be other miraculous liquefactions. Do any, save those of SS. Andrew, Januarius and Pantaleone, take place on expected dates? Is there any blood which liquefies and is not associated with the old kingdom of Naples?

I have searched in vain for antique stories of liquefying blood.

Blood of the victim in a vessel on the altar was the most I could discover (these liquefactions might derive from an early cult of unlettered times). In the dead olive tree which sprang to fruitful life we may surely discern a variant of the Adonis legend, when flowers sprang from blood of the slain victim. The blood of S. Pantaleone liquefies, as I have said, on July the twenty-seventh. Is it too doubtful a conjecture to connect this date with the blood which flowed from human sacrifice at the gathering of the harvest? A vegatative ritual, and the worship of trees, appear to be implicit in the saint's legend.

Pantaleone is a rare saint, whom I always come on with pleasure. I have paid a respectful visit to his church in Rome, a late structure which, except for its patron, is not interesting. Just outside Vallerano in Lazio is an exquisite church, plausibly attributed to Vignola. In one chapel I saw the painting of an unclothed young man, tied to a tree. I took him at first for S. Sebastian but, seeing no arrows fixed in his flesh, I recognised Pantaleone. The encounter with his bones at Bisceglie was welcome.

Superstition, ignorance, jiggery-pokery, idolatry: these are the kind of attributes which a stubborn free-thinker, or a free-churchman, might apply with happy indignation to the jolly, believing crowds who were enjoying themselves with gay abandonment when I first attended the miracle. I had seen in a poster, announcing the times of services, and processions, and music from a band, and fireworks at the festa, one particular attraction: 'The blood of our saint, glowing like a ruby, and testifying to his perpetual presence among us' — or words to that effect. Whoever saw in posters advertising an English fair — St. Bartholomew's at Newbury, for example, or St. Giles's at Oxford — so magical an enticement? To me, foreign in ways and belief and upbringing, the warm and noisy air was spiritual, together with the incessant loud talking and to-and-froing of the crowd, the crack of rifles at targets, the swaying, wobbling, luminous bundles of balloons, the drinks at café tables, the gold lights and the black impending darkness — to me all these became sacramental, as though the sanctified airs of the ancient cathedral had for the night flowed outward to glorify and enliven the merry-making company. These airs enveloped all the town; they entered the cheap, noisy little restaurant where we ate, involving the local young Italian with a French girl, towards whom his intentions were evidently anything but honest: and the jovial drunk at our table, who kept raising the clenched fist of communism, and mitigated the gesture with the crossed forefingers of a demochristian. Only as the hours latened and the crowd diminished, did it seem that the mystic flood was ebbing back into the cathedral, relinquishing, like a material tide, some all but palpable evidence of its flowing.

The last bus had been long gone. We set off walking with several friends down the steep dark valley. Invisible now were the cliffs and grottoes and pinnacles and buildings which in day so fantastically adorn the scene. At a dividing of the way, where some of our group were to leave us, we paused, and then, from far overhead, came the echoing bangs and stars and rockets from the last exuberant discharge of fireworks. The night became filled again with fleeting and whizzing jewels of light, outlining the black precipitous hills; the valley roared all around us. The latest of the crowds would soon be following. The saint was back within the shelter of his temple, to rest until the month of May when, issuing in procession again, he would refresh once more the faith and devotion of his followers.

CHAPTER VII

East from Amalfi

1. MINORI

The towns immediately to the east of Atrani — Minori and Maiori (Lesser and Larger) — evoke problems of nomenclature. They were once called Reginna Minor and Reginna Major; the nouns were forgotten, and only the adjectives remained, curiously Italianised in the plural.

Minori, once a bishopric, is the first to the east, lying at the mouth of a valley. The most attractive approach, if a little laborious, is to take the bus to Ravello and walk down. The way goes past the church of the Annunziata and through the porticoes of little churches which I have already mentioned. The territories of Amalfi are not poor in works of art; yet on this excursion one must feel, as so often in these parts, that, for the accumulation of beauty, art is almost a superfluity. The valley is steep on either side, and beyond is the mountain of the Avvocata, southward of which a gentle declining plateau stands over slopes which fall to the sea. Higher up, the roughly weathered rocks are ruggedly shaped into the profile of an old man. Far above is the church of S. Maria del Avvocata. According to Mansi it owes its name to a statue, discovered in a crypt, of *La Vergine nostra Avvocata*. This church stands beside the ruins of a monastery and is the scene, in June, of an uproarious pilgrimage, with festivities lasting throughout the night.

I took this walk from Ravello, not principally to get to Minori. I had noticed, looking down from the eastern verges of Ravello, a church with a handsome bell-tower, and a noble portico supported by antique columns. This was the parish church of the hamlet of Torella. The columns of the portico

143

have, as I found, good Corinthian capitals, almost certainly Roman.

On the way down I passed the lowest of the little Ravello churches, with a portico over the road. The portico has double vaults, supported on two ancient columns, one with a Romanesque and the other with an antique Corinthian capital.

When I got to Torella I found, of course, that the church was locked. An elegantly dressed lady was near and I asked if she knew where I could get the key. She politely and obligingly fetched it herself and let me in. The aisles are divided from the nave by three massive antique columns on either side. The capitals are Romanesque. One antique capital, upside down, serves as the base of a column. The stations of the Cross, and the figure of the Baptist over the font, are surprisingly good contemporary work by a sculptor from Minori.

I offered the kind lady a tip which she politely refused (this is something I have quite often experienced in south Italy); when I pressed her, she took the coin, thanked me and put it into the box for offerings.

Below Torella I passed another church, a tiny one, with its portico over the path; the portico consists of a single vault.

The most important monument in Minori is the Roman villa, which has been already mentioned among my generalisations on early art. Its most interesting part is the domed room which I discussed. For pure pleasure the bath is to be preferred with its vigorous, although rather coarse, mosaics of animals. Indeed, the villa is well worth a visit, but it lacks the painted richness of those lately excavated at Castellammare and, with Pompeii and Herculaneum at so small a distance, it is, relatively, of minor importance.

The parish church of S. Trofimena, protectress of Minori, was originally the cathedral. There was a church here in the tenth century. I was told by the priest that, of the present building, naves and aisle were of the seventeenth century, and transept and choir of the eighteenth. Most guide-books give a later date to its present form. However that may be, it is a nobly proportioned building. There is a good marble pulpit of the early seventeenth

15. Minuto: church of the Annunziata: frescoes of about 1100 in the crypt (page 103)

16. Scala: the cathedral (page 92)

century. This church, however, is attractive less for its form than for the curious legends of its patroness.

Trofimena, it is said, was a Sicilian, martyred in the fourth century under Diocletian or Maximian. Somehow — and this is not explained, though a miracle seems to be implicit — her body got to Minori, where it was buried, close to the sea. One day a woman was doing her washing in the river and, thinking the tomb of Trofimena a convenient place for the purpose, began to beat the linen on it. While she was doing this her hands fell off. Frightened and sad, as she is unsurprisingly described, she went home. Her neighbours asked her what had happened but she, fearing to lose her tongue as well as her hands, answered only by begging them to send for a priest. When she told him her story, and he had repeated it, a great crowd came with torches — for by then it was night — and went to the tomb beside the sea. Wondering whether it was a woman or a man who was buried there, they discovered an epitaph proclaiming it the burial place of Trofimena. (No explanation is given for the virgin martyr's grave having been unrecognised; one suspects a hiatus in the story, and that in fact the grave was new, and that the miraculously transported body had been as miraculously interred.) Some knew — how is not told — that there were pearls in the grave; accordingly the bishop of Amalfi was sent for, and in his presence the tomb was opened. Wishing to convey the saint to a sacred and fitting place, priests attempted to carry her away; her body at once became so intolerably heavy that they were unable to lift it. On this, the bishop of Minori called for many young maidens, who carried her with such ease that it seemed as if the saint were supporting them rather than they the saint. Amid prayers of the multitude the saint-afflicted woman recovered her hands. The body was taken to the cathedral, where the relics of S. Trofimena are still preserved and revered.

To judge from her posthumous behaviour, S. Trofimena, it would seem, must have been somewhat severe of character during her life. After all, she might have chosen less drastic means to reveal herself than by making a washer-woman's hands fall off. During the first half of the ninth century, Sicardo, Lombard prince of Benevento, invaded the Amalfitan republic. The bishop of Amalfi (the archbishopric had not yet been established), thinking that the relics of the saint would be safer in his cathedral, had them brought there from Minori. They found the body with, beside it, three small flasks of a sweet-smelling ointment. The body, exuding fragrance, was exposed in the cathedral of Amalfi. A woman coveting a piece of so precious a relic, cut off a bit of flesh, and blood ran out of the wound, as if from a live body. A little time after, the bishop saw, in a dream, the saint, who reproached him for moving her body and allowing it to suffer such indignities. 'Know,' she said, 'that you are shortly to die and your body, being torn out of the sepulchre, will be eaten by dogs.' Sure enough, the bishop soon died, and was buried in a tomb which he had prepared. The Lombards invaded the city of Amalfi and sacked it; seeing in the church some fresh plaster-work they broke it down, thinking to find treasure. They found only the rotting corpse of the bishop, which they left; dogs, entering the church, tore it out and devoured it.

The body of S. Trofimena was carried off to Benevento, by Sicardo (he had followed the example of his father, who stole the body of St. Bartholomew from Lipari); the citizens of Minori begged him to give them back their protectress, and he complied. She was taken first to Salerno, where she rested for a while; then, with rejoicing and grave ceremonies, she was restored to Minori.

Such pleasant stories should not be too closely looked into. But historical truth compels me to record that the relics of S. Trofimena are now contained in an urn made of alabaster from Volterra, and are preserved in the crypt of the old cathedral at Minori. In spite of her severity, she is a popular saint; many girls in the neighbourhood are named after her.

Minori possesses one rare antiquity. At the east end of the sea-front is a fountain, consisting of a stone basin into which two lions pour water from their mouths. Unlike the bull and lion on the fountain at Ravello, which stand above water-jets, these lions at Minori are mechanical parts of the fountain. It is usually referred to as Moorish, but the lions are Romanesque, and would not appear out of place carrying the columns of a Cosmatesque pulpit. Their present functioning might, I suppose, be due to later manipulation; I think it more likely that they are from the fountain of a Romanesque palace, Sicilian in luxury, like the Palazzo Rufolo at Ravello.

2. MAIORI

Maiori, unfortunately, is built on a wide bay at the mouth of a valley. I say unfortunately, because parts of the long, once un-developed sea-front are becoming crowded with ugly modern hotels and blocks of flats. Amalfi and Atrani, by the narrowness of their level spaces, have been so far safe from such pollution. Maiori's great boast, from the point of view of tourism, is a long sandy beach. On my first visit to the coast, I was persuaded to go with a party and bathe at Maiori. A boy in the party suddenly said solemnly to me:

'The water is dirty here.'

'Why?' I asked.

'Many dead people,' he answered grimly.

('*Molta gente morta.*')

In the previous autumn a fearful and fatal flood had fallen upon several towns of the coast, in particular on Minori, Maiori, Vietri, and one quarter of Salerno. It happened at about two o'clock in the morning, when almost everybody was in bed. Houses tumbled into the torrent, with all their occupants. There were two or three hundred deaths, and the sea became strewn with corpses. The body of an elderly woman from the valley above Maiori was found off Positano. In one house the whole front fell away and water swirled into the first floor. A father stood in rushing water at the back of his room, holding two of his children by the hand. One let go and was carried away, never to be seen again. Going for the first time to Amalfi, I was driven from Salerno. The lower part of Vietri looked as if bombs had been dropped along it.

It is curious how restricted was the disaster. Amalfi and Atrani and the coast westward suffered nothing at all. Most of the damage has been repaired, although a few destroyed houses are still visible in Minori. The rivers have been widened near the sea, and barricades constructed higher up, to prevent such a calamity ever happening again.

The chief church of Maiori was never in danger, for it stands some hundred feet up on the side of the hill, the church of S. Maria a Mare, St. Mary at Sea. This is the traditional story of the name. The dates which I have found are inconsistent, but the circumstances are clear.

At the time of the Frankish conquest and sack of Constantinople in the fourth crusade, a ship bearing Frenchmen and Venetians, and laden with loot, took refuge from a storm close inshore off Maiori. In order to lighten their endangered ship, the sailors threw much merchandise overboard, including a wooden image of the Madonna, upon which the ship was able to continue its voyage. (In this record a tradition is probably concealed, by which this image chose to be received at Maiori; we shall find such a tradition at Positano.) Henceforward the church, which had hitherto been dedicated to St. Michael, bore its present name. A very beautiful image of cedar-wood, often said to be the original, is preserved over the high altar. It is usually hidden by curtains, but the sacristan will readily open them. It has not the look of Byzantine work, and Signor Schiavo is no doubt correct in saying that it cannot be much earlier than the sixteenth century. There was a church here before the thirteenth century. Ancient masonry may remain, but what we see now is a baroque church, a noble cruciform building with a cupola. The nave is sixteenth century, with a carved ceiling of that period, and later paintings on it. The rest of the church is seventeenth- and eighteenth-century work, which was overhauled in the 1830s. As in many churches of the coast, apse and dome are decorated outside with coloured tiles.

My first visit involved the most gratifying disappointment I have ever experienced. I had read in a guide-book of a tenth-century bas-relief there representing St. Margaret, the Annunciation, the Nativity, the Resurrection, the Assumption and Coronation of the Virgin, and St. James. Promising myself the delight of Byzantine work, I went to S. Maria a Mare. The relief was not in the promised place. A priest was pacing slowly to and fro in the church, reading his office. I kept near to him, like a hungry dog. When he had finished his devotions, I asked him where I could see the carving. He took me to the small sacristy, and there it was on the wall. 'But,' I burst out, 'it's English!' 'Yes,' responded the priest, 'School of Oxford' — a term often used in Italy for what we call Nottingham alabaster. This — I guess its date to be about 1400 — is for design, and for quality of carving, one of the loveliest I have ever seen. It is a complete altar-piece and — a most rare feature — still has much of the original wooden frame with Gothic lettering on it (Pl. 20).

It is well known that, during the fourteenth and fifteenth centuries, there was a large export of such objects from England. During the disgusting iconoclasm of the Reformation, many were clandestinely sold abroad, with a nice balance of piety and avarice. At Capodimonte in Naples is a splendid altar-piece, with its frame and much original colour: examples, I believe, may sometimes be found even in the Balkans; for strangeness of place, the most amazing that I ever saw was at Reykjavík in Iceland, to which remote country it had been exported during the fifteenth century.

In the same room is a fine gilt wooden figure of the Madonna and Child, of the seventeenth or eighteenth century. I once, with proper patriotism, took an Italian friend to see that exquisite work of my mediaeval fellow-countrymen. We then admired the figure, and he told me that there used to be a traditional trade on the coast of carving figure-heads, and that the same craftsmen fashioned many of the church images. It must be added that some consider this image to be Spanish.

Eastward of Maiori the road runs up the hill to the high, rocky, intricately weathered promontory of Capo d'Orso. When I first passed that way, an Italian friend attempted to point out a rock shaped like a bear (*orso*); try as I would, recognition of the bear was beyond my powers of imagination, or self-delusion. One writer derives the name from a cave at the foot of the cliff, where waves in rough weather are said to make a noise like the growling of bears. Since there was once a great family in the neighbourhood called Orso, these ingenious speculations would seem to be unnecessary.

At the highest point an ancient round watch-tower has been modernised into a restaurant. The view from there seems un-excellable; eastward, to the left, on clear days, may be seen all the bay of Salerno (and, with binoculars, the temples of Paestum), its plain backed by mountains; and across the bay are mountains of the magical Cilento; to the right, westward, are hills and steep capes of the coast with, in the farthest distance, the Faraglioni of Capri rising behind the Galli, the Siren isles.

A little below Capo d'Orso, to the west, is a building which I used to take for no more than a fine and rather unusual example of the traditional peasant architecture. Some three stories high, it is built into a grotto, whose roof partially overhangs the structure. Crude buttresses sloping out give the impression of a creature leaning back under the rock for shelter. Picturesque I thought it, and no more. And then I discovered it to be one of the most remarkable monuments on the coast.

In 973 a hermit named Peter came to live in the cave here, accompanied by a young nephew of his, called John. On the death of Peter, other hermits joined his nephew. Their caves, half protected by walls, can be seen in rock faces below the road. On Peter's death a midget Benedictine monastery was established here, and the first abbot was called Tauro. It was dedicated to S. Maria de Olearia, which means roughly, Our Lady of the Oil. For the lover of art, the importance of this institution is that here is to be found the other series of paintings 'in the Greek style' which I mentioned in Minuto.

It needs a little trouble to visit the place, although it is scheduled as a national monument. On my first attempt I went into a part which I could see was inhabited. Somebody called me from above and, going up, I noticed small round arches supported on columns. This was something quite different from the local country cottages. I met a woman who, when I had explained what I wanted, told me to come back next day. I kept the appointment, and a little girl met me. She went to the outer edge of the road and shouted to her father at work below in the lemon-groves, near fearful abysses falling suddenly to the sea. He answered from far away. I waited a long time and was beginning to feel vexed, when at last he turned up with a large load of fodder on his back. He had not wanted to waste the long climb up. After that I was treated with the kindest attention.

A notice outside promises lamps with the best oil. In fact, only candles are provided, and it is wise to bring a torch, as I had forethoughtfully done on this occasion. We went up steep steps and into a pitch-dark cave, which is the crypt of the chapel above and was once used as a burial place. It has paintings dating from the eleventh century (Pl. 21). The most conspicuous and best preserved is in a recess; in the middle is the Virgin with her arms outstretched in an attitude of prayer — the *Virgo orans*. On one side of her is a priestly, on the other a military, saint. I am reminded by these, perhaps fancifully, of mosaic figures in the cathedral of Cefalù in Sicily. The ground is indicated with tufts of formal vegetation. In the angle to the left is the donor carrying the representation of a church. The painting is strong, and the drapery well rendered. Near by, in a niche, are three angels wearing Byzantine robes. Their faces are missing, having been stolen, I was told, by Germans, not during the war, but before it; the thieves were predatory tourists. Other, fainter figures can be seen on the walls. I do not think that much colour has decayed; but over the centuries, smoke of candles and of burning oil has covered the frescoes with dirt. A proper restoration would make this rocky chamber into a most impressive place. Many bones are lying about, and on a shelf is a row of skulls. I went back once with Signor Samaritani of Amalfi, to get photographs. He saw the skulls. '*È carino!*' he said, 'that's pretty!', and he took a photograph of them (Pl. 2).

Above this crypt is a miniature chapel. Outside is a courtyard in proportion, with three round arches against the rock. In the first arch is the admirably lettered memorial of the abbot Tauro. A circle of inlaid stone has been removed from it. This, I suppose, was carved, and had been stolen, perhaps by the German thieves.

The tiny chapel has a nave, divided from a northern aisle by a broad pillar and a small column. Nave and aisle have each of them an apse. Of decoration there is a painted colonnade in the main apse. There is also, on the pillar, the figure of a tonsured man; this unusual fresco is not Byzantine in style. I would guess it to be of the early fourteenth century, but I have never seen anything else quite like it in Italy.

Above the chapel is a little shrine, open to the air; it is barrel-vaulted, ending in an apse, and with a round arched entrance. Some authorities say that it was constructed by the first hermits. Since it forms a second story to the chapel, I cannot believe that anything of the kind would have been constructed by two solitaries. Probably it, with the chapel, is the earliest relic of monastic building.

On either side of the entrance are angels, with the hand of God above the arch. Inside, the little building was once completely frescoed. In the apse are the Madonna and Child, between St. Peter and St. Paul; above is the Lamb of God, between St. John the Baptist and St. John the Evangelist; in the vault overhead is Christ the Pantocrator. On the sides are a martyrdom, a miraculous resuscitation, and groups of figures. Enough remains to show that here were once paintings of fine quality, and purely Byzantine in style. There is Greek lettering.

These paintings have been attributed to an Amalfitan called Leone. From 987 to 1029 there was an archbishop of Amalfi named Leo; I suspect that patron has been mistaken for painter. It seems to me most likely that the artist was a Greek, both from the evidence of the lettering, and even more from the evidence of the style. He may have been one of the many Greek painters who were working at that time in Byzantine Apulia.

The condition of these paintings is tragic. They are disfigured by *graffiti* (one at least dates from the sixteenth century). Worse still, the painted surface is in a state of continual decay; many white patches show where colouring has lately fallen from the surface. In a few years, if nothing is done for them, these important frescoes will have disappeared.

It is generally and with justice thought reprehensible to criticise our hosts. Yet here I must condemn some of the more cultivated among the Italians. For many years past there has been a policy in Italy of tearing down baroque work in early churches. In many such cases, columns and capitals were often found to have been hacked and chipped so that the plaster might adhere properly. When the work of restoration is done, walls have to be rendered again and, in the end, all we can see of ancient work are columns and, with luck, a few complete old capitals. Will Italians not learn from English errors of the last century? Gothic churches, restored then with perverse pedantry, now look like purely Victorian buildings. These bleakly restored Romanesque churches of Italy, lacking all contemporary surface and the frescoes which once covered them, will look in a few generations like twentieth-century imitations of Romanesque. They seem, now, like places where nobody has ever worshipped. Worse still, such denuding is often carried out in churches which are structurally sound; the work, if it had to be done, could have waited a hundred years. For a twentieth part of the cost needed to de-baroquise a perfectly sound Romanesque church, the remarkable frescoes at Maiori could have been preserved. The paintings in the crypt are more or less safe; as for those in the uppermost shrine, probably only a few years are left in which it will be possible to see anything of their merit, or to feel their vanishing enchantment.[1]

It must be pointed out that the frescoes in the crypt and those in the shrine are clearly by different artists. It is equally clear that quite a different artist painted the slightly later frescoes at Minuto. One other series of such paintings is to be seen on the peninsula, though not in Amalfitan territory.

In Castellammare is the grotto of S. Biagio, with paintings of the eleventh century. They are more vigorously, but less delicately, painted than those at S. Maria de Olearia. To visit them you must go first to the Antiquarium Stabiano in Castel-

---

[1] In the *Provincia* at Salerno, the seat of provincial administration, there are some late nineteenth-century copies, in pencil and water-colour, of frescoes in the shrine.

lammare, the admirable little museum of excavated antiquities. You will very likely have to make an appointment for the next day. Your time will not have been wasted, for the museum is well worth a visit. There are Greek vases of the fifth and sixth centuries from the city of Stabiae, which was overwhelmed in Vesuvian ash at the same time as Pompeii and Herculaneum; these are a charming proof that the imperial Romans were, like many of us today, collectors of antiques. Not to be missed is a sarcophagus, carved with a procession of actors and musicians.

For S. Maria de Olearia it will be wise, as at Castellammare, to make an appointment before going there. At present the custodian is also sexton of the Maiori cemetery. However, it will almost certainly be possible to make arrangements with one of the family.

I have never visited any churches on the coast to the east of Maiori. At Cetara, once a nest of Saracens, the main church has an ancient bell-tower. A little inland is an apsed church which promises delight. The name of the town is said to derive from *cetus*, meaning a dolphin; one cannot but suspect some variant of the legend of Orpheus, who was once carried ashore from the sea by a dolphin. I have already mentioned, from farther east, the rococo buildings of Vietri; but this is getting out of Amalfitan territory.

To the north of Maiori is one of the most bewitching country-sides known to me.

3. TRAMONTI

Tramonti is a *commune* without a town to it, like a rural district in England. Although I have explored in it, there is much in that valley which I have never visited. The community is bounded east and west by lofty wild mountains; between these is an ascending succession of little, steep hills, planted lower down in the valley with lemons, and above with vines. These green pastoral hills, enclosed as they are by high, fierce crags, have seemed to me, ever since I first saw them, a perfect image of Bunyan's delectable mountains; they are the scenery of old romance, and crave the old language where words bear more than their common meaning — 'a faire field full of faire flowers and grasse' — 'a plentifull country' — 'a faire Towre by a maries on that side, and on that other side a faire meddow' (I quote from Malory). Tasso, be it remembered, was Sorrentine. And yet, it was from these gentle hills that the slaughtering flood descended on Maiori.

In the community are thirteen parishes, of which I have visited five. I have explored the valley in a car belonging to a friend. My discoveries — for such, so far as guide-book information goes, they were — may entice another to further searching.

I will first confess to a failure. Not far up the road, on the opposite side of the valley, can be seen a strange, sombre church. It has an old tower, and the main building stands on a high basement against the hill-side. Much of it is darkened by ivy. My companion, a native of the coast, told me that many years ago a priest had been murdered there, and the church was never reconsecrated. I mentioned it to an Italian professor of architecture who knew it; it dated, he thought, from the times of the Angevin kings of Naples. It must be two or three miles from the nearest road, and may very well be impossible to go into if ever you get there.

On my exploring trip, we turned off the main road and stopped first at the village of Polvica. This is the centre of the *commune*, with the municipal offices. A little to the north, on the summit of a steep hill, is the cemetery, with its church whose slim tower is a landmark visible in most parts of the valley. There is also a monastery at Polvica. I looked into the church where I met a young postulant who, at my request, took me up the tower. (At first I found him sulky but, since he turned out friendly, I suppose he was only shy.) The tower is tall and slender, ending in a domed turret, of which I was anxious to examine the construction. It is no more than a neatly moulded little dome like an inverted basin, This tower, together with most of the sanctified buildings around it, I should judge to be no later than the seventeenth or eighteenth century.

From Polvica we went on westward. I noticed an alluring

tower in a village called Figlino. This demanded a short walk from the road. Figlino was more rewarding than the metropolis of Tramonti. In the church, to the right of the entrance, close to the holy-water stoup, is a stone bas-relief of the Nativity, dating almost certainly from the sixteenth century. There are the trampled remnants of a fine ceramic floor. Strangers, I was informed, had once come here and taken a cast of the relief. The bell-tower, which had caught my attention, is a fine thing, with round-arched openings, and presumably Romanesque. The sacristan told me that the tower was now so frail that they dared not ring the bells. However, he suddenly asked me the time and, finding that it was just about mid-day, hurried off to ring the Angelus. I waited for the crash and roar of a falling tower, but nothing happened. Presumably it was only the pealing of larger bells which would endanger the fabric. Close to the church is an old palace, once a noble residence but now more than half derelict, although still partly inhabited, and with chickens picking about outside. This was evidence of grander life during old days in Tramonti. When the palace was properly lived in, there can have been no road near the village. This was the dwelling of a rich land-lord. Until the last part of the eighteenth century, the coast was always in danger of raids by Barbary pirates; the rich would have lived for safety either in well-defended towns like Amalfi, or in villages difficult of access like Figlino.

The next village I visited was Cesaranno, at the end of the side road. The church has been baroquised; over a vault below the floor is a slab dated 1534, testifying to the original antiquity of the building. Stations of the Cross are represented in old engravings. A very primitive painting of the Madonna, touching peasant art, dates from about 1900.

I ended my venture by eating at a small, simple restaurant in the village of Pietre. I and my driver sat in one corner of the little dining-room. A young man came in and sat diagonally opposite to us. He had already ordered his meal and, while we were waiting, he was given a plate of spaghetti. He looked across the room at us. '*Permesso?*', he said, 'May I?', and, to our '*Buon appetito*', he set to.

I have made on my own one other, brief church-hunting sally into Tramonti. The most southerly parish is Pocara. Mansi says that in the church are paintings by Luca Giordano, and adds that he was native of Tramonti (the claim seems unlikely; he was probably born in the neighbourhood of Cava dei Tirreni). I went to Pocara to look for these pictures. The church, of course, was shut, and nobody had the key. A lady near by said that in two days it would be open in the morning. I went back and, finding it still shut, I knocked at the door of the priest's house. I was received by a nervous girl, who seemed reluctant to let me into the church, but relented at my pleading. Her Italian was defective and I found her dialect difficult to understand. 'We're frightened of letting strangers in,' she said, 'as we've been robbed.' She showed me a charming angel holding a candlestick; the pair to it had been stolen. I think I managed to reassure her by saying I was well-known in Amalfi and Atrani and that I was writing a book about the country. Had her proper Italian been good enough, she ought to have known that mine had been exercised in the neighbourhood.

I am not qualified to give attributions to paintings. In this case it was a question of elimination. Of all pictures but one, it seemed impossible that they could be by Luca. The rest are charming, if a little uncouth, and probably the work of journeyman painters; some might well be of the sixteenth century. Of dated monuments, the oldest was from the early years of the seventeenth century.

If Mansi be correct, and there is work in the church by Luca Giordano, it is a baroque Annunciation in the north-east chapel. The picture, in a delightful carved and elaborate surround, is good and well painted. The church is fine, if a little rustic. The exterior of the dome looks as if the architect had seen a bad copy of a bad drawing of something by Bramante. The work around the west door is charmingly carved, and dated 1600. On the open space in front of the church a classical column has been set up, with an antique capital on it.

The church is on the hill, above the main road. When I got back, I found a group sitting on the wall by the highway.

They appeared glum and unfriendly. One I recognised as having directed me to the church on my first visit. I greeted him, and at once a friendly smile dawned over his face. Another had a trussed kid, to be killed and eaten, I knew, a few days later at Easter. 'I shouldn't like to be a kid at this season,' I said. At once the whole group broke into friendly conversation. I stayed a while reflecting, as we talked, how strange it was to find, within three miles of the tourist-infested coast, this pastoral, so easily misunderstood, shyness. Indeed, in the village, I had come on unfamiliar signs of old-fashioned courtesy. When I said 'good-day' to an old man sitting by the path, he had stood up before returning my salutation.

The road up through Tramonti ends in a short narrow pass beside the tower of Chiunzi. I know of few transitions more dramatic. Behind are the delicate green hills of Tramonti, walled by the high, wild, rugged mountains; at the crossing of the col, suddenly, Vesuvius reveals itself — the most beautiful, I often feel, of all mountains — rising in its splendid sweep above the plain and bay, with Naples beyond. Below are the towns about Pompeii and, across the plain, mountains which mark the fringes of the southern Appennines. Above the road are ruined fortifications. Lord over all is the tower, said to have been built in 1453,[1]

[1] Camera speaks of a republican castle at Montalto in Tramonti. The map shows Montalto as a mountain west of the valley, well away from any road, and a most improbable spot for defensive fortification. Many round towers date from the days of Amalfitan independence. It seems to me not unlikely that the old tower of Tramonti was in fact the strategically situated tower of Chiunzi. So important a safeguard would have been continually strengthened and enlarged.

This locality has been the occasion of a curious etymological confusion. My facts are from Signor Enrico Malato's recently published book on the dialect *Vocabularietto Napolitano* (Naples: Edizioni Scientifiche Italiane). There is an expression *Arrivare* or *andare* (go) *a Chiunzo*, which usually means to fail in an enterprise already undertaken. The common explanation is that there is a place between Gragnano and Agérola, which tricks the traveller into believing himself arrived — a delusion sadly familiar to walkers in mountainous places. A dialect poet of the last century, Gabrielli Quattromani, better informed geographically, assumed that Chiunzi was intended, 'where the horizon is so vast that nothing is left to be desired' and, translating Horace into dialect, uses the phrase in that sense. For this he is blamed by Signor Malato who, moreover, disbelieves that *Chiunzo* refers to a locality. He relates it to the Italian word *Chionzo*, which roughly means short and stocky, or dwarfish. *Andare a chiunzo* could thus easily imply the failure of a high undertaking.

with the permission of Alphonso I of Aragon, by Raimondo Orsino, Prince of Salerno and Duke of Amalfi; although these titles had lost by then all sovereign implication, the buildings here suggest that much autonomy, with military power, was left to feudal possessors of the dukedom and principality. The tower is visible from the valley through which run the motor-way and the railway to Salerno and the extreme south. The sight of this tower from the train has many times made me feel like an exile coming home again.

There is a simple café-and-restaurant here, where I have often stopped; it belongs to the proprietor of the restaurant in Pietre. Not far southward, on the east side of the road, are the woods which I have mentioned in the botanical chapter as a home of *Colchicum neapolitanum*.

I have explored, as may be calculated, only five of the thirteen parishes in Tramonti. Other obscure treasures must be there, like the bas-relief in Figlino. Tramonti has beauty enough to woo a traveller without the adjunct of ancient art. In the Icelandic saga of Grettir the Outlaw, it is told how he went into a region of glaciers and found, encircled by cliffs of ice, a temperate, green pastoral valley, where he remained in peace and safety for many months. Tramonti has something of the same ambience as that fabled hyperborean pasture of refuge. Ferocious and menacing are the high mountains on either flank of the valley, while the gentle, steep, pointed hills enclosed by them have a radiant Virgilian richness. There is nothing else like it in Amalfitan territories or, for all I know, anywhere else in the world.

It is a point of interest that the fierce north wind of Italy, the Tramontana, may have taken its name from this romantic small region. Of all valleys on the coast this is the least protected from the north. I have read that sea-faring Amalfitans accordingly called a *tramontana* any cold wind which fell upon them from the north, and that this name, in consequence, became usual throughout Italy.

CHAPTER VIII

West from Amalfi

Westward of Amalfi the disposition of the land alters. The Lattari mountains become higher, culminating in the peak of Monte S. Angelo a tre Pizzi, only a little under five thousand feet; guide-books speak of difficulties, and caution needed in the ascent, warnings confirmed by contours on the map; it is unlikely that I shall ever get to the top of it. The coast-line becomes more precipitous; the hills above are interrupted by cliffs. Moreover, except for Positano, there are no towns like those to the east. The hill-sides are scattered with hamlets, each with its church. Into many I have never been; those which I shall describe are worth visiting, and hint at unknown pleasures to be looked for in other parts of the neighbourhood.

Westward from Amalfi the road goes through a tunnel. A short way beyond is the Hotel S. Caterina, one of the older establishments of Amalfi. Opposite the hotel is a flight of steps which lead eventually to the church of Lone, a small parish which reaches down to the coast. The church is beside the new road to Pogérola, just where it turns into the valley above Amalfi. Once, at the house of some friends, I met the parish priest, who claimed to have in his church a painting by Andrea da Salerno; accordingly, one day I went there. The church was unexpectedly open; I went in and found the sacristan with his wife cleaning up the place. Although the church is Romanesque, with an apse, the interior is a quadrangular structure of the eighteenth century. I looked round and saw no pictures which could possibly be Andrea's. I asked the sacristan about it. The old picture, he told me, was behind the altar. I notice that the tabernacle was empty, with darkness beyond. I was then invited to stand on the altar

160

17. Atrani: procession of the *Battenti* (page 110)

and look through the opening. This seemed rather sacrilegious
to me, so, like Moses beside the burning bush, I took off my shoes
out of respect. Looking through the gap I saw dimly a Madonna
and Child. Of the fourteenth century this fresco seemed to me, and
one of the minor Giottesque paintings which must have once
adorned many churches of the coast. I profited by my lesson in a
church farther to the west. To describe its position, I must clear
up a confusion of nomenclature.

Not far along the road to Positano is the village of Véttica
Minore. Farther on is Praiano; included within its bounds is the
village of Véttica Maggiore. Now this last has been developed
for tourism with shops and lodging houses and hotels, and has
become much larger than Praiano itself. In ordinary talk, Véttica
Maggiore is generally referred to as Praiano.

As you come into the true Praiano, there is a diminutive apsed
church on the inland side of the road. It had enticed me for some
time, and one day I stopped to look at it. I got, luckily, the key
from a house nearby and was taken in. In front was a small,
elegant garden. The church was dedicated to S. Caterina, and is
the private property of a family whose name I have forgotten. I
found inside, as I had foreboded, a pretty eighteenth-century room.
It was possible to get behind the plaster-work over the altar. I
happened to have a torch with me. In the apse are the remains of
an early fresco, apparently of Christ in Majesty. I have no doubt
that similar frescoes are hidden by later work in many Amalfitan
churches.

The dominance of Véttica Maggiore over the once superior
Praiano is not a matter of modern times. Véttica has a fine
baroque church, S. Gennaro, cruciform, and with a dome of
coloured tiles. Inside is a number of satisfying sixteenth-century
paintings. It stands on a broad terrace, with a magnificent view
westward towards the extremities of the peninsula.

Positano, not far to the west, is in danger of becoming a mainland Capri. It is built over two valleys, whose contours beautifully
define the town. The municipal authorities have wisely forbidden
all buildings of a contemporary style, such as pollute half Maiori
and an enormous part of Salerno. Even a new luxury hotel must

follow the local style of architecture. The vision of Positano from the sea is dazzling. Yet, in its commercial entertainment of foreigners, it is losing its natural life in a way from which Amalfi and towns to the east of it are entirely free.

There are two traditional explanations for the name Positano. One, which I have mentioned in my historical appendix, says the inhabitants came originally from Paestum, once Poseidonia, which was corrupted to Positano. This reinforces traditions as to the origins of Amalfi. The plain of Paestum was terribly exposed to invading barbarians, whereas the rough coast would have promised situations easily defendable. I find the plausibility of this tradition a little unfortunate, for the other tradition is much more attractive.

During the iconoclastic period in Constantinople, a revered painting of the Madonna and Child was carried away for safety and taken to Italy. The ship carrying it was off Positano, when a voice from heaven cried: '*Posa! Posa!*' ('Put down! Put down!'), and the ship would not move. The painting was then taken ashore and placed in the principal church of the town, which thenceforward took its name from the event. The picture was, when I last saw it, completely over-painted; but the form is, to my mind, consistent with the eighth or ninth century to which, according to the tradition, it ought to belong. Pottery replicas may be bought in the town, with '*Posa! Posa!*' on them.

This church, the Assunta just above the sea, is, for all that can be seen of the main structure, a building of the eighteenth century. Some of the fabric must be considerably older; Romanesque fragments, including pieces of Cosmatesque work, have been built into the exterior of the north wall. There is at least one painting of the sixteenth century.

On the dignified campanile, which stands apart, is a very strange Romanesque relief. It represents a marine monster with forelegs and a coiled tail. Below is a wolf. Monster and wolf are each of them devouring a fish. Fish are on other parts of the relief. The significance of this work has never been satisfactorily explained. The monster comes from the same ocean as Jonah's whale. I have sometimes wondered, improbably, if it may not be an eccentric representation of the whale, with Jonah still inside it. Mansi accepts it as a fish which from early times was a symbol for Jesus. Yet why should that symbol be shown eating its own symbol? We can only enjoy the carving all the more for the mystery of it.

I had often noticed in Positano a church which I wanted to visit — a small apsed building, with a vaulted roof like that on many an old cottage in the neighbourhood. At last I found a man who could get me the key (he later refused a tip). Inside are ghosts of frescoes, and two good Roman sarcophaguses. It belongs, or once belonged to the family of Di Palma and is used, I was informed, only on Palm Sunday.

Another church in Positano puzzled me for some time. It stands to the west of the town at almost its highest point; it is round, and covered by a cupola. After years of curiosity un-satisfied, I found it was called the Chiesa Nuova, and is barely a hundred years old; it makes a fine land-mark and is visible from the sea.

The finest works to be seen west of Amalfi are on the higher road which branches off not far west of the town, climbing to Agérola and eventually reaching Castellammare.

Westward of Amalfi, on the steep hill-side, can be seen from the town a structure like a colossal, rather corrugated terrace, with a small, graceful tower on its inland edge. This is the convent of S. Rosa, founded towards the end of the seventeenth century, in the village of Conca. There was an ancient church here, but it would seem to have been reconstructed when the convent was built. Only the tower remains. The convent, long abandoned, has lately been made into an hotel. Its most curious feature is that it has been built of concrete, on the same principle as the character-istic old houses of the country-side. The great roof is an assembly of low, longitudinal cupolas.

On the same road you pass the village of Tovere, whose bounds, as with many other parishes about here, reach the sea. This has the most beautiful and graceful of all the smaller bell-towers in the coast. It has four slender, square stories, the fourth being narrower than those below it; above, narrower still, stands a round turret crowned by a flattened cupola. In principle this differs only in height and slenderness from many neighbouring towers; in grace and proportions it is faultless. Inside the church, to the west, is an almost detached, rectangular little chapel. Vaults of the roof are supported in the centre by a massive column. On the altar is a late Giottesque fresco of St. Peter between two saints. He is wearing the triple crown which, according to Signor Schiavo, must be a later addition, for it is of a shape which could hardly be earlier than the eighteenth century.

I have told how the late Archbishop Rossini of Amalfi showed me the collection of pictures which he had rescued from decay in country churches. One, he said — and I gathered it was the prize of all — he had not been allowed to take away. It was in Furore, and was by Antonello da Capua; '*not* da Messina', he said, and repeated 'da Capua'. The opinion of such a man on such a subject was not to be passed over. 'How do you find the church?' I asked. 'You walk up from the road,' he said; 'it takes about an hour.' He described the position of the path, and I recognised it from my knowledge of the coast road. I remember thinking then that it would be more comfortable to walk down.

The last time my mother visited the coast, she arrived on her eighty-second birthday. We motored from Naples by Castellammare and Agérola. I made the driver stop at the Bacco, the restaurant-bar in Furore, and we toasted her in the local wine, fitting stuff for the pious occasion. Wine of Furore is renowned as the best on the coast. The village is high up, on a southward protuberance of the mountain, so that the sun is all day on the ripening vines. Maybe the relative coolness of the nights delays fermentation just so much as to perfect the process. It is sold, bottled and labelled, in restaurants down below. It is still good thus, but few Italian wines will travel well unless laced with spirit and mixed with other wines. To drink Furore wine at its best, you must go to the Bacco; and there I went with a friend for a preliminary drink on our search for Antonello da Capua.

Furore has several churches, and I did not know which was

the right one. I told one of the sons of the house what we wanted. He knew about the picture. The church, he said, was some way down the mountain-side. Below the village is a rough road running west from the highway. At the end of this road is a flight of steps which leads eventually to the coast road. Not far down, on a little piazza, is the church of S. Elia. (This name may be puzzling to English readers. It means Elijah. The habit of sainting prophets is confusing to us; the full name of the church is, in fact, S. Elia Profeta.) We followed the easy instructions. It was a few days before Easter, and we found the church blessedly open, for it was being put in order. We went in. There was no question at all of asking which was the picture.

Having no idea of what had been ahead of us, what kind of painting, or, although guided by a respectable opinion, of what its quality was to be , we stood amazed in front of it without speaking. Who would have looked for such a work in this little church of a remote hamlet, and well away from the road?

An admirer of Ezra Pound once, after quoting a pretty passage, wrote: 'If this is not great poetry, I do not know what great poetry is.' I thought of adopting his formula, and writing: 'If this is not minor poetry, I do not know what minor poetry is.' In the case of this unheard-of Antonello, I can think of nothing else to say, after a second visit, and the study of a photograph, but: 'If this is not great painting, I do not know what great painting is.'

The picture, of the fifteenth century, represents the Virgin and Child enthroned between Elijah and St. Bartholomew. The Virgin wears a heavy and gorgeous robe of brocade, with the rough circle of a large formalised flower below her knees; above this is the Child with His face half turned away, and His arm held towards her left hand in which is an apple. There is a veil over her head, and her face has the unexpressive majesty which we are accustomed to in some great paintings of the period. Her throne is simply decorated and has a winged creature on each arm. Elijah holds a scroll, and St. Bartholomew his knife; their drapery is well designed and masterfully painted. The feet of St. Bartholomew are particularly to be noticed (Pl. 22).

Very little indeed is known about Antonello da Capua (he is

sometimes called Angelo Antonelli di Capua). He is described as a painter and embroiderer of Naples, of the mid-fifteenth century. He is recorded as having, in 1472, executed some paintings in a room for King Alphonso I of Naples, and, in the following year, other works for the Duchess of Termoli. Of the altar-piece at Furore, Camera says: 'In 1482 he painted on a panel a splendid picture, in the Greek style, for the parish church of S. Elia in Furore, representing the Blessed Virgin, with the prophet Elijah and St. Bartholomew the apostle. At the foot it is dated 1482, and by the rector of that church he was paid sixty-four ducats, a very considerable sum in those times, when for such work very little was paid.'[1]

There is a peculiar addition above, not earlier than the eighteenth century, representing God the Father among angels. The background to this group has been worked so as to leave an almost rococo outline to the original gold base. These intrusive figures, which fit into the baroque frame, were probably executed when the picture was put into its present position, at which time, also, the panels must have been adjusted as we see them now.

Strange things have been done to the painting. The ground across the tryptych is not consistent, and the relative positions of the panels must once have been different. A friend has even doubted whether the Virgin was by the same hand as the attendant saints. Almost certainly the panels were once separated by parts of a frame. What happened to the rest of it? There must have been a predella, and probably figures in small panels above.

It is too easy to over-rate our own discoveries and, for my friend and me, this picture was near enough to a discovery as makes no matter. This is indisputably by far the finest painting on the coast; beside it, the most charming and lively works by Andrea da Salerno seem a little debile. It would never surprise me if Antonello da Capua were one day declared a ghost, and his picture attributed to some known and eminent artist.

We talked for a while with the priest, who knew well enough

---

[1] I have already mentioned Camera's curious qualification for this work 'in the Greek style'. The reference for his information is 'Protocol. del notajo Salvatore de Cunto di Amalfi, il di 10 aprile an. 1482, Indiz. Ia. fol. 112.v.'

what a treasure he had in his church. He told us of two Englishmen who had come to see it, after a disappointment when they
had mistakenly gone to a church of S. Elia in Tramonti. (If this
comes to their notice, I should like, as agony-column advertisements put it, to get into communication with them.) I asked the
priest if I might come back and get a photograph taken of the
picture and, having been given his consent, we left.

The photographs caused me trouble such as I have rarely
experienced in my sight-seeing. Later in the same year I went
back with Signor Samaritani. We made the same journey, and
arranged for the car to wait for us on the lower road. The church
was shut. When Signor Samaritani began to ask for the key, a
strange air, almost of enmity, began to be felt. He was sent from
one to another. A story was told of photographers nearly setting
fire to the church with their flashes. One supposed possessor of a
key said that it had been taken away; besides, the painting was
very precious, and it would be too great a responsibility to open the
church. 'I'm Samaritani!' he said, with a tone in which pleading
and authority were about equally mixed. (Anyone within ten
miles or more of Amalfi, who wants his photograph taken, goes
to Samaritani.) He cried out, he pleaded, he clasped his hands
together in attitudes of prayer; his name had kindled a little
warmth, but no bending of an inflexible resistance: for resistance
it was, since there must have been someone living near by,
responsible for cleaning the church, and who had the key.

During all these difficulties I had stayed to watch over his
apparatus. Some small boys were playing football on the level
space in front of the church. They were being very seriously
overseen by a young man of about twenty, who kept skilfully
imitating a metal whistle. The game was often interrupted by the
ball going over into a terrace planted with lemons. Once it
stuck high up in a lemon tree, and for nearly five minutes the
boys threw stones at it until at last they brought it down.

Signor Samaritani gave up and asked for the priest's address;
he lived near the sea in Praiano. Before we set off, he made me
walk a little way to show me a stupendous view of the coast
westward. Then we set off down the slope to where, far, far

below, the car would be waiting for us. As we went down I perceived the faculties which make him so excellent a photographer. The texture of stones, the colour of quarried rock, the light on an old building, all made him bubble with ecstasy. I pointed out clumps of cyclamen in flower; his face glittered with joy. Suddenly, when I was a few paces ahead of him, he said: 'Stop! I want to photograph you with that tree.' On the slope above was a splendid umbrella pine (Pl. 1). He hurried back up the steps. He motioned me this way and that. I could not indulge what little of vanity is left to me in my sixties. No doubt he may have said to himself that I was '*Carino*' ('Pretty') — like that row of skulls in the crypt of S. Maria de Olearia.

The path follows an almost precipitately descending gorge, the Vallone di Furore. Were there no church at S. Elia, and no masterpiece, it would be worth going along that rough road to walk down this way. Soon on the descent we found ourselves enclosed by profound slopes which hide the view up and down the coast; rock and rich vegetation bound the path; olives, cistus, olorous herbs, small fig-trees twined into the stone, cover the rich slopes; from time to time the gorge is visible with vertical cliffs. The climax is fittingly the end of it. The deep ravine is crossed by a splendid, single-arched bridge; the sides are precipitous, and clean sand reveals how far the sea runs inland beyond the bridge.

Apart from the eventual advantages which we were to get from our visit, our diversion was of use to Signor Samaritani. We had two or three miles to go.

'Do you know,' he said to me, 'the rock called the *Madonnina* ?' (little Madonna). Some one had asked for a photograph, to go into a book or an article. This pillar of rock stands on the outer side of the road and, being about thirty feet high, the diminutive, interpreted literally, is anything but suitable (it is used here as a sign of affection, and not of size). The outline is that of a slim figure, facing the sea, and holding a baby. It is rather as if Giacometti had left unfinished a colossal statue.

'Do you see,' he pointed out when we stopped for the photograph, 'how the Babe always has a bush growing out of it?'

We found the priest's house easily enough, and were made hospitably welcome with glasses of brandy. Very soon we had arranged to go back the next Sunday, and take photographs before he said Mass at 9.30 in the morning. He told us how the picture had not gone away to be restored. It was a repetition of the defence of their Byzantine doors by the inhabitants of Monte S. Angelo. People came from the Ministry of Fine Arts — doubtless at the instigation of Archbishop Rossini; they had immense cases with them for the panels, and an escort of *carabinieri* for the defence of the treasure. People of the hamlet crowded about the church in protest and defence. Meanwhile, unknown to the intruders, there were men among the vines and lemons with loaded shot-guns. Luckily the passive resistance was effective; otherwise there would certainly have been a real, bloody battle, with lamentable consequences in the criminal courts.

The priest defended his parishioners. 'It might never have come back,' he said, and other events might be held to justify him. At Tarquinia there used to be a superb Madonna and Child by Filippo Lippi. During the war its custodians were warned that the Germans were after it, and it was sent to Rome, where it still is, in the Galleria Nazionale. 'They would say,' the priest went on, 'that it must go to an exhibition, and perhaps another, and when would we have it back again? And the painting above, which is later; we do not want to lose that, unless, of course, there is something like it underneath.'

Pedantic answers there are in plenty; yet, against the love which he and his parishioners feel for their picture, what can be decently said? Parts of the picture need cleaning — in particular the Virgin's head — but my unskilled eyes could see no evidence of dangerous decay.

Taking the photograph was an odd experience. We carried all the apparatus into the choir; the priest removed Crucifix, flowers and candles from the altar. A small camera was set up, and several exposures were taken. All the time members of the congregation were coming in and sitting down. Not feeling confident of his first results, Signor Samaritani set up a large, old-fashioned camera — one of those without a shutter, and which is operated with a cap over the lens. He tried it in various positions and looked each time at the hooded screen. Everybody was sitting quite still and staring ahead as though we were not there. Then the tripod was put on three chairs, necessitating a fourth for the photographer. At last he finished; we took everything to the side of the church; I put the chairs back in their places. At once the congregation burst into *Ave Maria*.

The church has, for holy-water stoup, a Roman cinerary urn. This is not at all unusual around Amalfi. The urn at S. Elia, carved with foliage, is beautiful above the average. We collected together all the apparatus, said a grateful good-bye to the priest, I gave a small offering for the church, and we left. As we were going out, I showed the urn to Signor Samaritani and, carrying some of the load, went on ahead of him. Looking back, I saw him opening the doors wide, and politely motioning away some young men in the entrance, half attending the service. Then he photographed the urn (Pl. 23).

Sightseers may take advantage of my experience. It is most unlikely that anybody in the neighbourhood will let you into the church; the admirable priest, if you visit him, may not be at home. If you go to S. Elia at about half past nine on a Sunday morning you will almost certainly be able to eventually see Antonello's painting.

It takes about twenty minutes walking down to S. Elia, and half an hour up. This time we did not make the long, lovely descent to the coast road. As we started back I said: 'It was very inconvenient the other day, but there is something touching in the devotion which these people have for their picture.'

'Yes,' he said: and then added dryly, 'it shows an ugly lack of trust.'

CHAPTER IX

I Promessi Sposi

We all know stories of times past in England, when marriages were arranged like business contracts, and a marriage for love could seem almost an impropriety. There were exceptions as, during the seventeenth century, in the case of Dorothy Osborne with its happy ending; but John Donne's marriage, with its consequences so terrible at first, illustrates the more prevalent attitudes of the epoch. Although things are beginning to change there now, something of the kind persists in the old territories of Amalfi (I have little doubt that the old rules are very much more respected still farther south, in the wilder parts of Apulia, Calabria and Lucania). I do not mean that young people are forced to marry against their wills, just to satisfy the tyranny or avarice of parents; but those parents still have a terrible power in the matter.

I knew an Englishman with a house on the coast. He told me one story with which he had been particularly concerned. A young man who worked for him a long time became engaged to a girl from a family of fisher-folk, living in a village some distance away beside the sea. Being employed by a generous foreigner, the young man — let us call him Giuseppe — had an air of prosperity about him; the girl's parents were delighted at his proposal, most correctly made by asking permission of the father before anything was said to the girl. They drank to a life-long friendship by crossing their arms as they did so. 'You are an honourable man,' said the father; 'you spoke to me before you spoke to my daughter.'

'Everything went on as well as could be,' said my friend. 'The parents asked me to their house. One day the girl came to mine, visiting me as though I was a parent of her betrothed. She gave me a bunch of flowers, and formally kissed my hand.

'Gradually, it came out that the parents had thought the young man to be much richer than in fact he was. It appeared that they had been planning for him to buy a house where they might all live together. The young man's ideas were very naturally and very reasonably different. He could, in fact, perfectly well support a wife. He could hardly have supported her parents as well, and in any case he had no intention of doing it. A coolness developed. The girl wrote to him to say that her father had accused him of not having saved any money, where another man in his circumstances would have plenty put by. "Tell him," she begged, "that you have lots in the bank, that you'll get a house, and ask them to live with us. It won't matter after we're married." But it would not do. When the parents realised that he did not intend to provide them with a home, they made the girl break off the engagement. "It is not my fault," she wrote to him, "but I must obey my parents. If it is our destiny to be married, we shall be married." "Destiny" is a potent word in these parts. In the end she asked him to send her letters back; she would let him have his. She must obey her parents, she said, but if it was their destiny . . .

'He asked me what he ought to do. "Say," I advised him, "that you'll only send her letters back, if she writes swearing by God and her mother (that's a very strict oath round here) that she doesn't love you, and doesn't want to marry you." It wasn't any good. "I must obey my parents," she wrote — they weren't seeing each other by now — and then more about "destiny".

'I found out that they'd been suggesting, as part of their excuse, that my relations with the young man hadn't always been strictly proper. Strong in the certainty of my innocence, this gave me a lead as to how to treat them. At last, we realised for certain that the marriage would be quite impossible. Giuseppe asked me to take her letters back, and get his in return. "But don't," he said, with native pride, "try to get anything out of them for me."

'I went down to their house. They gave me an effusive and hypocritical welcome. I refused rather severely the offer of coffee which convention demanded. I told them of Giuseppe's message, and then I accused them of slandering me.

' "Who told you that?" the father shouted with sham indignation. I didn't answer, although my authority was good enough to be certain of it. I said: "Do you swear by God that you didn't say it?" and they blasphemously swore that they'd never said it. "Do you swear by God that you never believed it?" And they perjured themselves again. Then I said, "If I find out who said it, I shall bring an action against them for calumny. And I pray that the pains of hell may come on the people who said such a thing." Some misfortunes have come on them since then, and I'm pretty sure they'll have believed that it was the result of my curse — together, of course, with their blasphemous perjury.

'It was a miserable scene. We talked a long time. The girl had fetched Giuseppe's letters for me to take back to him. All the time she was looking through the letters and weeping. In the middle of her weeping, she got up and made some coffee. Since it was she who had done it, I took a cup. At last I left, and gave her my blessing for what it was worth, as a sort of counterblast to the curse I'd put on her horrible parents.

'Both the young people have got married since then. Giuseppe happily, I know. But for her — I don't know. I liked her and don't like to think of her as unhappy. But her parents are now among the very few people I really do hate. They're a horrible, despicable, covetous, unfeeling, selfish couple. I sometimes actually hope that my brutal prayers may come true for them.'

After hearing this story I can never look down without something like horror at the little fishing village where the frozen-hearted couple lives.

It is not only parents who can bring about such disaster. Another young man I know fell in love with a girl who his family — brothers and sisters: the parents were dead — did not think good enough for them. They were descended, it is true, from one of the old noble families of the neighbourhood, but, although prosperous, no longer lived like gentry. All are in decent occupations, and I look on them all as good friends of mine. Their treatment of the young lover was brutal. They would not feed him; they would not talk to him; the womenfolk would not do his washing. He went home only to sleep. Knowing him as a plump man, I came out one year to find him cadaverous and with drooping cheeks. He thought of getting work in England, and I was asked by friends of his if I would sometimes put him up at my house. I, of course, agreed. One day the girl asked me if it was true that he was going to England. I said to her — evidentaly suspicious that something was up — that I did not know; all I could say, I went on, was that, if he came to England, he would always be welcome at my house.

I must interject here that the word she used was not *Inghilterra*, England; what she said was *Londra*, London. London means England for most people in the south. I have often been asked if I had met somebody's brother or son who was in London. Once this turned out to mean Southampton, and once Liverpool. Even this is hardly as crazy as the case of a man who told me that he was going to work at the Essex Hotel in Liverpool. Happening to be in Liverpool I thought of looking him up, but there was no such hotel in the telephone book. In the end I discovered that he had gone to a hotel in Essex, to which he went from Liverpool Street Station. This geographical confusion seems to reveal an adolescent, almost childish, simplicity, once so characteristic of all Italians, as in the case of Piero di Cosimo who lived alone, never washed, and lived chiefly on boiled eggs; or Sodoma, with his house full of strange pets, including a raven which answered knocks on the door in his owner's voice.

The family is, in the south, and very likely in other parts of Italy, a strict, enclosed community, with huge implications of loyalty. If anyone deviates from the expected behaviour, there rages up in savagery the herd instinct. A man I knew had fallen in love with a married woman. Divorce and marriage were not impossible — they were both working out of Italy. So far as I had any influence, I discouraged this. Careless as many of them may be in church-going, the great rules of the church have immense power. Far worse than fornication or adultery is re-marriage after divorce; there is added to all the guilt of those sins the profanation of a sacrament. The project my young friend was considering would have separated him very seriously from his family. They knew the danger and were naturally worried; but I discovered that they were imputing countless other faults to the potentially erring son. He was considering a deed they could only be ashamed of; he must therefore be harried away with volleys of false accusations.

I have remarked about my south-Italian friends that they boil at a lower temperature than most Englishmen. A frenzy of anger implies much less with them than it would with most of us. I did once lose my temper with a close friend (he was much angrier than I); we shouted at each other. Next day I felt ashamed and said: 'I raised my voice too much. I'm sorry.' For a moment he could not think what I was talking about, and then, suddenly remembering, he said, in a tone of surprise: 'But that doesn't mean anything with friends.'

The family became reconciled to their shrivelling, love-lorn brother I have spoken of. The erring one, who never erred in the end, was acquitted of his uncommitted sins. One man did not take the long expensive journey to be at a relative's wedding. The injured bride vowed — and meant it at the time — never to look him in the face again. Look him again in the face she did, and not long after. I have wondered sometimes, in the awful pity which I have felt for friends unfortunate in love, whether I may not have been troubling myself too much with pity for them. And yet my plump friend really did become thin. Another young man, distracted with love gone wrong, ate hardly anything for many days on end. And two stories I was told reveal how far their passion may distract young people of the coast.

There is a high cliff beside the road between Amalfi and Atrani. A young man whose girl had left him for another, to prove his manhood and desirability, dived over that cliff, about sixty or seventy feet, into the deep sea. No great harm resulted except, I was told, that blood came out of his ears. Another such case ended less happily.

Along the road, a young man thumbed a lift, and then, not long after, asked to be put down where there is a fearful cliff by the road. His girl had given him up. He climbed over the wall and hung for a while by his hands above the void. 'Keep away! Keep away!' he shouted when the motorist and passengers tried to get hold of him. But then, as his grip grew weaker, he called for help, too late, and he fell and was killed on the beach below.

A young south Italian in England — friend of Italian friends of mine — tried to kill a girl who had brutally chucked him for another man. It was evident that there had been unbearable provocation, for he was given only three years, and was not expelled from England.

Things of this kind happen all over the world, of course, and few of us there are, unhappily, who have not known the agony of broken affections. And yet I do not think there are many Englishmen who become possessed with such excess of wildness as often seizes the southern Italian. There is a proper word for it, this violent, outward manifestation of trouble — *sfogarsi*, which may be rendered as 'disfume oneself' (blow off steam is a parallel but weaker image), a ridding oneself, somehow, by strong physical action, of the heat and passion which has so disturbed the heart.

Body and spirit are thrown into the exercise. The gestures of an excited conversation seem to drain away the malignancy of excitement. A shaking of the right hand, palm towards the body covered with clenched fingers except for the extended index, shaken and thrown towards the adversary, level with the face, whether materially present or imagined: more quiet, a gentle movement of the extended hands, held together as in prayer, and then suddenly, with a hunch of the shoulders, turned outwards, palms away from the body: a violent knock with the forefinger on a table. The variation of voice is not of pitch, as with northern races, but of speed and volume. The purge is often complete, and so it was that my friend, when I made my apology, had quite forgotten our accomplished rage.

The puzzle for an Englishman is to guess how serious is the cause of a tremendous explosion. Once the son of a friend took out his father's motor-bicycle without permission, ran into a wall, and buckled the front wheel. I happened to be in the house when the delinquency became known. From the next room I heard the father shouting for quite five minutes. 'Poor Giovanni,' I thought

18. Atrani: procession of the *Battenti*
(page 110)

19. Giant Fennel
(*Ferula communis*)
(page 120)

(that was not his name), 'he really is catching it.' A little later I found that Giovanni was not in the house at all; the father was telling his wife what he would say to him when he came back. It was a summer of hot nights, and Giovanni stayed out until next day. The solo of rage had fulfilled its clinical function. Nothing more was said.

The *sfogarsi* (I can give it no other name) is also, I think, a help in circumstances of miserable bereavement. In England, a friend of mine had just lost his father, and we were talking about it, with controlled calm, in the company of an Amalfitan. 'I can't understand you English,' he broke out; 'we should all be crying now.'

I once went to the funeral of an old lady in Amalfi. Almost everybody who went in, bearing touching bunches of flowers, kissed the coffin. She was to be buried in a family compartment, like a large cupboard. Not many months before, a son of hers had died. When we arrived for the end of the ceremony, the place of disposal was open and the son's coffin was visible. Kneeling against the open vault, in black draperies, was the widow, wailing loudly. For the proper arrangement of both coffins, the son's was humped out, like a trunk out of a luggage-van. The widow, with a great shriek, flung herself on it, and kissed it. Her wild manifestation of grief, although the expected behaviour, was, I am convinced, true. After the funeral, I said to a son of the dead lady: 'How is your poor sister-in-law?' 'Quite all right,' he answered cheerfully, as though the question had not needed asking. The widow had split the fury of her grief, like water, in the cemetery, and so had freed herself of its agony.

Sfogarsi is surely a wise undertaking, whether in the trivial vexations of domestic life, or in the deep sufferings of bereavement. The required English calm in situations of agony all but unbearable is leaning too close to the flame, and leaves bitter ashes. I suppose we cannot, in such affairs, alter our ancient manners; yet we would be foolish to consider ourselves thus the better of unbraced Italians.

'Damn braces; bless relaxes,' wrote Blake. The southern spirit may blaze too easily into passionate scenes, yet it flows as easily with kindliness and hospitality. Arriving once with friends at two o'clock in the morning, we were met by the brother of one; he carried us off to his home, where his wife got up and cooked us a big meal, such as one would expect in the middle of the day. Never have I gone into a house without the offer of coffee or strong drink, and usually both. In the case of the latter I have observed a curious custom. Often I have been offered my drink — vermouth or spirits — in two glasses. At first I thought that my host was to share it; but no, it was all for me. Intimate friends have not been able to explain this.

It might be thought that such openly feeling people would be without the verbal gentilities with which many English untastefully veil functions of the body and places reserved for them. Propriety is international. However, it has its dialects, and some southern delicacies have sounded comically in my ears. At a festa I asked a friend where to find a public lavatory. He took the question gravely and then, after quiet thought, enquired: 'Big act or little act?' I never see without delight the notice to the lavatories of Atrani, *Gabinetti di decenza*, cabinets of decency.

A wise man said to me that we can understand something of people's nature from their language. I have wondered if this may be true of the Amalfitans. Can we see in their familiar dialect a light on their behaviour in love or anger? This is a question I cannot confidently answer.

Many people far more competent in Italian than I would find their general talk incomprehensible, as, indeed, would many Italians from other regions. I myself understand very little of the local form of Neapolitan dialect although, after a good many years of listening to it, I am at last able, usually, to know the subject of conversation. Much that I have learnt to understand of the dialect is archaic Italian. In the speech we discover vestiges of ages long gone by.

Its first obvious attribute is a disfiguration of classic Italian. The musical beauty of that language consists largely in the many vowel endings; almost all of these are suppressed. For example *sono* becomes '*son*': the name Antonio becomes Anton, with

the last syllable ringingly prolonged — Anton-n-n-n. 'Sit down',
is, in proper Italian, '*s'accomadi*'; I have often been welcomed with
'*s'accom-m*'.

Archaic is the regular insertion of 'i' before 'e': *tiempo* for
tempo: Salierno for Salerno. O turns easily into u, so that Sorrento
becomes Surriento. Another ancient usage is a transposition of
the consonants in the diphthong gn. *Mangiare* (eat) becomes
magnare. Stranger is the insertion of an m before b: *Ubriaco*
(drunk) becomes *Umbriaco*. This may happen with combinations
of words. In the Cilento is a village called S. Mauro la Brucca;
I have heard the last two words pronounced *lambrucca*. This even
gets into print. Near Sorrento is the small town of Massa Lub-
rense; I have seen the sign on a bus Massalumbrense. Perhaps the
oddest transformation of all is of d to r; a local, in excitement,
will shout out *Maronna!* instead of *Madonna!* (But the most
cursory study of correct Italian reveals a very curious interchange-
ability of consonants.) Another peculiarity of pronunciation
involves the diphthong gl which may be transliterated ly. *Aglia*
(garlic) is properly pronounced something like *alya*: an Amalfitan
will say *aya*. I have teased a local friend about this. Say *Italia*, I
tell him, the last syllables being almost indistinguishable from
aglia properly pronounced. He says it normally. But when I asked
him to say *aglia* he can never say anything but *aya*.

Il (masculine 'the') is never used in dialect, only *lo*. This
accords with the language of Dante. However, in the dialect,
there are odd consequences. Lo is turned into *o*; and then the *o*,
as I have said, is turned into *u*. I once heard the sound *uragazz'*;
it took me a little thought to realise that this came from *il ragazzo*
(the boy). This is how the change came about: *il ragazzo — lo
ragazz' — lu ragazz' — 'u ragazz'*. One day I was sight-seeing and
looking for our goal, the driver asked for the cathedral. '*U duomo?*'
he said. I imagined at first that this must be an intrusion of French:
'*Où duomo?*' Then I realised that it involved no more than the
metamorphic process — *il — lo — lu — 'u*. 'The cathedral?' he
had said.

An English friend asked me: 'Do you know the dialect word
lancop — meaning "on top"?' I did not know it, but, with a

sound so devoid of Latinity, I guessed it to be, not a word but a compressed phrase — *la in cop*. I was confirmed in this by what I heard from a workman. He was up a ladder and, calling for something from his mate, he said 'Ca cop'. I then realised that the latter was indeed a separate word. *Ca* I must interpolate is the dialect form of *qua*, here. Qu in Italian is pronounced as in English. The dialect form is perhaps derived from a French pronunciation acquired in the time of the Angevin monarchy. *Coppa* I at last discovered means, in Neapolitan, top or summit. Long ago the word was good Italian; Dante, in the *Purgatorio* speaks of the sun falling on his *coppa*, meaning part of his head.

S before c becomes sh: thus Scala is pronounced Shcala. Double s often assumes the same sound: *qua in basso* (down here), becomes something like *Ca bash*.

I think it likely that I have picked up more dialect usage in my speech than is genteel; but I have much difficulty in following the local speech. To grasp at the trend, I have to add the cut final syllables. to notice the few local words I know, and then turn it all into Italian before I begin to understand what has been said. By that time the talk has usually got ahead of me. And there is the added difficulty of words not heard in proper Italian, and verbs differently conjugated.

As an example of local words, I will give one which I have heard so often, and have so often used myself, that I am in danger of uttering it in northern Italy, where it would be quite incomprehensible. *Palamido* is the name for a coarse fish of the mackerel group, much like the horse-mackerel of British waters. It is used — and I have never been able to guess why — to signify stingy. The fish is prepared for the table by being dried for several hours in the sun, and then fried. It is not appetising. I cannot think that this process has any bearing on the colloquial use of its name.

I could give other dialect words told me by my most frequent companions of the coast. The list would be too long to interest, and too short to instruct. I will only point out the deductions which can be made from my scanty account of the dialect. It is largely archaic, with intrusions from French and Spanish and, at

least about Amalfi, probably from Arabic.[1] Whether or not it
illustrates a corporate personality of Amalfitans, their way of
speech, in spite of its ugliness, is not inappropriate to the country;
an antique tongue is fitting to so ancient a community.

Proverbs as well as language distinguish a people. I will end this
chapter with a few:

To get into Paradise, you must climb one step at a time.

Better the egg today than the chicken tomorrow.

In the day look around; at night shut the door.

The next, I cannot interpret.

Who has taken fire, lives; who has taken bread, dies.

Relatives are like boots: the closer they are, the more they
trouble you.

The last, which rhymes, must be given in Italian:

A San Martino
Ogni fusto è vino

'On St. Martin's day every flask is wine.' There was a belief
that wine should not be bottled before St. Martin's day. My
friend, when he told me this, hobbled round the room like a
decrepit ancient. 'Don't, don't put the wine into bottles before
St. Martin's day,' he quavered in the pleading voice of an old
superstitious person.

---

[1] At least one alleyway in Amalfi is called *rua*, from the French *rue*. This word
is, I believe, not infrequently to be seen in Naples.

Since writing this I came across Signor Malato's *Vocabolarietto Napolitano*, which
is alluded to in Chapter Seven. He traces many dialect words to old Italian and
to Latin, both classical and mediaeval; Spanish and French are also invoked and
in a few cases Greek, Lombard, Oscan and Arabic.

CHAPTER X

Feasts of the Saints

On one August visit to the Amalfi coast, I ended my journey by the delectable sea-trip from Naples. It happened to be the fifteenth of the month, *ferragosta* — the most crowded and confused of Italian holidays, and also a most sacred occasion in the Roman church, the feast of the Assumption.

At Capri the boat had discharged most of the encumbering, noisy, jostling gay crowd, all urgent and restless in the pursuit of a few hours' joy.

> *Fleeting is the festal day, and to the feast*
> *Follows the common day; all human things*
> *Are snatched away by time. . . .*

So, roughly translated, Leopardi, who saw in momentary joy no more than the certainty of mortal disillusion. As I surveyed the jolly throng of passengers, fellow countrymen of Leopardi's, I wondered if the taste of later hours would be to them, as once to him, intolerably sour. I doubted it. Tremendous though he might be in his poetry of gloom, I cannot think that he sang the common sentiments of Italians; still less could he be thought of as speaking for the exuberant, affectionate southerners.

While we were waiting at Positano for passengers to embark and disembark, some rockets went off on shore, honouring briefly the reception in heaven of the Madonna. The principal church being of the Assumption, and contains that ancient, miraculously received painting of the Virgin. In towns where the most important church is dedicated to the Madonna, her Assumption is naturally the occasion of an especial feast. As the ship moved away, her siren sounded several times in homage to the Mother of God and Queen of Heaven.

I had often been told that the festa of the Assumption at Maiori was the best on the coast and thither in the evening I went with a friend.

Imperial processions of coronation, jubilee, great obsequies, even a lord mayor's show, with all the pictorial splendour of their presentation, are best seen by daylight. For the progress of saints, night-time is the proper scene. Shadows and half-lights make numinous and alive the passing image; its appearance is mystery, its recession the evanescence of a vision.

When we arrived in Maiori, Our Lady at Sea was moving along the main road, close to the shore and the low waves. Slowly, waveringly, carried by hefty men, head-high, she approached: finely shaped waxen features, crown, a long head of hair with curls like a judge's wig. Her garments were rich and sumptuously embroidered, in the style of the eighteenth century. She was near an open church, one of many she had to visit that night. She was put down, while the procession paused and a salute of fireworks went off. Circles of coloured stars, shoots of silver, sharp explosions, filled a nearer division of the sky. Again and again, like nets cunningly thrown, cones of sparkling light shot outward and downward. The Madonna stood in motionless dignity. Then, in the return of silence and under a black sky, she moved on through the yellow lamplight.

We climbed, rather breathlessly, up the steps to the lofty church. At intervals, spring-times of blossoming fire soared into the sky, marking each repose of the Virgin. More and more people were coming into the church and crowding the terrace outside, where we waited and watched.

At last, out of the darkness below, came the heralding canopy, twisting up the zigzag stairway. Children of the choir followed. Below was the road to Tramonti. Opposite, across the deep street, glowed, in the light of gleaming garlands, warm-coloured houses built in the manner of two centuries ago. Beyond, towards the sea, illustrating the filth of our own age, glimmered ugly blocks of contemporary flats. On roofs, figures wandered vertiginously, black against radiance, some running along terrifying edges.

A stir and a murmur in the waiting crowd presaged the advent of Our Lady at Sea. Her bearers running, with a pause at each turn, she dashed up on to the terrace. There she turned and gazed out over the gulf. At once, for her delight, a cascade of silver light glinted brilliantly for a while from a roof across the valley. It failed; she entered her church; the ceremony was over.

We went down to the shore, where we met a friend with two Italian Americans, over on a visit to their maternal coast. One, born in Maiori, was well acquainted with the customs of his native town. The hurrying of the Virgin represented, he gave me to understand, the speedy carrying to her chosen sanctuary of the sea-surrendered effigy. 'It's much the same in Positano, I suppose,' he said magnanimously, though a little grudgingly. I agreed with what he seemingly felt. A picture, although carried ashore by heavenly command as it befell at Positano, should not, I considered, rank equally in divine protocol with a wooden image which, with whatever supernatural aid, had found its own way to a hallowed and hospitable sanctuary.

Then began, with its long glories, the epilogue of the feast. There is, I have been told, a competition for the best display, each being contrived by a different group of people. The passion of honourable striving is often manifest in dark figures, fleetingly glimpsed as they scurry up and down behind jets and sprays of fire. Eagerness may bring disaster. It is still told how in Maiori, some years ago, a large bursting firework blinded a boy and destroyed his hands. Indeed, I have been assured that he is still alive today in his dreadful mutilation.

I was happy not to be a judge that night. 'One star differeth from another in brightness'; all seemed equal in beauty. Lovely — and natural, it seemed, as the northern lights — a heavenly display such as legend might have allowed to accompany holy appearances; soaring lights, now from one part of the beach, now from another, filled various quarters of the sky, soaring, spreading, dispersing, falling, colouring and enamelling with brightness the faintly starred night.

This I felt, as so often before, was an occasion when life on the coast approached its zenith. It was not a mere spectacle as on the

Fourth of June at Eton, or in old days at the Crystal Palace; it was not the visible delight of it which so totally beguiled me; the ambient faith of the people, pagan it could be called, with its multiplicity of spiritual beings, lares and lemures of all the parishes in the neighbourhood — this it was which made so bewitching the apparent beauty of whirring lights; the fires, like lit candles on the altar, were sacramental; in the hidden ritual of it all, it seemed to me, while loud explosions heralded, one after another, the close of the celebrations, as if I had been looking beyond the bounds of mortal life.

Popular amusements can illustrate the character of a people. Many are devised to delight the perpetual adolescent in man. An ordinary Englishman, in Italy for the first time, might easily think childish the Italian enjoyment of saintly processions and their accompanying fireworks, forgetting that he himself is equally childish when he sits watching a game of professional football. Italians enjoy football as well as any Englishman, but we have no such holy processions and displays. It was not always so. In his poem beginning 'Farewell, Rewards and Fairies', Richard Corbet, the friend of John Donne, wrote these stanzas:

> *Lament, lament old Abbies,*
> *The Fairies lost command,*
> *They did but change priests' babies,*
> *But some have changed your hand;*
> *And all your children stol'n from thence*
> *Are now turned* Puritans,
> *Who live as changelings ever since*
> *For love of your demesnes.*
>
> *At morning and at evening both,*
> *You merry were and glad;*
> *So little care of sleep and sloth*
> *Those pretty ladies had;*
> *When Tom came home from labour,*
> *Or Ciss to milking rose;*
> *Then merrily went your tabour*
> *And nimbly went their toes.*

Witness those Rings and Roundelays
Of theirs which yet remain.
Were footed in Queen Mary's days
On many a grassy plain.
But since of late Elizabeth
And later James came in,
They never danced on any heath
As when the time had been.

By which we note the Fairies
Were of the old profession,
Their songs were Ave Maries,
Their dances were procession. . . .

In looking at a few south-Italian festas we shall not only understand something more of those for whom they were contrived, but we may also gain some conception of sacred pleasures in England long ago.

I have sometimes been asked on the coast what festas we have in England. I can only bring up Guy Fawkes Day, with its fireworks and burning of the guy, atavistic vestige of human sacrifice. Our bonfires and fireworks are fun; but little of mystery remains in the celebrations. A lapsed Roman Catholic once asked me about the Anglican church. When I told him we did not invoke the saints, he exclaimed: 'But the saints are the poetry of religion!'

With all the secular circumstances of an Italian festa, the saint is lord over all; his image, borne in procession, becomes sacramentally alive. Whatever lighter or graver sins they may be planning that night, onlookers regard the moving effigy, for the time at least, as a live creature, the jealously esteemed protector of their community.

I have been to many festas, large and small, on the Amalfi coast. Much they have in common. In all the larger municipal festas, there will be a band. The best — I do not know why — come from Apulia, the most popular being apparently from Lecce and Gioia del Colle. 'We shall have the most beautiful music in all Italy,' I have been informed on such occasions.

After the procession a long concert will follow, with very long intervals. (In one town, I have been told, the public clock was put back, to trick the band into supplying extra music.) The village of Pogérola, on the hills west of Amalfi, has the peculiarity of providing singers as well as a band.

The climax is the display of fireworks which always ends with a prodigal discharge of rockets. The exhibitions must be very expensive, and a large part of the cost is met by contributions sent home from emigrant citizens. Each community disparages the festas of another. 'They're all thieves there,' I was told of one town. 'Nothing worth looking at,' was said of a festa invariably resplendent. A lady from Amalfi is said to have gone to the festa of the Magdalen at Atrani; in the rival town she put up an umbrella hoping, either by some sort of sympathetic magic to induce rain, or else to frighten visitors away with the assumed prospect of it.

She was trying to mar what in my opinion is the best spectacle of all.

At Atrani the deep, precipitous, narrow valley opens on to the sea in a rough triangle, standing on its apex and perhaps four hundred feet in depth. Towards the end of the display, with echoes bellowing from cliff to cliff, with roll and roar and reverberation from depths far up the hollow valley, rockets blaze into showers of stars, first singly, then more and more at a time until the whole vast opening is streaked with racing lights against their reflected glow on the wall of smoke which floats behind them (Pl. 24).

The smallest festa I have ever seen was in the diminutive hamlet of Sanbuco, no more than a church in a cluster of houses, nestling into the valley east of Ravello. The church is Romanesque and not much larger than a cattle shed. There were formerly three apses, but the northern one has been replaced by a very small sacristy. Inside are two images of the Madonna, one of which cannot be later than the early nineteenth century; the other, a thank-offering from a named donor, must derive from late in the same century. This is *La Madonna della Pumice*, a puzzling name, which seems to mean 'of the pumice'. The o in the proper word *pomice* (Latin *pumex*) would turn naturally to u in dialect. But I had noticed, in one of my rare readings of Horace, that he had written in ode eleven of book one

quae nunc oppositis debilitat pumicibus *mare Tyrrhenum* —

which may be rendered 'which now wears out the Tyrrhenian sea on opposing cliffs' (*pumicibus*). Mr. John Sparrow, Warden of All Souls, has told me that Horace uses *pumex* for rock generally. La Madonna del Pumice might well be translated the Madonna of the Rocks. In strict Italian, so far as I can find out, *pumice* is not used for 'rock'. An ancient Latin meaning, lost to the national language, appears to have survived in dialect.

I went there in bright sunny weather, on the Monday after Easter Monday. Deciduous trees had not yet put on their green; stretches of chestnut, with their tangles of grey twigs, lay across the hills, like luminous drifts of mist for ever motionless. A service was in progress; at its conclusion a few rockets were let off. I then went to watch an egg-rolling contest which is played at this festa and is, I was told, permitted only then.

Each player has a hard-boiled egg, with marks or colour distinguishing his own. They play on a smooth place in the path. Each man puts down a small stake. Eggs are rolled from the edge of the slope; they must not be pushed. The first player whose egg touches another's collects the pool.

They tossed for starting by a method known as *la morra*. Suppose Tom, Dick and Harry, having agreed to play in that order, must toss up to decide who shall begin. They first agree where to start the count. Let it be Dick. Each throws out a hand with one or more fingers extended. Let Tom have put out two fingers, Dick one, and Harry four. The total is seven. Starting with Dick, it will be seen that the count ends with him; he goes first. This, in the particular game, is unlucky; the later you roll your egg the safer you are, and the better chance you have of hitting another.

There is a simple game played by the *morra*; it is only a matter of betting on odds and evens. I had mentioned the practice to a friend who lives in central Italy. He questioned a local citizen and reported to me: 'Angelo says that it is an adult game and was, in his childhood, played at all the *osterie*. You call out a number while showing a number of fingers, and the game is played at great speed. Somebody not playing marks down the points. He said that the players calling out at this great speed made a noise almost like music. It is, I gather, unlikely that we shall see it being played, as the game was banned by law — Angelo thinks by Mussolini — as it was easy to quickly produce a knife, and stabbings were frequent.' (At each turn they each threw a hand out from behind their backs.)

In the cathedral museum at Salerno is a series of twelfth-century ivories of scenes from the old and new testaments. They are local work, Byzantine in style, and used to be considered panels of an altar front; later opinion judges them to have been part of a throne. At least two artists were involved, the new testament panels being finer work than those of the old.

In most representations of the symbols of the Passion, we find the dice with which the soldiers cast lots for the garment of Our Lord. In the panel of the Crucifixion at Salerno, the soldiers are playing the *morra* (Pl. 25). Monsignor Arturo Carucci, custodian of the museum, has written a monograph on the ivories, in which he says that the soldiers are generally represented as playing the *morra*. For myself, I have noticed this elsewhere only in some fourteenth-century frescoes at Tuscania, in the chapel of St. Francis. Defective observation on my part is very likely to blame.

The egg is commonplace as a symbol of the Resurrection. In this game played at Sanbuco we have come back to the liturgical nature of festal proceedings. This quality of sacred celebration I noticed in the first procession which I ever saw on the Amalfi coast. It was at the festa of the Magdalen in Atrani. At one stage the penitent saint was carried to the beach, resting at intervals to the sound of loudly exploding fireworks. Eventually she was set down close to the sea. At once many boats approached for her benediction, converging towards her like swans towards food thrown into the water for them.

Less beautifully, but even more lucidly, I comprehended this absolute blending of the natural and the supernatural at the

Ravello festival of S. Cosmas and S. Damian. Their festival, which is not elaborately carried out, lasts for more than a week. During the period, garlanded cars of pilgrims may be seen on the roads. The sanctuary is a grotto, low down in the cliff to the south-east of Ravello. Ancient in origin, the sanctuary has been restored so much that nothing is discernible of antiquity. The chapel is a squared-out cave, with large open windows in the wall of rock.

I saw two tiny coffins hanging up. The saints were twins who as doctors sometimes, it would seem, like Pantaleone, assisted medicine with miracle. The coffins had been prepared for dead children who, on invocation of the brothers, were restored to life.

The service of benediction was in progress, and I attended the rest of the ceremony. A man was looking in through one of the windows. At the elevation of the Host he gave a signal. The band struck up, while a salvo of rockets banged and blazed into the sky. Fireworks had become liturgical. Our reformers, however theologically justified, threw out a very big baby with the bath-water.

CHAPTER XI

Ultramontane Amalfi

It was natural that the domains of sea-trading Amalfi should extend along the southern coast of the peninsula. Strange is the extension of the republic northward, beyond the mountains, to where are now the towns of Gragnano and Léttere. I have never discovered when those towns were annexed, together with intervening country. History provides a plausible explanation.

In the sixth century, once he was secure on the throne of Constantinople, Justinian resolved to recover the western empire — north Africa, Spain, Italy and much of France, which were in the possession of barbarian conquerors, Gauls, Vandals and Goths. It was the last who possessed Italy. The emperor's reconquest began with the invasion of Sicily in 535; after eighteen years of gains and losses, during which Rome changed hands five times, the campaign was completed in March 553. Teias, king of the Goths, was with his army near the mouth of the Sarno, at the south of the Bay of Naples. Let Gibbon tell the rest:

'Teias maintained this important post, till he was deserted by his fleet and the hope of subsistence. With reluctant steps he ascended the *Lactarian* mount, where the physicians of Rome, since the time of Galen, had sent their patients for the benefit of the air and the milk.[1] But the Goths soon embraced a more generous resolution: to descend the hill, to dismiss their horses, and to die in arms, and in the possession of freedom. The king marched at their head, bearing in his right hand a lance, and an ample buckler

[1] Gibbon appends a note: 'Galen . . . describes the lofty site, pure air, and rich milk of mount Lactarius, whose medicinal benefits were equally known and sought in the time of Symmachus . . . and Cassiodorius. Nothing is now left except the name of the town of *Lettere*.'

in his left; with the one he struck dead the foremost of his
assailants; with the other, he received the weapons which every
hand was ambitious to aim against his life. After a combat of
many hours, his left arm was fatigued, by the weight of twelve
javelins which hung from his shield. Without moving from his
ground, or suspending his blows, the hero called aloud on his
attendants for a fresh buckler, but in the moment, while his side was
uncovered, it was pierced by a fatal dart. He fell: and his head,
exalted on a spear, proclaimed to the nations, that the Gothic
kingdom was no more.'

A few cities of Italy still remained in Gothic hands, but from
that day until the early twelfth century, on its conquest by the
Normans, the republic of Amalfi, although in fact independent,
was formally vassal to the Byzantine empire. Is it an unwarrant-
able supposition the Romans of Amalfi — for such they were —
had assisted at the battle, and had remained in possession of those
northern territories? Their extent is historically indeterminate. A
Doge of Amalfi, in 1033, issued a proclamation 'from the castle
of Léttere in the territory of Stabia'. I quote from Camera who
says, in a note, that many other documents of the time describe
Léttere as being in the territory of Stabia — that is of Castellammare. Was the latter town, or a part of it, at some time subject to
Amalfi?

These outposts of Amalfitan empire are most conveniently
reached by the road through Agérola. The climbing road is
usually in full view of the coast and the sea; sometimes it darts
in and out of narrow valleys, with fractured rocky cliffs, like
Cyclopean walls; through the parish of Furore, the road coils its
way up in enormous loops and then seems to pause before
turning inland.

Here we are in different country. Green from the moisture of
hill mists and of rain are fertile fields, and among them many
large chestnut trees. Agérola is a big village of houses with pitched
roofs to throw off rain and snow. Coming from the low domes
and flat roofs of the sun-smitten coast, we might almost fancy
ourselves in another continent. I have been told that at Agérola,

20. Maiori: S. Maria a Mare: English alabaster of the Assumption (page 149)

21. Maiori: S.Maria de Olearia: eleventh-century frescoes in the grotto-crypt. (page 151)

in the Good Friday procession, a live man used to be tied to the Cross. I have also been told that it has a *pizzería* of exceptional quality.

Subject at one time to Amalfi, Agérola is now, unhistorically, in a different province. We have passed from the wide-flung province of Salerno into that of Naples. In consequence letters from Amalfi to Agérola, having to go through the provincial capital, may take two days, while the bus gets there in an hour or so.

At a short distance from Agérola, where I have found no antiquities of interest, the tunnel is reached which points at Vesuvius. I have stopped at the far end of the tunnel for a perfunctory botanical search. I found there, for the first time in the south, a plant I know well from north Italy, the elegant, unguent-scented, yellow-flowered sage, *Salvia glutinosa* (it is hardy and I have naturalised Italian plants in my wood at home). The woods above are probably good ground for flower-hunting.

From the tunnel the road winds down among steep woods, mostly of chestnut and the local ash. Forests of these hills supplied timber for ships of the Amalfitan fleet. We are in a damper climate, and vegetation is richer than to the south. Primroses are abundant here in early spring. The woods are regularly cropped, providing poles for the pergolas on which vines and lemons are grown. As the road descends northward, a valley opens to the right. On a promontory from the eastern flank is a church, with campanile and portico. According to a map, this is S. Maria a Monte Pino; it is mentioned by one guide-book, but only in the directions for a walk. It appears to be Romanesque and, although involving a long walk, it should be worth visiting.

The first village is Pimonte — a corruption of Piedimonte as, over two and a half centuries ago, Pansa referred to it. It is not far from Gragnano. The church stands on some level ground, a little above the centre of the village. A guide-book mentions a Madonna and Child, of about 1500, by Protasio Crivelli. Imagining Protasio to be a relation of his great Venetian namesake, I was anxious to see it. I found near the church a boy who got me the key. I wandered round, and three polite, smartly-dressed men followed me. At first I could not see any picture of the Madonna and Child, until at last, to the right of the entrance, I saw them in fresco, rather faded; the painting is beautiful, though by no means of the greatest merit. The three men stood by me while I looked at it. They seemed curious.

'That is by a Venetian painter,' I said rashly; 'he was the son of a great artist.'

They seemed to be impressed. Unluckily I had misled them. Protasio Crivelli was a Milanese who died in 1506; at Capodimonte in Naples there is a painting by him of St. Martin and the beggar.

More enjoyable than this fresco are effigies of saints, dressed in robes which cannot be later than the eighteenth century, or even earlier. There is a splendid image of St. Michael — to whom the church is dedicated — transfixing the devil in the shape of a man with a serpent's tail. This form of the devil, conquered by St. Michael, can be seen in an altar-piece in the cathedral of Ravello.

The three men left while I was looking round the church. When I went out they were dismantling a stall on the flat space in front of the church. They were not, as I had supposed, prosperous inhabitants of Pimonte, but itinerant merchants who had been selling wares at a festa. Whatever their trade, they were friendly and good-mannered; I was glad to have met them.

Although the road is long from Amalfi to Gragnano, a foot-path of no more than about eight miles long crosses the peninsula from Scala. This passes the site of the now vanished hermitage of S. Maria dei Monti, where for a time S. Alfonso dei Liguori lived in retirement. I had many times thought desirously of doing the walk, and an old friend from Atrani, Mimi Gatto, promised to show me the way. (The first name has no implications of effeminacy; it is a diminutive of Domenico.) On the morning fixed it poured with rain. A second time this happened. Before another planned start Mimi was suddenly called on to do work he could not get out of. I felt like a frustrated lover; it seemed my destiny never to visit S. Maria dei Monti.

By old custom many people, on Easter Monday, go to S. Maria dei Monti for games and picnics. This jollification is called *pasquone* (pronounced in dialect *pascone*). Weather and possibility contrived at last that my excursion had to be undertaken on Easter Monday. With cheese, bread, salami and a bottle of wine, we set off from Scala a little before 8 o'clock in the morning.

'We could take a steep way straight up the hill. It would be all right for me,' said Mimi; 'but not for you,' he added in consideration for my years and frailty. 'There's a better way, although it's longer.'

We went up past S. Pietro in Campoleone, restored but with its rustic narthex destroyed, and the remains piled horribly around the edges of the piazza, like walls of terraces. Soon we passed the hamlet of S. Caterina with a partly Romanesque church, level with Campidoglio and to the east of it. Then we were in open woods. I saw mistletoe on an apple tree — for the first time on the peninsula and an omen of promise richer than I knew. *Cyclamen repandum* was blossoming here and there.

I know before starting on a mountainous excursion that a time will come when short breath and thumping heart will almost make me wish I had never set out. After about an hour, just when shameful thoughts were upon me, we heard tinklings from a herd of goats. It was a good excuse to sit down. They came up past us. The billies were belled. Their broad collars were wooden, bent, I presume in steam, and incised with geometric patterns such as decorate archaic vases.

'There's nobody with them,' said Mimi in surprise. Very soon, however, the tiny herdsman appeared, a boy less than ten years old. He was too shy to talk, but as he went off into the wood he began singing an ancient song, one of those which it seems can never have echoed within the enclosure of walls. It was a cry of the forest and the mountains.

The going was laborious. I was sage enough not to ask how far we still had to climb. Nor did I look up to deceptive summits but encouraged myself with the sight, now far below us, of Ravello. We came out of the woods on to the bare hill-side. The failing end of a sirocco was blowing its damp air into wisps of tattered cloud against the cold mountain. All was sunlight. We were on the side of a broad, steep valley; shouting and singing came out of it.

'They are going up from Scala or Pontone,' said Mimi, 'and will be there before us.'

Earlier he had remarked on the absence of company. 'Nobody walks now,' he had said; 'at one time there would have been many people coming up from Ravello.'

I stopped to rest, and we were joined by a stalwart young man, an acquaintance of Mimi's. He told us how, in summer, he would stay up on the heights for weeks, in charge of his flocks. Mimi told him where I was staying. He asked me to arrange so that he might collect the waste herbage there to feed his beasts with. Many people keep three or four sheep, and a cow or two. These live in stalls. Children or women of the family cut anything green from wall or bank as fodder. You may often see them shouldering huge green bundles. I said that this little harvest had already been allowed to another. On this he expressed — enviously, I think — contempt for the named beneficiary.

He pointed at heights to the east. An English battery, he told us, had been there during the war (some Germans were holding out at Chiunzi, above Tramonti).

'My father was frightened of the Germans,' he said, 'and he went to the English. He waved a handkerchief, and shouted "Don't shoot!". After that I used to take the donkey and fetch water for them.'

'How old were you?' I asked.

'Four,' he answered.

We went on together, and soon I wanted to rest again. It was better, said the shepherd, to go on slowly, never stopping.

'My heart is beating too hard,' I said, 'and I must sit down.'

He looked alarmed, evidently expecting an embarrassing collapse. I said my heart was all right, but I needed a rest. He went on and Mimi, I felt, was pleased with his absence.

'There it is,' he said, and pointed to a summit gratifyingly close. Quite soon we were at the top, about 3,000 feet high (Pl. 26).

We found a youthful party — the same, I think, as we had heard chattering and singing on the steep ascent. They had an album of records, and were playing a gramophone. We rested a while and looked down into the hollow slopes of the mountain, and on to the sea glittering far below. To the left were the woods and slopes where we had come; to the right, huge cliffs; in front, the steep valley. All was filled with luminous air. I had expected to have come on the sight of Vesuvius and the Bay of Naples. Instead, to the north of us were small pastures and open woods.

'I should like to stay up here for a month,' said Mimi, 'away from people and the town,' and he talked about the malice and gossip he had heard and put up with. I told him stories about the same pests in my own village.

'What! Does it happen in England too?' he asked in a tone of surprise and disillusion which flattered most undeservingly many of my compatriots.

We set off down towards the north, and soon came to flat pasture lying in a shallow basin. Thin woods were around it, and, over much of the turf, black stalks of last year's mulleins made a miniature dead forest. It might have been a nook in Kent except that above the trees were cliffs of bright grey rock.

Many young people were there (Pl. 27). Some were playing football; some were lying down in groups. There were a pony, a donkey and a mule on which boys were galloping bare-back. Beyond the flat turf was a house. We sat down on the still dewy grass, in the fringe of the trees, and drank a little wine. Very soon I suffered a sharp botanical exasperation.

A party came towards us across the field. When they were near, I saw that a girl among them was carrying a large bunch of poet's narcissus, a flower I had never considered seeing in Amalfitan territory. 'Can we ask her where she got them?' I asked Mimi. My question did not need answering. A friend of his, a youth from Scala, called Pantaleone, came up. He, too, had a bunch of the narcissus. We gave him a glass of wine and I asked him where they grew. Some way off, he answered, on Monte Cerreto (this rises to above 4,000 feet eastward of S. Maria dei Monti). I asked if we were likely to find it on the way down to Gragnano. 'No,' he said, and offered me some flowers.

I said it was bulbs I wanted, and then saw in his bunch one which had come up with the flower. This, when I asked for it, he very complacently gave to me, adding some flowers. At least, I reflected, in a few years I might raise a small assembly of the plant.

At one time I had an obsession for these flowers, and had collected varieties in southern France and in the Alps. Botanists divide them into several species, many or few according to the temperament of the classifier. At home, from Pantaleone's gift, clumsily dried, I identified it as the type species, *Narcissus poeticus*. I had never before seen it wild.

Pantaleone was in charge of the animals on which heavier burdens, such as records and gramophones, had been carried up. 'You should come and spend several days here in the summer,' he said. 'You can get the key of the house from the mayor of Ravello. The food would be carried on a mule, and it would be used to fetch water from the spring.' Every spoken description of S. Maria dei Monti ends with 'There's a spring there.' Its waters, you will be told, are finer and lighter than any other waters, and are sovereign for stirring the appetite.

While we were talking, a look as of desire came into Mimi's face. He was gazing at the footballers, and I recalled how I had often seen him kicking a football about on the quay at Atrani.

'Do you want to stay here, or to go on? We will do just as you please,' he said, with all the courtesy of a professional guide. It was early still, and I did indeed want to stay, to look about me and to savour the jolly company. Ecstatically he joined a game.

I can hardly call it football. The games put me in mind of the croquet in *Alice in Wonderland*. In the middle of the field was a group intending serious sport but, so far as I could make out, with only one pair of goal-posts, close to where I was watching. At either end games even less consistent were in progress. Sometimes all the balls were in one group and nobody seemed to care which he kicked. The goal, when a ball was available, was shot at from either direction. Players left the games or joined them as they pleased. This simplified things and imposed no limit of time. Somebody, it is true, in the more coherent game, occasionally blew a whistle; it seemed no more than a fitting musical accompaniment, for I could not discover any response among the players.

Panteleone asked me if I liked football. 'No,' I answered, and told of my miseries at school where I was twice given a beating, not for playing lazily but for playing no better than I could, which was very badly. 'Never since then have I liked football,' I concluded.

The party of the narcissus was close by. They were playing records on a gramophone which turned waveringly, and the sounds were distressing. I wondered why it disturbed me so little and then, while I surveyed them, the answer came to me.

The southerners are most of them comely above the average. In movement or in repose they have the gracefulness of fine animals. These, sitting or reclining, had grouped themselves without thought into a composition which asked little mending. Thus, I thought, would they have set and ranged themselves, had one been playing a lute or a guitar while another sang. No matter the wailing mechanic notes of the gramophone: no matter the flash holiday clothes: I was seeing what Giorgione had seen before he painted his *Fête Champêtre* (the one girl among them, to be sure, was not in the nude). I thought of snatching a photograph but the sight of the camera would, I knew, stiffen them into false and rigid poses.

I noticed, a few feet away, a spot of lilac. It was a belated flower of *Crocus imperati*. Thus awakened, I made a little botanic tour. A Dutchman's pipe (*Aristolochia*) was sprouting up everywhere, with its strange tubular flower. The turf was starred blue and white by the Apennine anemone. *Scilla bifolia* was there, and leaves of the dwarf *Colchicum neapolitanum*.

I walked across to the house. From its form I should judge it to have been adapted from a chapel. On the wall someone had written up: '*Viva S. Maria. Viva S. Maria e Gesu.*' 'Long live Saint Mary. Long live Saint Mary and Jesus' — the formula of political *graffiti*. Above was a tiled panel of the Madonna and Child, dating from the 1950s. The manufacture of ceramics has for centuries been an industry of the Amalfi coast. Although hideous and vulgar things are so often made nowadays, the ancient tradition is strong and lively, and lovely things are made too, such as this Madonna.

A biologist had asked me about moles in south Italy. It had been suggested, he said, that they might live entirely on the surface, without making mole-hills. The question answered itself for me now. I saw mole-runs and mole-hills. I did not see any large mounds such as they nest in at home.

After an hour or so Mimi was evidently resigned to no more football, and we left a scene which was, in the strictness of truth, idyllic. The landscape through which we went was still, save for the occasional distant vision of fierce cliffs, calm and pastoral. A translucent haze diffused sunlight into shadowed places. Here came the flocks and herds in summer. Many bushes of broom had been nibbled by goats into neat topiary shapes. Shrubs and trees were around us, and innumerable varied stars of the anemone. The way was easy. Whenever we met someone, Mimi asked about the way to Gragnano. Answers were curiously discouraging: it was rough, steep, long, difficult, even, it was hinted, dangerous. Since people certainly came up from Gragnano, I did not let myself be too much dismayed. In any case, the walk in this high, quiet country, among the pointed mountains, was entrancing. I would, I resolved, enjoy myself while I could.

A steep rocky path beyond the leveller champaign, and with drops below too vertiginous for my liking, brought us down to the shady spring. A small, cold stream gushes out of a hole in the mountain. The spot is marked on the map Acquafredda, cold water. We unpacked our provisions and, almost ritually, I filled a glass with the water and drank it. I am not, I trust, a victim of too easy persuasion. Yet, after my relish of the limpid draught, I began to understand how, in torrid countries, there may be connoisseurs of water as in the temperate West of wine.

Wine we drank with our food. A party from Ravello turned up, friends of Mimi. Our little party became gay; they offered me some of their own wine, delicious, heavy and the colour of amber. Ours they refused. Indeed Mimi would not drink much. I could not bring myself to throw any of it away, so finished it, and we filled the rinsed bottle with water from the spring. Our friends from Ravello knew how to find the path to Gragnano; again there were implications of warning.

At the top of the path from the spring we were faced by a vast slab of almost vertical rock, like the wall of a fortified city. Our way was across the inner shoulder. I had horrid visions of traversing a ledge along a similar cliff. Perhaps apprehension appeared in my face.

'Can you do it?' asked Mimi.

'We'll try,' I answered; 'if it frightens me too much, we shall have to go back by Scala.'

Pilgrims in allegory come on signs to confirm their proper way. We scrambled easily up the rock and then, almost at once, I saw a small yellow pansy; it was *Viola lutea*, which is to be found in many sub-alpine pastures and is native in England. This is the only true mountain plant which I have seen on the peninsula. Heartened by the propitious discovery, I got to the top. The path was rough, and the declivities below it were very steep and very deep; but nothing to drive me ignominiously back by the way we had come. The path was very long, winding gently downwards, in and out of valleys; sometimes the sea was visible to the north; sometimes we were enclosed in a huge hollow of the mountains. Woods, in all the bright freshness of half unfolded leaves, were still bright with anemones. Suddenly I shouted, abrupt in my excitement: 'Bring me the bag and give me the fork!'

In earth above me I had seen, for all Pantaleone's warning, the narcissus. I collected as much as I needed. Afterwards, looking at the map, I discovered that we were then on the flanks of Monte Cerreto. Curiously enough the narcissus was then flowering hundreds of feet above us, while these were still in bud.

The path is an old, dilapidated mule-track and must once have been firmly paved. Now all the stones were in unstable confusion. Gone was the coolness of mountain air. Twice we stopped and drank the spring water. The way was through a country of beauty and magnificence, steep mountains of forest, with rock breaking through in cliffs (Pl. 28). All day the sun had been brilliant, inflaming a thin golden haze which glowed into sunless valley and shadowed precipice. Tired and tireder though I might be, I had nothing to complain of. I reflected how rains and interruptions, by wrecking my earlier plans, had forced me to S. Maria dei Monti when people were at *pasquone*, and just at a time when unlooked-for flowers were to be seen. We were, throughout all our progress, as I told Mimi, crossing territory of the Amalfitan republic where it was widest. We had walked up from Scala in two hours; three it took us before we reached the first houses near Gragnano. A man passed us.

'Have you come from S. Maria dei Monti?' he asked.

'Yes,' I answered, adding boastfully, 'we came up from Scala.'

Gragnano is renowned for two of its products. It has a large export of pasta; in the nearest town to my home in England is a shop which sells much pasta from Gragnano. Far more excellent is the wine, a heavy, red wine, slightly aerated. This is undoubtedly the best wine made on the peninsula. An indistinguishable wine is also made in Léttere. The wine of Gragnano was accidentally the occasion to me of an unusual mortification.

I have always been as careful as I could not to correct my natural English accent in speaking Italian. The danger is that otherwise I would pick up a strong Neapolitan accent; I should become like an Italian who had learnt his English in a village of Lancashire or Durham. Well! I was passing through Gragnano with two friends, and we went to a vendor of wine and ordered a bottle. While we were drinking, a man, learning that we were English, brought me a letter to translate. It was from the Ministry of Labour, and addressed to a youth who was looking for work in England. I gave the general meaning in Italian. 'It's wonderful,' said another man; 'he's turned an English letter into Neapolitan dialect!'

I have not mastered the dialect; yet this intended praise must imply that, in other parts of Italy, my speech will sound more peculiar than the average foreigner's.

I had hitherto seen no more of Gragnano than the main street.

This has no pavements and is gay as a market. I had noticed nothing of artistic merit in the place; yet it was, I felt, pleasing to the eye and of great charm. Our way from the mountains had carried us to the east of the town, where happy discoveries were to be made.

For a while we walked beneath relics of the old tufa walls of Léttere, once the grander city. Lower, we came to a street of small, massively built mediaeval houses. Mimi, by profession an electrician, has missed his proper vocation. He is a born guide. Over parts unknown to him, he had looked after me with delicate care, often, in rocky places, showing me just where to put my feet. Now, he companionably enjoyed the beauty of these houses, and he was later to notice beauties of architecture without my pointing to them. (In one matter alone he fell short; he could not, he confessed, take any interest in wild flowers.) At last we came to a square in Gragnano which I had never seen before. We drank beer at a stall, and looked round. There were several small palaces, modest but beautiful, and some with good iron-work on them. In England I would have dated them late eighteenth century, or Regency. In Italy, as I have often found, such judgement may be a hundred years too late (this is particularly true of church monuments). Whatever their period, these palaces have a quiet nobility such as I had not found in other buildings of Gragnano.

I had lately read of a church which was said to contain an imitation of Raphael's Transfiguration, by a sixteenth-century Sienese, Marco Pini, who did much work in the south. It is the church of Corpus Domini. It was locked. There was compensation in the wooden doors, fine carved work of the late Renaissance. I did not have to content myself, however happily, with these. Mimi took charge. The priest was out, so he went about asking various people, including a policeman, where we could get the key. All were polite, but none could tell us. Then he saw a priest; he was only there on a visit, he told us, but he had been into the church.

'There is a copy of Raphael's Transfiguration which I want to see,' I asked.

'How did you know?' he asked in startled astonishment. I admitted to having got my information from a guide-book.

'The copy is *exact*,' he said, and then told us where to find the sacristan. So we got into the church.

I looked round in vain for the familiar composition and eventually had to ask for it. The copy is not exact, although the design, and in particular the drawing of the figures, would seem to be much influenced by Raphael. It is astonishing that Pini should have paraphrased only that part of the painting which is nowadays allowed to have been executed by Raphael. The Transfiguration alone is represented, without the scene below of the demoniac boy. The church has a rich and delightful decorative ceiling, painted by an unnamed artist of the mid-eighteenth century.

All this was an accession of richness to a day which had already so immensely enriched my conception of Amalfitan lands. My destiny, so stern at first, had in the end allowed me far more than I would ever have dared to hope for.

Even these discoveries did not disturb my old conviction that the chief artistic glory of Gragnano is to be found in a little primitive village on the fringe of it.

A short way inland is a small hill, like an island in the valley. The hill was at one time covered by a large castle, and the village is called Castello. Remains of the castle are to be seen in many of the buildings. The small church, of the twelfth century, is one of the most charming in all the Amalfitan territories.

There is a road being made into Castello; the only time I was ever driven up it, the exhaust pipe got broken. On my earlier visits it needed about half an hour's walk, down into the valley and up again. I first went that way in autumn, and cyclamen flowers fringed the terrace-edges by the path like lobelias or alyssum in a cottage garden.

The church is at the far end of the village. Beside it are two colossal cypresses, of which the inhabitants affirm that they are older than the church. Tragically, the larger of the two — an immense tree — was destroyed by killing frosts early in 1963.

The portico is, in principle, like the demolished one of S.

Pietro in Campoleone, in Scala, but here both design and
construction are superior. It is a wall pierced by three pointed
arches, of which the central is the largest. Over the last is a
Renaissance carving of the Madonna and Child. Above are
fragments of mosaic; there is evidence that they were once parts
of a Cosmatesque pulpit. The curves of the arches are decorated
with masks, startling to me as an apparition. Such masks are
quite often to be seen in English Norman churches. At Avington, not far from my home in Berkshire, is a fine series; such are
also to be seen on the west door of Iffley near Oxford. The masks
at Castello differ from these English counterparts only in not
being beaked; they come from the same world of the spirit,
and emphasise the ecumenical nature of Christian art in the
early middle ages. Good carved tombstones have been set in
the inner wall of the portico. The nave of the church is divided
from the aisles by four antique columns on either side. There
was once a ceramic floor; beautiful fragments are still visible.

Against the west wall is a little Romanesque baptistry, pointed
arches on four classical columns of which one is twisted. The
font is of the early sixteenth century and bears, amazingly, the
Medici arms. My amazement at this was abated when I learnt that
Giovanni di Medici, afterwards Pope Leo X, became in 1510 —
adolescens, as the report puts it — Archbishop of Amalfi.[1]
Though he may never have visited Amalfi, his office can explain
the appearance in Castello of his family arms.

On my first visit, I was shown into the church by a young
builder who was working next door on the priest's house. The
previous incumbent, I was given to understand, had been an un-
fastidious Sicilian; his successor required something better, and
the house was being put into order. There is a small Romanesque
campanile which I wanted to investigate. I expected to go up a
staircase; instead I was taken alarmingly up ladders on the
outside.

---

[1] The date is probably wrong, for he would by then have been thirty-five. I have
read of him that 'he received the tonsure at the age of seven and was soon loaded
with rich benefices and preferments'. We must assume, I suspect, a more juvenile
consecration.

From the highest point I noticed long avalanches of mud through wooded slopes of the valley. I recalled how, not long before, under tremendous rain, the deep viscous soil had flowed down like lava and overwhelmed a village near by. I asked about it, adding: 'You must have been safe here on this hill.' 'It was terrible!' he said. 'It began early in the morning. There was a fog, and we could see nothing. There was a tremendous noise which went on for a long time. Nobody knew what was happening. It was like the end of the world.'

While I was on my way back, I stopped at a small bar for a drink of beer. It was soon apparent that, in this lost village, a foreigner was a very strange creature. I asked when a foreigner had last been there. A French lady, they told me, had come to Castello about nine months before. I asked the price of the beer, and was charged rather more than I would expect to pay at a smart establishment. I was about to challenge the amount, and then thought, No! They must have heard of vast riches brought to other places by tourists. What was I in Castello but a tourist? What else could they do but overcharge me? It was more touching than vexatious. And I must in fairness add that on a later visit I was asked an entirely reasonable price.

On another occasion, with friends, I met the priest for whom the house had been modernised. He took us round the church and enjoyed our appreciation of it.

'There is something much more interesting in my garden,' he said; 'I think it may be to do with the cult of Aesculapius.'

He showed us, beyond his vegetable patch, the stone figure of a man, with a snake around his legs. It was a twin to the figure which holds up the reading-desk on the larger pulpit in the cathedral of Salerno. This, with the small pieces of mosaic on the portico, is all that remains of the probably magnificent Cosmatesque pulpit which I have postulated.

To the south of Gragnano is Léttere, last refuge of the last king of the Goths. In the tenth century it became a bishopric, under the archbishop of Amalfi; the diocese was small, comprising only Léttere, Gragnano and Pimonte.

The town itself, that ancient Roman health resort, seems to be of little interest, with no obvious monuments of decayed grandeur. But to the south, on the lip of the steep valley, is the castle.

I was advised to visit this by the Ravellese painter Giuseppe di Lieto. Rarely have I had better advice. North of Léttere is a small valley, and beyond it is an elevation, whose farther flanks fall very steeply to the plain. On this is the castle. It has a central keep, and along the walls are three round bastions. Apart from the magnificent Castel Nuovo in Naples, this, though smaller than them, is almost the only building of its kind in Campania comparable with the great castles of Apulia. It was built by Amalfitans not later than the tenth century. It was also worked on by the Angevins (Pl. 29).

On the south edge of the little valley, between the castle and the main hill, is a quiet restaurant. I sat on its terrace and drank frothy Léttere wine. While I drank I gazed at the magnificence of the castle, which stood up as though it had emerged from hiding, so unexpected is the vision of it. Its keep and outer walls can, in fact, be seen from the valley beyond; from there, with its image diminished by distance, it would be difficult to guess at its true splendour.

Quietly enlivened by the local wine, I went into the castle. Some men already there warned me to be careful; there were holes, they said, with deep cisterns below them. This is true and, since all the floor is overgrown, it would be easy to fall through unawares. Whether they are cisterns or dungeons, I cannot tell. The minute risk is worth taking. Apart from its own beauty, the castle is most dramatically placed. Through one void window can be seen Naples and the sea; through another Vesuvius; north are the plain and the high inland mountains. But I would rather not go near to these last windows, for just outside is a fearful drop. On the east side of the inner walls are remains of a plastered apse, evidently of the chapel; still may be seen, very faintly, ghosts of old frescoes.

Eastward of the castle, and enclosed on the north side by a wall, are the ruins of a church. It has the wreckage of a good baroque door. Beyond is a chapel, crowned by a low dome on pendentives, with all the facing lost. I tried to make this Romanesque. The walls on which it rests have the remains of baroque frescoes, and this chapel is almost certainly of the seventeenth or eighteenth century, built after the church had gone to ruin. I found the same problem in a derelict church on the inland fringes of Pogérola above Amalfi. (An architectural expert, of course, would never for a moment have been puzzled by either.) These pauses in judgement indicated a fact which I never remember having heard mentioned. The Gothic architecture of Italians was always an unsympathetic aberration. (This is a strange fact when we remember how marvellously were Gothic forms adopted and transmitted by Giovanni Pisano; but the only fine, pure Gothic buildings in Italy were designed by foreigners.) Italian artists can never lay their classical spirit, nor should they attempt it. The legitimate succession of Italian architecture is from the Romanesque, with its antique origin, through the perfection of the early Renaissance, with its many domed buildings, to the baroque. Countless baroque churches are cruciform, with a dome over the crossing; the same is often true of Romanesque churches. Most of the baroque domes are on pendentives, as are many Romanesque domes. Sometimes the dome rises from a polygon defined by pillars, as with the sixth-century S. Vitale in Ravenna and — let me give the incongruous comparison — the Italianate seventeenth-century St. Paul's in London.

It is likely that this ruined church was the old cathedral of Léttere, whose bishopric was established in 984. In 1570, according to Pansa, the cathedral having become ruined, and being without dwellings near it for citizens, priests and even the bishop himself, Pope Pius V authorised the establishment of a new cathedral in the town; one reason given for the Pope's compliance was the old cathedral being remote from habitation and exposed to the depredation of thieves; relics and treasures were moved to their new security. The position and state of the old church are accordant with all this.

The finest existing part of the old church is the tower. Although dilapidated, most of the structure is complete. It is very like the campanile of Ravello cathedral and must also date from the

22. Furore: S. Elia: altar-piece by Antonello da Capua (page 165)

thirteenth century. In its days of perfection it could have been the more beautiful of the two. The Saracenic decoration is more elaborate; though much of the inlaid stone-work has gone, the old patterns are easy to trace. And still, a noble ruin beside the most noble castle, it stands and testifies to the old, long-lost glories of Léttere, once a bishopric and a strong outpost of the Amalfitan republic.

CHAPTER XII

Amalfi Outremer

In the year 866, Sergius, Duke of Naples, seized the bishop of that town, his uncle Athanasius, and imprisoned him in the Castel del'Ovo which stands on an island, now joined to the mainland by a short causeway. At the request of the emperor, Ludwig II, the Amalfitans with their fleet rescued the captive.[1] In gratitude the emperor gave to Amalfi Capri which had formerly belonged to Naples. This transfer of authority disturbed the Byzantine emperor who was nominal sovereign of southern Italy. He protested without effect; Amalfi, for all her Byzantine vassalage, took no notice, but took Capri.

It has been said of Amalfi that her imperialism was commercial and not territorial. She had spread her dominion, it is true, along the south coast of the peninsula, and northward, as we have seen, beyond the mountains to Gragnano and Léttere, and even farther; but Capri and the Galli, or Siren Isles, are all that she ever acquired in the way of possessions overseas.

The Galli are three small islands off the south-west shores of the peninsula. They are sometimes referred to nowadays as the Siren Isles, for here was the abode of the sirens, and here passed Odysseus, roped to the mast, so that he might listen to their unmatched song, with no fear of following the irresistible and fatal

---

[1] It is to be doubted if the bishop deserved rescuing. On the death of his nephew, a brother of Athanasius, another Sergius, succeeded to the dukedom. He fell under the Pope's displeasure for allying himself with Saracens, and Athanasius, conceiving an appetite for temporal power, had him blinded and sent to Rome, where he died miserably. No sooner duke, than the bishop commenced aggressive campaigns, allying himself for the purpose with Saracens. Ignoring both papal protests and excommunication, he maintained for some considerable time this outrageous conduct.

call. At the extreme end of the peninsula, on the Punta Campanella, never a part of Amalfitan territory, there is said to have
been a temple dedicated to the sirens.

I once heard, narrated rather incoherently, a legend accounting
for their name, Galli, which means roosters. It was told me by
an amiable, elderly Italian lady who spoke an enthusiastic but
most imperfect English. I am therefore not quite confident about
her story. (For all my shortcomings in the language, we had much
better have talked in Italian; but it would have seemed rude not to
answer in English.) However, this is what I coherently deduced
from her obscure tale. At one time cocks used to arise out of the
sea off Positano, and crow. The perplexed and frightened inhabitants consulted a white witch who told them to throw stones at
the cocks when ever they appeared, upon which they would sink
back into the sea again. This advice was followed for some time.
One day it was neglected, and the cocks turned into rocky
islands, the Galli.

I have never been to any of the Galli. The chief island is now
again appropriately associated with music and magic, for
Léonide Massine has built himself a house there. In 1919, when I
was still a schoolboy, I lied to my house-master, saying that I had
an appointment with my dentist in London. He believed me; I
was allowed to go, and that afternoon I went to a matinée of the
Diaghileff ballet, my first vision of that incomparable body. One
ballet which I saw then was *La Boutique Fantasque*, a new work
of Massine who appeared in it. I was to see it many times again,
and I never lost the immediate, entranced sense that here was
one of those rare works of perfection with which we are so seldom
blessed.

These islets, hardly to be thought of geographically, swim in
seas of legend and of art. Hear Browning as he celebrated
them in *The Englishman in Italy:*

> *there slumbered*
> *As greenly as ever*
> *Those isles of the siren, your Galli;*
> *No ages can sever*

The Three, nor enable their sister
To join them — halfway
On the voyage, she looked on Ulysses —
No further today;
Tho' the small one, just launched on the wave,
Watches breast-high and steady
From under the rock, her bold sister
Swum halfway already.
. . . Then stand there and hear
The birds' quiet singing, that tells us
What life is, so clear!
The secret they sang to Ulysses,
When, ages ago,
He heard and he knew this life's secret,
I hear and I know!

Well may legend have given them a living birth!

The Galli must have been valuable to Amalfi, as look-outs and outposts of defence. But when I look at them I think, not in strategic or historical terms, but rather of old legends, and of the great artist who has made himself a retreat there, and who has enriched so many lives with the fantasies of his genius.

Capri was a different matter. It brought wealth, no doubt, to Amalfi. More important, it must have been of enormous advantage in defence against Naples and Sorrento, with both of whom she was sometimes at war.

Norman Douglas, in *Siren Land* records that, after this transfer of sovereignty, Amalfitan names first began to be known in Capri (here implying not only imperialism but, more reprehensible, colonisation). This is probably fallacious. It was the nature of Amalfitans to settle abroad in close commercial communities; many were already established in Naples and Salerno and other large cities; it is most unlikely that there had hitherto been not even a few of them in Capri.

The transfer, whatever its imperial impropriety, was geologically appropriate. As masters of the new imperialism might say, the island of Capri — like Goa, Gibraltar and the Falkland Isles —

was essentially a part of the neighbouring land; it is made of the same limestone as the southern coast, and this, according to modern codes, would justify a claim to sovereignty.

In form the island is pre-eminently beautiful, with its town saddled between cliff and height, and with all the rococo extravagances of cave and arch and pillar on its vertiginous declivities. Such features proliferate along the mainland cliffs, enhanced there to dignity by the higher mountains behind them; in Capri, by compensating contrast, lesser elevations leave on the lovely rockwork a spirit of almost frivolous fantasy. Small wonder that this diminutive and naturally exquisite island has been for so long a resort and an all-but shrine for, as one guide-book puts it, 'artists, emigrants and eccentrics'.

This curious and long-continuing community has been drawn for ever by Norman Douglas in *South Wind*. His story is set in the years just before the First World War, and among the characters are portrayed, in part at least, people who had been alive at the time.

I first visited Capri with a friend, the two of us undergraduates at the time, in the summer of 1922. We had been enticed out by Sir Compton Mackenzie, who had leased a villa there. This stood in a melodramatic position above four hundred feet of cliff, beyond which rose the gigantic obelisks of the Faraglioni, three vast precipitous rocks, one attached to the land, the other two standing in the sea. Close by is the lesser but still imposing islet of Monacone. (The view of these rocks is reproduced on innumerable tourist posters.) One night, at full moon, a party was given at the villa, a party which has been fixed for posterity by Sir Compton in two of his most brilliant books, each of them set in Capri, *Extraordinary Women* and *Vestal Fire*.

Men of distinguished names were there: Marinetti, the futurist poet; the great musician Casella; and Reggie Turner, the intimate friend of Wilde and Max Beerbohm and Norman Douglas. Bastard of some still unidentified magnate, Turner had a face of extraordinary ugliness, with a continuous twitching of the cheeks and blinking of the eyes. Did this betoken a wound, never properly healed, which he received from Wilde's disaster?

He had a trick, at emphatic points in his talk, of raising both hands, palms outward, and rolling up his eyes. I have seen the same gestures in Max Beerbohm and, modified, in Berenson who, after talking about Wilde, would look up, raising one hand, and say: 'Ah, dear Oscar!' I have long suspected that these gestures were caught from Wilde. I was told in Capri an anecdote about Turner when he was devotedly attending the death-bed of Wilde. (It may well have been printed since then.) Wilde said one morning: 'Oh Reggie, I have had the most dreadful dream. I dreamt I dined with the dead!' 'Well, Oscar,' responded Turner, 'I'm sure you were the life and soul of the party.'

Other guests have always been nameless to me, young men whom, since they were about thirty and I barely twenty, I reckoned as middle-aged. There was a plump, jolly woman in her forties who, it was said, had left England because she had been caught keeping a brothel. A short, neat woman of about the same age was so demure in her manner that she seemed out of place. There was also a group of Neapolitans who, since apparently none of them could speak English, kept apart from the Anglo-Saxons.

At supper I sat next to Reggie Turner. I have long realised that he was, if not the wittiest, at least the funniest, talker I have ever listened to. Of such talkers the plain record of their utterances must always be defective, not only in likely failures of verbal truth, but in the complete omission of tone and pace and gesture and visible expression. I remember laughing that night, helplessly and exhausted at his enormous fantasy of the original Siamese twins. One, he said, was costive, and the other too free in his bowels. Each took remedies and blamed the other for his intestinal embarrassment. The mountain of invention culminated in one becoming married, and eventually divorcing his wife with, for co-respondent, his brother, who promptly married her. During the meal he looked at me, a little tipsy. In those days I wore a single eye-glass. 'When I first saw you,' he said, 'your eye-glass went straight to my heart like Cupid's dart.'

Of course, during all this time there was the expected music — accordion, guitar and singer; and, of course, at one moment came *O Sole Mio*. 'That song will never die,' observed a very serious young man, who believed he loved art, and whose favourite painter was Tuke. Reggie Turner blinked his eyes with, it seemed, a significance of more than habit. But the half-expected comment unfortunately never emerged. He confessed afterwards to the naughty impulse, and we lamented its suppression.

When eating was over, Marinetti was asked to recite, which he very complacently did. I had heard that his poems truly merited the much-abused term 'futuristic', and I looked forward to something strange. Disobligingly he began in French, with some poems in prose by Baudelaire. However, he concluded with a poem of his own, on an aeroplane. I could then understand very little indeed of Italian; but I made out that the lines were disjointed (free-verse, remember, was still rather outrageous in 1922); and the poem ended gratifyingly with pure sound — a long, buzzing z-z-z-z-z! rising in pitch and signifying, I suppose, the ascent of the machine. When he had finished, one of the Neapolitans got up and read from a paper something I understood not a word of. After that, I did not notice much more of Marinetti. He had been burlesqued, at which the great man took the very greatest offence.

We went out on to the terrace, warm in the unchilled summer air. The full moon broke and trembled over the blazing sea, and plated with brightness the black-shadowed monoliths of the Faraglione. At intervals Casella played very good-naturedly, on a tinny piano just inside the house, Albeniz and Chopin. (Unlike Marinetti, he modestly performed nothing of his own.) 'I have just discovered a delightfully vulgar work by Albeniz,' he said in French after he had finished playing. The music of the Spaniard, still contemporary and new to me in its manner, added an exciting life to the gathering. And this, but for these grand musical interludes, was becoming ever more frivolous. Somebody, with a mixture of cruelty and fun, asked a young man if he would do his dance. With just a pretence of bashfulness, he assented. As he passed a friend I heard him say, in a tone of bogus resignation: 'They've made me do it again.' The dance was a swaying affair of leaping and bowing. He had hardly started when the plump, alleged brothel-keeper followed, unseen by him, mimicking his movements. This immensely enlivened the whole performance. At the end she flopped down beside me panting, and said: 'There's no fool like an old fool.'

Her example was followed a little differently, by the quiet, short woman, who had seemed too demure for the company. She went round, kicking her legs up shoulder-high. She was obviously very drunk. This gave me a sense of history, for I concluded she must be the original of the alcoholic lady in *South Wind*. I was wrong. The original was dead. Thus did even so loose a society as that one rediscover, tribally, the lost functionaries which it required to preserve its proper character.

At last, at about three o'clock in the morning, we went away, back along the cliff-path from the villa; among olive groves men were at work, profiting by the counterfeit day of that blazing moon. Some forty years later I walked, grieving and in horror, along the same path.

I have been for many years passionate in the search for rare narcissus. Now, in the old standard *Flora Italiana* by Giovanni Archangeli, there is recorded a *Narcissus aschersonii* of which the only site given is 'On the rock of Monacone near the island of Capri'. It is described as one of the tazetta group, and with small flowers, few to the umbel. His first edition gives it as a separate species; in his second edition of 1894 he gives it as a sub-species of *Narcissus tenorii*; the flowering time of this is said to be March and April. The latter is now a name of doubtful authority and, as I have already said in my botanical chapter, there is no satisfactory classification of the whole group, and much of Archangeli's naming has long been out of date. Still, there was always a hope that there might be on Monacone a proper species of extraordinary rarity. Accordingly, in one leap year, the weather being fine and the sea calm, I went to Capri on the 29th of February. This was my first return to the island after about forty years. In this season I found the place dead. The larger hotels were shut, and the cafés empty. I walked down to the Marina Piccola, the little harbour on the south of the island opposite to the main busy

Marina Grande. Few people were about. I asked at a café if they could tell me where I might find a room. Kindly and without charge they telephoned several places and found me accommodation. They also, knowing by then what I was there for, found me a boatman who would take me next morning to Monacone. I met him as arranged in calm and sunlight.

He was charming and intelligent, in late middle age. He listened to my talk about botany, and the flower I was after. Very strangely, for an Italian, he knew what I was talking about.

'There's a flower like that to be found on Capri,' he said.

I knew this, I answered, but the Monacone plant might be something peculiar to that rock. During our progress he told me of a beautiful blue flower which it was impossible to transplant. In this I recognised the lovely *Lithospermum rosmarinifolium*; a friend who lives at Antibes has told me that even self-sown seedlings in his garden will not stand transplanting. Almost all desirable species of this genus suffer from the same lamentable failing.

'You are passionate about botany,' he said (he used the expressive word *appassionato*, which can imply anything from deep love to enthusiastic interest); 'I am passionate about geology'. And as he rowed on he pointed out to me various peculiarities of rock formation. He rowed me up to a cleft in solitary, sea-girdled rock, where the transient light revealed a stain of deep amethyst, deep as in the famous and profitable Blue Grotto.

My enjoyment of the scene and the situation was a little diminished by a problem. The flanks of Monacone are very steep and in places vertical. Would I be able to get on to the overgrown top of it? I asked him about this, and added that in my old memories of the rock there were steps on it.

'Yes,' he said very reassuringly; 'it is easy. Those are Roman steps.' (An emperor's favourite is said to have been buried on the summit.) I made myself as easy in mind as I could. In our passage it was mainly the uninhabited splendours of Capri which were visible. Only now and then could I descry implications of horrible change. There is a precipice, hollowed by a huge cavern; on its pointed summits are the picturesque ruins of a castle. These, I discovered with dismay, are now masked by the vulgarity of a large sun-parlour.

We passed the Faraglioni soaring stupendously out of the sea. I thought of the blue lizard which lives on one of them. It may be no more than a local variant, bred in isolation (a naturalist of my acquaintance discovered a colony of black lizards not far from my home in Berkshire); however, according to Norman Douglas, it differs in small structural aspects from the normal species. An endemic animal on one rock enhanced at least the possibility of an endemic plant on another near by. I became tense with hope. And then, in front of us, loomed, alarmingly, precipitous Monacone.

Facing us was a cleft of steep rocks which seemed to me frighteningly steep. The Roman steps were indeed visible, but far above, near the top. The boatman took me in close to the rocks and said: 'That is the way up.' There followed a succession of purgatorial humiliations, the fiercer for my knowledge that near at hand might be the rarest of narcissus.

I scrambled up the steep jagged rocks until I came to a cave with its entrance roofed by a flat stone, large as a good-sized table, and just level with my chin. If I could get up on to it, I reflected — and the proposition was doubtful — I would probably never get off it again without tumbling dangerously down the spiky rocks. I went back to the boatman.

'I can't get up,' I said.

'You go into the cave,' he said, 'and there is a hole you can get up.'

I went into the cave. Water was on the floor of it, and there were many rounded stones. It must once have been at a level where the sea flowed. Light came in through small openings, far too narrow for a man of my size. I went abjectly back again.

'I can't get through these openings,' I said.

'You must go to the back of the cave,' he instructed me.

Back up I went and in, and sure enough, at the farthest point and going up about eight feet, was a chimney. Chimney-climbing is an activity I had never tried in my life before, but my floral passion carried me bravely through the ordeal. I came out on to a cosy, bright nook on the face of the cliff. Not far above were the ancient steps. I could see the herbage of the rock and, though no narcissus were apparent, flowerless plants would, I knew, be easily discovered.

Ahead of me was a curious formation like a gutter along the edge of the cliff — a narrow ledge with a depression on the inward side; the flat rim was about six inches wide. This was evidently the way I must go if I was to get the narcissus. The ledge went on thirty or forty feet to where a cleft ran up to the steps. One thing I did not like: as it widened it sloped outwards at an increasing angle. I said to myself: 'I'm close to the narcissus,' and set out: there, for the ledge overhung, right below me was the sea. I dare say the drop was only of some forty or fifty feet; to me it seemed infinite and, like a frightened beast, I froze. The boatman waved encouragingly to me. '*Non posso*,' I bleated; 'I can't.' 'I will come up,' he shouted back. He made the boat fast. The view from my lofty post, a little out to sea, must have been stupendous. Close were the Faraglioni, and as close the intricately broken precipices of the main island. I regarded nothing of this. All I saw, as I shrank back into the security of my cleft, was that terrible thin way, and the sea shivering brightly far below it. In a short time the boatman was with me. He looked along the ledge.

'If I held your hand,' he said, 'do you think you could do it?'

'No,' I said simply, with something like tears in my voice. And then, pulling myself together, I said: 'If you can do it, would you be very kind, and take my bag and my fork, and get me a few plants?'

He looked along the ledge and then said, with curious firmness: 'We'll see if there's another way up.' On the way down I tumbled out of the chimney. A spare pair of spectacles fell out of my pocket and rattled down irretrievably among the stones. I bruised one thigh; at the same time, I knocked the top joint of one finger and, to judge from a swelling which lasted for many months, probably chipped the bone. My drenching on the watery floor was a small misfortune.

We got into the boat. Humiliation almost extinguished disappointment.

'I feel so ashamed,' I said; 'if the way had been two or three metres high I could have got up easily.'

'You needn't feel ashamed,' he responded; 'as soon as I looked down, my head started spinning.'

We rowed round the rocky little island. At one point only did access seem remotely possible. But it would involve swimming and, for all my botanic enthusiasm, I did not choose to make such an attempt in the cold waters of February. 'That's that,' I said to myself; 'I shall never know if there really is such a species as *Narcissus aschersonii.*'

'If it is really important,' said the boatman after the disillusion of our circumnavigation, 'there is a boy here who could get the plants for you.'

I have never understood his postponement of this admirable plan. My fears and failure and fall had added, it is true, much drama to the search; suspense gave relish to success; but for all his good-heartedness I doubt if he could have been moved by motives so delicate. Happily he rowed to a beach near by where some boats were pulled up. The boy was found — quiet, shy, about seventeen years old — and I promised an agreed payment. We rowed back to Monacone. He climbed up those laborious rocks as though he were walking on the level; emerging from the chimney, he went along that awful ledge and up to the steps like a rabbit. Soon we saw him digging. He made a conscientious job of it, walking all over the top of the islet. As I watched him, I realised how little I would have liked searching on the steep turf, descending to cliffs which to me, from above, would have seemed enormous. Even to watch him at it made my head, like the boatman's, spin. Soon he was down again with a good load of bulbs. When we put him ashore I gave him, in my joy, more than his promised payment. This left me with only a note too large for the boatman to change. I changed it in a bar at the Marina Piccola by ordering myself two large brandies. I needed them. I was trembling.

Narcissus aschersonii may be disposed of now. In his first edition, Archangeli described it as having small flowers and few. In his second edition, as I have already told, he classified it as a variety of a species, now probably unacceptable, *Narcissus tenorii*, giving the flowering period as March and April; he still speaks of small flowers.

My plants from Monacone had ripe seed and had probably flowered at least two months earlier. In their appearance I could see no difference between them and seeding specimens of the autumn-flowering narcissus which grows round Amalfi. It was only the accident of a leap year which dated my excursion in February; I have seen the spring-flowering tazetta blossoming in early March. Had there been two narcissus on Monacone, one flowering in autumn and the other in spring, a few specimens of the latter would certainly have been blossoming at the time of my visit: and the boy would as certainly in that small area, have seen and collected some of them. The probability remains, therefore, that my narcissus is the only one growing on the rock. And my plants, so far as I could judge, were indistinguishable from the autumn narcissus which I know already. Monacone is not beyond a bee's flight from Capri, and it is likely that, had a marked variation evolved, it would, in a few generations, have been obliterated by the genes of the dominant local form. Only in remote isolation is a variety likely to turn up which, inbreeding, may eventually evolve into a form deserving of a specific name; Monacone is not remote enough for such a process to be probable. My suspicions were to be confirmed.

Back in England I sent bulbs to various experts, among them being my friend Mr. John Gilmour of the botanic gardens at Cambridge. Some time later he wrote to me saying that my bulbs had flowered and that they were the ordinary tazetta. I answered him, deprecating the use of the word 'ordinary', but accepting the identification which confirmed my own opinion.

To discover a rare species of plant, or to confirm its existence, is glorious. To expose a presumed species as no more than a ghost is not botanically useless, and that I had done.

I had two or three hours to pass for lunch and wandering after my return to the Marina Piccola. For the refreshing of youthful memories, full of delight and a lost happiness, I sought the way through the olive groves. There was nothing but a broad path between small villas, lodging houses and cheap hotels. In place of the simple vine-shaded café where we used to jovially meet, I found, when I went in for a sentimental drink, a large, flashy, expensive saloon. In old days, although tourists rich and poor resorted there, Capri had its own spirit as a community. But now that spirit was no more than a dummy in an automatic machine, able to move into a mechanic life only on the insertion of coins. Vestiges of the true life remained in my companionable boatman, in the kind people at the café who had found me a room for the night, and in the boy who so boldly climbed Monacone. As a corporate creature, Capri was no more.

Dead in the colder seasons, Capri becomes intolerably crowded in summer by visitors who, if English, call it Caprí, reversing the proper accent, and look upon it as the ultimate goal of their longings. Venice in summer is, I am told, as intolerably crowded, yet it remains Venice, and Carpaccio is always Carpaccio. I would never seek now in Capri the company I found there in my youth. Sir Compton Mackenzie's party will never be repeated or rivalled — the best party, I sometimes think, that was ever given in Capri since the entertainments of Tiberius.[1] Yet, though

[1] I am not imagining orgies such as were attributed to that emperor when he ruled the world from Capri. Perhaps they took place, perhaps not. In the last few decades there has been a movement to rehabilitate Tiberius (like Richard III), a movement largely initiated by Norman Douglas. Most comments made nowadays infer disbelief in his alleged enormities. One wickedness told about him was that he kept in large tanks a flesh-eating sea-eel which was said to become particularly tasty if the flesh was human. To these fish, the uncharitable tradition affirms, he would have live slaves thrown, his sadistic enjoyment being titivated, no doubt, by gastronomic anticipation. I like to think of Tiberius in Capri as a wise and benign old man. But not long ago I saw something which had rather horrid implications. At Sperlonga, on the coast a little to the south of Gaeta, there was lately excavated a sea-side residence of Tiberius. The discoveries included sculpture of the finest quality. Among the structures found was a fresh-water tank fed from a nearby spring. A small museum contains the removable discoveries. In one show-case I saw a long flat piece of bone. 'Is that from a horse's head?' I asked the attendant. 'No,' he answered: 'a crocodile's.' Tiberius may have kept the crocodile in his tank for ostentation, as so many potentates used to keep exotic animals. But one wonders.

the habitable parts, once so picturesque, have become a holiday camp for people of all classes and of all incomes, most of the island can never be built over, and its form, so marvellous and so deservedly famous, survives.

In San Marino is a church decorated by an excellent Umbrian artist called Niccolo da Foligno. I once looked for it with some friends. The idea of searching for works of art in San Marino was so odd that we were not able to find the church. It is equally odd to look for works of art in Capri, but the endeavour will be well rewarded.

The vestiges of Roman palaces in Capri are very important. Unfortunately their treasures of art have been removed, and they were dreadfully robbed both by the French and the English, in order to build fortifications during the Napoleonic wars. Of later buildings the most interesting is the small church of San Costanzo.

It was built during the tenth and eleventh centuries, while Amalfi was still independent. The form was of a Greek cross: nave, choir and transepts were equal in length. Over the crossing is a dome, tall and turret-like outside. Across the west end is a closed narthex or portico. Originally there were apses to the choir, to the transepts, and to each end of the narthex. Those to the north have gone, and the choir was replaced, under the Angevins, by a Gothic structure, rib-vaulted, and with some good carvings. The church is of the same family, architecturally, as the early Sicilian-Byzantine churches of Palermo and the early churches at Ravello. Columns of fine marble were removed by one of the Bourbon kings for use in the chapel at Caserta; they were replaced by granite columns. In spite of alteration and restoration the church is still alive with the magic of that most magical school of building.

Up above, in the town itself, the parish church of S. Stefano is a late baroque structure, built on the site of an earlier church; the architect was Neapolitan, but he was given much help by an Amalfitan — let his name be noted — Marziano Desiderio. Most notable inside is part of a Roman floor from the great imperial Villa Jovis; this has been laid in front of the altar.

There are also two tombs of Giacomo and Vincenzo Arcucci, by Michelangelo Naccherino, whose magnificent effigy of St. Andrew at Amalfi has already been praised. These, it is said, were originally in the church of the Certosa. There is also in S. Stefano a painting of which it is said that, having been thrown over a cliff by Corsairs, it returned, of its own accord, miraculously to the church.

A road descends south from the main piazza towards the fishing port of the Marina Piccola. (On my youthful visits we used to take a boat here to a beach where we bathed among monumental fragments of a Roman villa.) Not far eastward, reaching almost to the cliff edge is the Certosa, or Carthusian monastery. This is worth a visit. Founded during the second half of the fourteenth century, many misfortunes befell it. In 1553, and again in 1563, it was sacked and wasted by corsairs; suppressed in 1807, it was used, in turn, as a prison, a hospital, and barracks. It has been decently restored. Over the entrance is a good fourteenth-century fresco of the Madonna and Child, enthroned between saints. On my earliest sight of it, this was assigned by our guide to Giotto. Since, at the time of its painting, Giotto had been dead at least a century and a half, the attribution was a little reckless. Close by are graceful cloisters of the fourteenth century, a last, live breath of Romanesque, with old columns and capitals, some of the latter being antique and some, in style, Byzantine. There are larger cloisters dating from the late sixteenth century, and altogether admirable. On my first return after four decades I had seen, only a few days before, the tremendous cloisters at Padula in south-eastern Campania. Even with that splendour still brilliant in my memory, I found myself enraptured by the cloisters of Capri. Apart from its intrinsic merits, this Certosa is interesting in that the old parts were built, as at S. Rosa near Amalfi, by the same method as all rustic cottages of the country. The walls are of concrete, and the roofs domed.

After my tour of the Certosa, my guide took me to a belvedere. I looked each way in delight at the still unsullied cliffs of the island. 'At any rate,' I said to myself, with the smell of archi-

23. Furore: S. Elia: Roman cinerary urn (page 170)

24. Atrani: festa of the Maddalena (page 187)

25. Salerno: twelfth-century ivory in the cathedral museum: the soldiers playing at *la morra* for the garment of Christ (page 189)

tectural abominations foul in my nostrils, 'you can't build on a precipice.' Some work was going on close at hand. 'That,' said the guide proudly, 'will be a new luxury hotel: with a lift going down to the beach.'

Unique, and most enchanting of all works of art in Capri, is the tiled pavement of the church of S. Michele in Anacapri (in the visits which I have made, this church was opened only in the afternoons). The church was built in 1719 from the design of the Neapolitan Domenico Antonio Vaccaro (who may have designed the steps of Amalfi cathedral); it is octagonal with a dome, and opening all round into shallow chapels. The ceramic floors of these chapels are adorned with cherubic heads and wreaths of fruit and flowers.

On the main floor, still in perfect condition, is pictured on tiles the earthly paradise; it is formally the expulsion, but Adam and Eve and the Angel take up only a small part of it. The rest is a vision of trees and water and sky and birds and animals — some fabulous, like the unicorn; some nobly real like the lion and the horse. Such compositions were often painted during the seventeenth century, in particular by members and followers of the Breughel family, sometimes in collaboration with Rubens. I have seen a good many such pictures, but never so bewitching a presentation as this in Anacapri. The work was carried out posthumously from a design by Francesco Solimena, to my mind the greatest of the late Neapolitan painters. My knowledge of this fact once made me look a little foolish.

I had been there some time in an ecstasy of attention, when an elderly Italian lady came in with two or three girls. She walked round, chuckling deliciously with delight. 'Oh,' she kept saying, 'the fantasy of the artist! The fantasy of the artist!' Such lovely enthusiasm had to be shared, and I pointed out to her two cases where a monkey was offering fruit to a bear. Then, obligingly as I thought, I told her the name of the designer and his school. We left Capri by the same boat, and I went and talked to her. One of her young companions then told me that she was a curator of a castle in north Italy which houses a magnificent art collection. With great delicacy she gave me to understand that historical matters were what she was mainly concerned with; but this, I think, was only to save me from embarrassment.

Altar-pieces in the chapels at S. Michele are contemporary Neapolitan work, all but two being by an artist from the remote and romantic Cilento, Paolo de Matteis. The custodian hopefully assigned them all to Francesco Solimena. One is an Annunciation. I have owned for many years a red-chalk drawing of this subject in which the poses of the Virgin and of the Archangel are very close to those in this painting. With the lunancy which may possess any collector, I began to half-believe that I might be the owner of a drawing by Solimena. The indulgence of my new faculty for looking at baroque painting soon stifled my ridiculous hopes. These figures — the Virgin who turns kneeling at a *prie-dieu*; the angel on a cloud and honourably saluting the Annunciate — these are of a convention as generally employed as the hierarchic Virgin and Child, derived from Byzantium, and which we see in countless early Italian paintings. Although the baroque theme has not the tremendous implications of those older works, nor did it survive so long, it was nevertheless a fine invention. It seems to have been conceived during the high renaissance; it came into full use towards the end of the seventeenth century.

It is happy to find this pavement in Capri, for otherwise there would be nowhere in the ancient territories of Amalfi any work of Solimena's (unless we depend on a brief domination by her of Salerno in the tenth century). This is strange, for he was born close at hand in Nocera Inferiore.

I have to confess that until only a few years ago I could look at very few Italian paintings of the seventeenth century. Then one day, in the cathedral at Capua, I saw on its side, a large painting of the Assumption. (The cathedral was destroyed during the war, and all the undamaged furnishings had not yet been put back; most splendid of all is a Romanesque paschal candlestick.) This painting pleased me and I asked the name of the artist; it was Francesco Solimena. After this little retreat there soon came utter surrender. In Naples, the resplendent baroque church of the Gesù Nuovo has over the west door a large and magnificent fresco — all light and tremendous movement — by Solimena of the expulsion of Heliodorus from the temple. The most bigoted mediaevalist could not, I believe, stand up to the impact of this masterpiece. Since then, in the company of two like-minded friends, I have made a number of excursions from Amalfi, in search of paintings by Solimena.

The nearest is not far away at Nocera Inferiore. In the cathedral, called the *evescovada*, is a chapel with its dome decorated by Francesco Solimena, in partnership with his father Angelo; the chapel is at the north-west end of the building. A priest was praying at the rail of the chapel; he got up and said: 'That is by our famous painter Francesco Solimena in' — fourteen hundred and something. Having uttered this error of three centuries, he went back on his knees. Angelo's work is dull by his son's, but here the inspiration of the younger dominates the whole decoration. The place is worth visiting for its own qualities. The cathedral forms one side of a fine courtyard, which is entered under a noble and massive baroque tower.

At Salerno, Solimena is best seen in the church of S. Giorgio. There is a fine altar-piece (in a chapel of the south aisle) of St. George and the dragon. Better are frescoes in the short north aisle; these are damaged, but movement and the beauty of brushwork — particularly in his treatment of vegetation — are still powerful. (Neither these frescoes nor the little dome at Nocera Inferiore are mentioned in any guide-book that I know; they are figured in the monograph by Signor F. Bologna.) This church possesses a dome by the father, Angelo Solimena — good work, but spiritless beside his son's.

If anybody, who feels as I lately did about such things, might think of venturing into the world of seventeenth- and eighteenth-century Neapolitan painting, he would be well advised to begin with the Gesù Nuovo in Naples, or with S. Michele in Anacapri. If these are impossible, I should not fear to recommend the frescoes in S. Giorgio in Salerno. It would be instructive to look at the dome, which is attractively decorated by Angelo Solimena, and then, as soon as possible, to visit for comparison the marvellously superior dome at Nocera Inferiore, infused with the genius of his son.

The vision of Solimena's floor can always obliterate a little for
me the wealthy degeneration of Capri. On my botanical visit I
had not seen it, and of Capri I felt as though I had been seeking
out a dear friend, not seen for many years, and had found only his
grave. My journey back had been like a journey from dead lands
to a land of living people. I crossed to Sorrento at dusk and got
into the Amalfi bus. Soon after we left, a man started playing
an accordion, for amusement and not for gain. He was near me,
and I asked him if he knew a tune which had haunted me for a
long time and which, having a poor ear for tunes, I could not get
right. This was the hymn to St. Andrew, sung and played in
Amalfi at the feast of the saint. He did not know it. The conductor, who was from Amalfi, sat on the accompanying seat
and hummed the tune. 'Is that it?' he asked; I said it was and
that I wanted to find somebody who would write it down for me.
At Positano the bus filled up, some of the new passengers being
acquaintances of mine. I was still chatting with one of these
when the conductor came and said that he had found someone
who could write down for me the hymn of St. Andrew, and he
introduced us.

My new friend was the proprietor of a small shop in Amalfi
run by his wife; he taught music at a school in Positano. In a
few days I went to his shop where he wrote down the tune. His
wife said: 'In old days, when many English came here for the
winter, they got women from Amalfi as nurses for their children.
They used to sing the hymn of St. Andrew as a lullaby.'

Back in Amalfi I felt rather like Dante when, departing out of
hell, he saw again the stars. The metaphor is too strong, of course,
but never before had I realised why I loved the place with so dear a
love. It was winter still, with perhaps no more than a dozen
foreign tourists in the town. Amalfi went on living its own life.
'Mon dieu!' I said to myself in Verlaine's words, *'Mon dieu, mon
dieu, la vie est là!'*

CHAPTER XIII

Ghosts and Legends

―――――――――

Many clever, or would-be clever, men have examined the legends and superstitions of an alien people and have professed to draw the most profound conclusions from them. It is not my intention to attempt anything of the kind. Yet, when we know what fantasies a people is ready to believe in, we feel, without being able to explain why, something of their communal character.

I look on myself, perhaps unreasonably, as a most reasonable man; I have had, as I have already told, both a scientific and a legal education. In larger matters of the universe I long preserved a balanced doubt, resiling from decision one way or the other in regions of the spirit where logical consideration has no validity.

Yet, I confess to a crazed uneasiness if I happen to see the new moon through glass, or find that I have cut my nails on a Friday. I am aware of a certain bravery if I walk under a ladder without spitting, however concealedly, or crossing my fingers. A ringing in the right ear gives me satisfaction, in the left discomfort. Such matters are of the smallest importance to me; yet I cannot pretend to feel, though against my reason, no force in them at all. I am in no position to look down on, or to laugh at, those people who hold superstitious beliefs in more poetic detail. Few of us, very few indeed, can justifiably do so. That Italians touch iron where we touch wood does not prove them less rational than we are. If I spill salt I can hardly refrain from throwing it over my shoulder, or at least making a cross in it. How can I, in fairness, mock at those who maintain that wine accidentally spilt brings good luck, or spilt oil bad? Who can but be pleased at the warning that, if you count enough stars, they will suddenly transfer themselves in equal number as freckles on your face?

I asked an intelligent Amalfitan friend, from a family I know well, if he could tell me any old superstition.

'We do not believe in superstitions,' he answered, very seriously.

'I know,' I replied, mendaciously, 'but there must be memories of them.'

People are coy about their native superstitions, and who knows what poetry is lost to mankind in this silence? I cannot believe that my friend had nothing to tell me about the vast, dark underworld of local credulity. A person infected with the Evil Eye may be morally of the most excellent character. He will not, in the ordinary course of things, act vindictively. Yet allusions to the subject can be unwise.

It is difficult for an Englishman to realise how near he may be in Italy to a chaos of charms and terrors. Whatever the force of a claimed scepticism, there are risks not to be taken.

Staying with friends in northern Italy, I came back from a botanical walk with, among other things, the herbaceous elder, *Sambucus ebulis*. It was the first time I had seen it (the plant is rare in England, though very common in Italy) and I wanted to make sure of my identification. The next day, I seemed to notice a curious look on the elderly, amiable maid who looked after me. I had forgotten that our common elder, *Sambucus niger*, has many ugly associations — among others, the supplying of sticks for witches' brooms. By bringing bits of elder into the house, I had probably done something rather sinister.

I once detected the same look on the face of a man near Amalfi. He had admired my ring, and jokingly asked me to give it to him.

'I won't give it you,' I answered facetiously, 'but if I drop down dead, you have my permission to take it off my finger.'

'No!' he said, suddenly very serious.

He may just have thought that this was a joke in bad taste; but I had the impression of having done something which might encourage dangerous influences.

It took me a little time to begin to pick up old stories. Curiously, even among those who have got to know me well and to trust me,

I have heard very little about the Evil Eye, that superstition so dreadful in Italy, and which must be powerful in my southern community. Everywhere are evident defences against the menace. Hanging from men's belts, round children's necks, at the back of bars, on lorries, behind buses, you will often see horns of coral, a sovereign remedy. Alternatively, you will see dummy hands, making horns, by extending the first finger and little finger. This defence is very ancient. In the museum at Benevento is an ancient statue, perhaps Etruscan, of a man making horns. 'He is making the *contr'occhi*,' said an attendant laughing; his expression means literally 'against eyes', and only against Evil Eyes would any action be needed.

A family used to live next door to some particular friends of mine, and in that family there was a remarkably pretty little girl. One day we were chatting gaily together when I saw her making horns at me. The parents noticed too, so, to pass it off, I laughed and said: 'What a naughty girl!' Afterwards the mother came up to me apologetically and said seriously: 'It's not her fault. When I take her for a walk, people often say to me, "What a pretty little girl," and I have to make her do it.' For the Evil Eye works, of course, by its possessor expressing honest good will towards the victim. An Anglicised family from Ravello came, with a baby, to visit their Italian relatives. The baby got ill, and the Italian grandmother, instead of attempting any proper medical remedies, sat beside it, letting drops of oil fall into a small basin of hot water. I was given to understand that this was a remedy against the Evil Eye. However, an Italian friend of mine, born half-Neapolitan but long resident in Tuscany, suggested to me that this was more probably a form of divination; from the behaviour of the oil might be deduced the nature of the evil.

The same friend told me how somebody, feeling ill, would cry out in anguish: 'I have done no harm to anyone! Why should this happen to me? Who can be wishing me ill? And I have never done harm to anyone!'

This refers to the casting of evil spells, and it may have been the suspicion of such a spell, and not fear of the Evil Eye, which led the grandmother to the divination of oil.

Medicine and magic were for a long time closely associated; indeed, when we consider the quack remedies wildly believed in today by many educated people, the association, it would seem, has not yet been entirely broken. As in most parts of the world, there are wart-charmers in Amalfi. I think the oddest medical charm I ever heard of was used on a friend of mine when, as a baby, he had mumps. The remedy was milk of a nursing mother, injected from her nipple into his ear.

I suffer at times from mild arthritis in the left knee. Once, when it was troubling me, I was taken to a friend who had, I was told, a power in his hands of curing such troubles. He examined my knee and said, rather unfeelingly as I thought: '*Roba vecchia*' — 'old stuff.' 'I can't do anything now,' he went on, 'while the sun is up. Come back in the evening.' My knee quickly got better of its own accord, and I never troubled him. I regret this. I should like to have seen what he did.

A suspicion of were-wolves lingers on. I know by sight a man credited with the condition. I have heard, too, a vague story of someone going up a flight of steps with no door opening on to them; a man seen descending from above passed by in the form of a dog. A friend remembers seeing, as a child, a figure hooded in black, and followed by many dogs; his mother threw a bucket-full of water over the apparently human creature, who ran away growling.

A friend from the coast, now at work in England, has provided me with a number of stories. He usually got them a little wrong, but I cannot regard this as a defect. Changes are the essence of live tradition; in the small deviations of my young friend are illustrated, almost vegetatively, the growth of a flourishing folk-lore. I had just seen, as I have described in a later chapter, the miraculous liquefaction of the manna of St. Andrew. He suddenly said, very solemnly: 'A miracle happened here not long ago.' 'What happened?' I asked, and he answered: 'A dead lady came out of the tomb.' He then told me the story, which I have since heard from other sources.

A youth was just setting off on his motor-bicycle, a Vespa (it may have been a Lambretta; the name of the make was mentioned, but I have forgotten which it was). He saw a young lady and asked if she would like a lift. 'Yes,' she answered, 'if you'll be passing near my home.' His destination suited her and she got up behind him. When they were close to the cemetery, she said: 'My home is near here.' (It cannot have happened in Amalfi, where you have to climb over four hundred steps to the cemetery.) It was cold and she had on only a thin dress, so he offered to lend her his coat. She thanked him and said: 'If you go to my mother tomorrow, she will give you back your coat,' and she wrote down an address.

Next day he went to the house and asked the mother for the coat he had lent to her daughter.

'I have no daughter,' she replied.

'But look,' said the young man, 'here is the address which she wrote down for me.'

The mother looked at the paper, 'My daughter is dead,' she said. 'Come with me.'

So they went to the cemetery and there, hanging on a cross over the girl's grave, was the young man's coat.

My informant added a curious epilogue; the youth was so horrified at having given a lift to a dead girl that he himself died within two days.

The story is of interest as being a very late variant of the Leonora story, famous in the romantic epoch, when the girl, bewailing the absence of her crusading lover, saw him arrive on horse-back. She got up behind and, after they had galloped some way, he turned round to look at her and disclosed, instead of a living face, the dry, white bones of a death's head.

I was told the story again by a friend from Salerno when I had betrayed my scepticism about ghosts. It is true, he assured me, and had happened in his own town (a scene topographically more possible than Amalfi). As an unanswerable answer to my sadducism, he told me another story.

In Salerno, a man was knocked down by a motor-car, driven by an elderly lady, with her daughter as passenger. He was not hurt and, after the most friendly apologies, they took him to their house where they made him some coffee. He talked with them, and smoked, and eventually went away. When he got into the street, he found that he had left his cigarette-lighter behind. He went back; the house was dark, and he started knocking at the door.

'What are you doing?' asked a passer-by; 'the house is empty.' He told his story.

'The house has been empty for a year,' said the passer-by: 'it used to be lived in by a mother and daughter, who were killed in a motor accident.'

The man persisted in his story, so at last they broke the door down. There was nobody in the house, but on a dusty table they found three coffee cups with dregs in them, and the missing cigarette-lighter.

On my first visit to Amalfi I was told a ghost story more domesticated and simple, together with a variant on the same theme. In a populous neighbourhood I know well, a girl was believed by many to have had a ghost for her lover. He visited her carnally, so it was said. Since to his other attentions he added the gift of a real ring, there were not wanting those who thought her story might allow a more material explanation.

Nearby another ghost conceived, but chastely this time, a passion as strong for another girl. The family were to move house, and the ghost threatened to kill his beloved if she went away. When she was finally leaving, she felt his hands over her face, holding her back (in another version he took her by the hair). Unfortunately I could never find out what happened in the end, either to the girl or the ghost.

The first teller of the motor-bicycle story said to me one day: 'Not long ago two *carabinieri* saved two children here.' 'What happened?' I asked, expecting, nastily, details of an attempted sex crime.

'Two strangers came,' he said (I do not remember if he used the word meaning foreigners, or one which signified no more than strangers to the neighbourhood); 'they took the children to the Torre dello Ziro, and the *carabinieri* followed and saved them.'

He was talking about the great tower on the hill between

Amalfi and Atrani. I began to suspect his meaning. I have never been into the tower, for this involves wriggling about eight feet through a claustrophobic tunnel in the wall. My informant had already told me that there was a well in the tower, reaching to below the level of the sea. (This is the tower in which, as I have told elsewhere in the book, the Duchess of Malfi is said to have been murdered by her brothers. Its present form is traditionally attributed to the licentious Queen Giovanna II of Naples.) Once, so he told me, an owner of the tower had himself let down into the well on a rope, hoping to find the treasure reputedly hidden there, under the guard of devils. When he got very low down, below sea level, many voices shouted at him. He managed to signal, and was brought to the surface, without any treasure, and nearly dead.

There is another story, in the little book on Ravello by Carlo Lacaita.

A Sicilian, living in Ravello during the first half of the last century, claimed the power of discovering hidden treasure. He was persuaded by eager and avaricious acquaintances to search the Palazzo Rufolo. After the recitation of proper charms, a wall opened to disclose a descending stair-case; in the revealed vault were four golden statues and heaps of precious things. Before they could take anything, a bearded figure, richly clothed, said they must first bring him the soul of an innocent, three-year-old infant. In the 1840's three men of Ravello were condemned in Salerno for murdering a child, with the intention of winning treasure. An account of their trial was printed at Salerno in 1857.

The memory of this story gave me the clue.

'Were they going to murder the children, so that the devil would give them the treasure?' I asked.

'Yes,' he answered, 'but the *carabinieri* saved them.'

The Ravellesi wizard survived — a little differently — into modern times. The painter Giuseppe di Lieto, in origin from Ravello, has told me that there used to be, in these parts, an elderly, benevolent man, who was said to sleep in a cave, on a rectangular bed, made of stones. He possessed a book, like a very large Bible, and full of charms.

Anxious, as others have been, to find hidden treasure, he one day drew the prescribed circle and read the effective charms. The devil appeared and asked for the soul of a pure creature; so the magician killed a chicken. The devil expressed dissatisfaction, and the next night a dog was sacrificed. Upon this the devil became enraged and demanded the soul of a pure girl. The good-hearted magician, unlike the murderers of Ravello, could not bring himself to sacrifice a child, so he never got the treasure.

Devil-guarded treasure is common talk round about Amalfi. I remember being near the ominous Torre dello Ziro, in company with a local family. The young people squeezed themselves in; but the mother stayed outside with me and said seriously: 'I'm not going in; there are devils there.'

The devil in these parts takes the form of a snake. I was once at the cemetery of Amalfi, which is just below the tower. 'Up there,' I said, joking, 'is the treasure guarded by the devil in the form of a snake.'

'Yes,' said one of the company, and then told me how two men had gone to look for treasure. They went into a promising cave, and turned up a stone, and found a snake — an ordinary, live snake — underneath it. This would be the guardian devil, they thought, and the treasure must be there. In great terror they killed the snake; they did not find any valuables.

An intelligent friend of mine, Raffaele di Palma from Pontone, has told me more about these matters. If, he said, you uttered the correct charm, the devil would appear as a snake. It would then stand up on end, and you must be careful not to say anything holy, and therefore offensive to the devil, or you would be whisked away. If you said nothing, the devil would then show you the treasure. I have been told that you must barter your soul as well, but I suspect this of being a corrupt tradition; more generally believed in was the necessary sacrifice of a pure soul (which would in any case put one's own soul in the devil's grasp).

Two men, so Raffaele told me, once got as far as calling up the devil. The snake appeared, and then stood up on end, like Satan in Eden.

'*Madonna mia!*' cried out one man in a panic, and '*Dio mio!*' the other, upon which the first immediately found himself on the beach at Positano, and the other on the mountains beside Agérola.

The ghost on the motor-bicycle probably derives, as I have suggested, from a northern tale, brought into the south, perhaps, by Norman or Lombard.

'In Naples,' said Berenson to Count Morra, 'I experienced an ecstasy like that of the Annunciate in the face of the Angel. The miracle is that civilised life in Naples, as in almost all Italy, has lasted for three thousand years. In other parts it is not so. There are voids centuries long.'[1]

In stories of treasure and the sentinel snake we are carried into vertiginous gulfs of the past. What is this, but, still alive in our own days, the story of the Hesperides, with the apples of gold and the serpent incessantly on guard? 'The apple tree, the singing and the gold.' No Norse or Anglo-Saxon story is of such vast antiquity; Leonora, beside this, is *parvenue*. Here, alive still, however debile and comically altered, is a legendary sign that southern Italy of our days has still something in it of Magna Graecia.

It is perhaps from the Greeks that a belief in retributive fate has come down. I have been told of a policeman who was given to wantonly killing pet dogs. Eventually he died in hospital, horribly, of a painful disease. This was considered a natural and proper consequence of his cruel behaviour. I have also been told of a graver case. Some years ago, on the coast, a man was murdered by stabbing and then robbed. The murderer was suspected, but there was not enough evidence known against him. He lived on in misfortune, without friends, going about alone. And then, I was assured, came confirmation of his guilt. He went to hospital for the amputation of a limb, and died during the operation.

'It must have been him,' said my informant; 'they say "Who kills with a knife shall die by a knife".'

There are stories which seem to have origins less ancient yet more alien and stranger in their quality.

---

[1] Umberto Morra. *Colloqui con Berenson*. Garzanti, Milan, 1963. Page 58.

'Did you ever hear the story,' a friend asked me one day, 'how Jesus was hidden in a lupin seed? But the Jews found Him, and put Him on the Cross.'

I had certainly never heard the story, and mentioned it to Giuseppe di Lieto, who had told me about the gentle magician. He had not heard it in that form.

'It was a stone-pine, as I have heard it,' he said, 'and that is why the stone-pine moves so little in the wind, and makes so little noise so as not to betray Jesus.

'You can see the hand of Jesus in it,' he went on and, fetching a cone, he took out one of the seeds. This he broke open, revealing inside a white germ, splitting at the end into five miniscule shoots. 'That,' he said, 'is the hand of Jesus.'

I have pondered much over this story. In the Gospel story, there are occasions when Jesus evaded his enemies and 'passed through the middle of them'; but the only occasion when he might have been hidden for any length of time would have been before the flight into Egypt. Can it, I often wonder, have a Muslim origin, in some unfamiliar story of the prophet Jesus? There was, as I have told, over many years, a Saracen colony on the coast at Cetara, and over the mountains at Nocera Inferiore and at Pagani. Moreover, the Amalfitans had much commercial intercourse with Mohammedan countries.

> *Where the White Hand of Moses from the bough*
> *Puts out, and Jesus from the ground suspires.*

Freely as he translated, Fitzgerald, according to his published notes to Omar Khayyám, was properly translating the names of the plants in question. Here, from a Muslim source, is at least hinted some vegetative association with Jesus.

An Italian friend from Meta di Sorrento knew the stone-pine story as one alive on the peninsula, but he had never heard of the lupin seed. This latter, obscure version illustrates how fecund still are the growth and modulation of legend in the neighbourhood of Amalfi.

'Did you know,' my Sorrentine friend asked me, 'why the olive tree is always twisted? When,' he went on, 'the Roman soldiers were seeking wood for the Cross, they went first to the olive trees and each, as they approached, writhed itself into the shape we see, that they might not be used to crucify Jesus.'

It is a commonplace of history that south Italy as a whole — that is the old kingdom of Naples and Sicily — has never known native rulers. Even in Roman times the population was largely of different stock, Samnite and Greek; Goth and Vandal passed through; Lombard, Norman, French and Spaniard conquered and ruled. I may be wrong in my suggested attributions of the few legends I have recorded. Yet it is not unlikely that a community so mixed in origin, Northern and Latin and Greek and, for a small part, Asian, should have preserved legends of their diverse forebears.

Sublimity cannot be attributed to all superstitions. There is in Italy a state lottery, the *banco lotto*. All you have to do is to choose three numbers; if you choose right, your reward can be very large indeed. Many superstitions may be involved in the choice. Mansi, in his discourse about Pantaleone, declares it very wrong to use saintly demonstrations in playing the *banco lotto*. Booklets are available which attach particular numbers to dreams and to unusual events; most who gamble on the lottery use these interpretations of petty auguries.

I have friends whose front door opens on to a steep flight of steps. I had been eating with them one evening; as I was leaving, I stumbled and fell against the wall opposite, and rolled harmlessly down about fifteen steps. My host's brother was there, and I still have in mind a picture of him, with his hands to his face, and an expression of intense alarm.

He plays the *banco lotto*. On his next entry, he put in the numbers for fright and for fall; I do not know what prodigy decided the third number. Had I cut myself and bled, he would have put in the number for blood — and he would have won. 'That was the time you lost me twelve million lire,' he sometimes says, and I am never quite sure whether there may not be, in his humorous reproach, a particle of serious blame.

CHAPTER XIV

Two Beetles

<hr/>

All my life I have had the enthusiast of a botanist, however defective I may be in a strictly scientific approach. In other branches of biology I am humiliatingly ignorant. This chapter recalls all that I have carefully observed of wild life about Amalfi.

I have a brother with an obsessive interest in mice and kindred animals. He asked me to bring him a mole from Amalfi. I spoke about this to a friend who worked on the land, and asked if he could get me one. 'Easily,' he answered. About a week before leaving, I asked him about it and got a different answer: 'Very, very difficult.' It was my brother who had suggested that in these parts the moles may not make mole-hills, a question which answered itself at S. Maria dei Monti. Rats and mice, too, would be of interest to a specialist. These animals, I am advised, can be preserved by gutting them, and stuffing the aperture with cotton-wool soaked in formalin; pure alcohol, easily obtained in Italy, might do as well. There is always a chance that you may find a new species, or at least a definable sub-species.

There are still wolves in the inland mountains, but I have heard no recent records of them from the Lattari range. Once, from a car, at night, I saw two enormous foxes cross the road.

Mentioning this to a man, he told me that foxes were sometimes eaten on the coast; the head must be cut off and the body left in water for several days, after which the flesh becomes quite palatable, and not unlike rabbit. I had been told in Amalfi that in Bologna, after much the same treatment, cats were eaten. Cats as food in the gastronomic capital of Italy! The proposition being impossible, I ranked the fox-eating story as a variant of the

26. Below S. Maria dei Monti, to the south (page 196)

27. S. Maria dei Monti on Easter Monday (page 197)

same fable. Confirmation of its accuracy was to follow. A friend of mine found a fox dying on the road, killed it and gave the body away. Afterwards, thinking it might have been poisoned, he warned the recipients against eating it.

The peninsula is indeed an all-but island, and doubtless a resting point for many migrating birds. The passing of the quails is a famous occasion. I have never seen it, even when the delicious bird was in season. Men stand along the coast road to shoot them. (The use of blinded decoys is now unlawful.) My eyes are neither sharp enough, nor sufficiently educated in ornithology, to make my observations of much value. Birds uncommon in England which I have certainly seen are the black tern and the Mediterranean gull. Had I not been warned by an experienced ornithologist that with such birds even expert evidence is doubtful, I would have claimed Savi's warbler on the Montagna di Pontone, and Cetti's warbler, which is to be expected all over Italy, on Stromboli.

In that island, among the most beautiful and strange which I have ever visited, I had an ornithological adventure from which I later profited on the coast. I was there with a friend and, on our walks, we kept seeing large, dark birds. I was for their being ravens; he suggested at first some kind of falcon, but was coming to my opinion when — his eyes are far sharper than mine — he said: 'The head is more like a hawk's than a raven's.' We had no bird-book with us, and tried to notice whatever features might help a later identification. We then noticed that there were two species of big dark birds. We distinguished them by their tails. In one they were squared, as if they had been neatly cut across; in the other they were bluntly pointed. I had a book in Ravello and when we got back again we discovered them to be respectively the griffon vulture and the black vulture. I lament not having been able to savour, at the moment, my first sight of a free vulture. The griffon vulture is by tradition the bird which tore at the ever-renewed liver of the enchained and punished Prometheus.

Back on the coast, on my last day of that visit, I saw, from the road above Maiori, a griffon vulture. Poetically appropriate, a fennel was in sight, vessel of the heavenly fire for whose charitable theft Prometheus was tormented age-long by that huge, insatiable bird.

Among insects, I need not speak of butterflies; who has not studied them, however little, at some time or other? It was invincible fascination, and nothing of science, which forced me to watch the two beetles whose antics I am now to describe.

One bright day of spring, I walked up from Amalfi to Pogérola, through the woods where interesting plants are to be found. At the top, I went to the eastern lip of the mountain to enjoy the spectacle of Amalfi, buildings, glittering bay and precipitous valley and, radiant over all, the splendid bell-tower of the ravished cathedral. Beside me, warm in the brilliant sun, was a little steep grassy slope. I noticed a sparkle of reflected sunlight from black shiny objects — a scattered crowd of slowly moving beetles.

Looking carefully, I saw that each was climbing backwards, untiringly, and with unconquerable patience, up the incline, and rolling with its hind legs a spherical lump of something. Near the bottom of the slope was a pat of dung, dropped, I suppose, by a passing donkey. Beetles were carving bits out of it with their jaws, and then clutching the prize with their hind pair of legs, and rolling it slowly up the slope. In the process the wet lump rounded into a ball, which became firm when dust dried the outer surface.

I stopped and watched — watched for a long, long time — with feelings at once of homage and of exasperation: homage for their strong assiduity, exasperation at the instinctive stupidity of these insects. One, I remember, tried to roll its load upwards over a twig in the grass. Again and again the dusted ball of dung rolled over and the beetle, clutching the burden tight with all its legs, rolled back down the slope with it.

Behind me was the tremendous panorama of cliffs, and of sea dazzling in a shimmer of amethyst; churches were near which I had come to look at; woods were around where I intended to collect cyclamen, and perhaps to enjoy the sight of unfamiliar orchids. I could not break away from the spectacle of those untiringly toiling beetles. 'Go to the ant, thou sluggard!' the Bible

Two Beetles

enjoins us; 'Go to the dung-beetle, infirm of purpose!' would make a fine annexe to the famous phrase. Backwards up the slope this tribe of a midget Sisyphus rolled their malodorous burden. After every set-back they would set obstinately off again with something more than resolution. The beetle, I understand, eventually hides the ball as food for the progeny of the eggs that she lays in it. Long, long though I watched, I never saw the consummation of their tremendous labours, although some were already a good three feet away from the source of their treasure.

Overhead flamed the hot sun; far below the sea sparkled in a galaxy of broken stars; around were fishing boats which at night, with the lure of their flares, would waver like little full moons on the black surface, floating each on its hemisphere of luminous water; in between were crags and fierce precipices, and steep declivities of woodland. In front of me twinkled on the warm slope the lucent black carapaces of the untiring beetles. Platitudes unfolded in my mind like weeds. What was the force, the passion, which compelled them into their strange and long activities? Was I, when I searched ecstatically for new flowers, or for works of art still unseen by me, was I — could it be? — sharing an ecstasy with these labouring insects? In my quivering hopes at the sight of land botanically promising, or of a building likely to house lovely objects — in the enjoyment of such hopes, though limbs might be aching and breath short — did I partake of a passion like the dung-beetle's?

Indeed, in that clambering crowd images of human behaviour, not always commendable, were to be found. There was one crook and parasite who kept trying to steal the properly acquired possession of another. At each attack the deserving owner clutched her private property with all six legs, and kept still. An odder, and to me rather awful, example I saw on another occasion.

Far-fetched interpretations of human behaviour are very much in the fashion now. A professional psychologist lately gave his opinion that the real reason for Khrushchev breaking off the famous summit meeting was, not that spy planes had flown over Russia, but that, as a child, he had seen his mother smash his pet cat to death against a wall. I am sometimes afraid that I may once, though with very much kinder intentions than mother Khrushchev, have done harm as dreadful to the psyche of a dung-beetle.

I was walking with a friend on a different Amalfitan hill, when we found a group of dung-beetles at work on a path. Their source of material was dryer, and therefore tougher, than that which I had seen worked on near Pogérola. One poor beetle was having the greatest trouble in removing his lump. We decided charitably to help and so, with a stick, feeling like good Samaritans, we cut through the bit which was causing so much difficulty. The beetle let go, and lay quite still, in what seemed like a trance, and from which, although we watched for a long time, we never saw it emerge. What spiritual and moral injury might we not have inflicted on it, we wondered as we set off, haunted with dreadful obsessive anticipations of a long, dull, dungless, barren life for a psychotic beetle, never to be again, throughout all her days, quite right in the head.

Somebody, the thought came to me, said that the English policeman — or was it workman? — is a weight-lifter, while the Italian is a ballet-dancer. When I think of Italians directing traffic with the most delicate gracefulness, their manipulation of the corded, imperative whistle, as it swings in a perfect arc, and the visual perfection of movement in twist of wrist and hand; and then of the majestic Englishman, holding up the traffic, or waving it on with slow and precise movements of monumental arms — when I think of all this, I have to admit a large truth in that saying. The northerner seems to labour at his best with an immensity of muscle; he is a figure that we see ideally portrayed in the paintings of Millet and Van Gogh. For the labouring Italian — and the lazy Italian workman is an Anglo-tourist fiction — the lifting of heavy burdens is an affair of balance, and implies, in his beauty of movement and pose, the etherial inward spirit which has given us all the art of his country. From the sight of an Englishman shouldering heavy loads we divine a character of huge, heroic, long-suffering endeavour, the manifestation of such a spirit as sustained the people in 1940. In the course of such cogitations there seemed to me something un-Italian about the dung-beetle, although S. Bernadino of Siena, in his preaching, alluded to this exemplary insect for moral instruction.[1]

There is another beetle, one of a dazzling group to be discovered in most warm or tropical regions of the world, and which can be taken as entirely concordant with the beauties of the Italian spirit. I first saw it in the valley of the Dragone.

I had been visiting, with a friend, a house in Pontone. This village, as I have said elsewhere, can only be reached by foot-paths, and we had taken the shortest, and roughest, which leads up from the road to Ravello. We were hospitably entertained with coffee and vermouth and spirits. Conversation turned to wines of the neighbourhood, and our hosts brought in a bottle of their own. An open bottle has to be finished; hospitable politeness requires that guests drink the largest part of it. An empty bottle on the table looks unseemly, so another was brought, and then, of course, in due time, another. I was not properly drunk when, in the darkness, we left, but I knew well enough that I had been drinking. My companion was worried over me; in some places, it is true, a tumble on the steep rocky path might have meant a long and painful roll down the mountain-side. I went perfectly well past all the difficulties of the path; it was not until we reached the easy road that I stumbled and fell harmlessly on my knees. I had this excuse, that my attention was distracted by something I had just seen in the utter darkness of the wood. Suddenly, for a short time, all around, but in one space only, the thick night was illuminated with little flying sparks. They darted about us and in a few moments we had left them behind. That evening I saw no more fire-flies, nor any more during that visit. It was late in April.

To write at all about the display of fire-flies is dangerous for

[1] At least once the dung-beetle has been linked to thoughts of sublimity. 'Do you know Fabre?' put in Lord Beveridge. 'He suggests that the beetle rolling a little ball of dung before him, in a dry old field, must have suggested to the Egyptians the First Principle that set the globe rolling. And so the scarab became the symbol of the creative principle — or something like that.' D. H. Lawrence: *The Ladybird*.

anybody who knows Ruskin's description in *Praeterita*: 'The fire-flies among the scented thickets shone fitfully in the still undarkened air. How they shone! Moving like fine-broken starlight through the purple leaves. How they shone! Through the sunset that faded into thunderous night ... the fire-flies everywhere in sky and cloud rising and falling, mixed with the lightning, and more intense than the stars.'

I have never seen fire-flies under a thunder-storm and may therefore perhaps, to some extent, in treating of this matter, be pardoned for falling short of Ruskin. Yet how can I not speak of them? In the southern month of May nothing, not even the variegated vision of fine flowers, nothing can be seen more amazing than, multitudinously flashing, fire-flies in swarms of myriads — something, it would seem between the regular bright beauties of nature, and the man-made fireworks which, about a month later, will, on sacred anniversaries, begin to flash and thunder among the beaches and hills and valleys of the steep mountainous coast.

Naturalists, it would appear, are undecided as to the function of these lights. All observation is against their being a courtship display, a guide or a stimulant to still-virgin mates. The most persuasive argument I have read interprets this magical activity as a communal display. It has been found that some gregarious animals, in particular those which, like certain sea-fish, congregate in vast numbers, distribute themselves according to the distribution of their food; in lean years they are far apart, and in prosperous times relatively crowded. Their medium of communication is, I believe, not known. The fire-fly's language is light; not hunger for love, nor anger at rivals, illuminates this beetle — for a beetle it is — but a need for propitious distribution of the courting community.

Goethe, I have been told, complained when he learnt how scientists with prisms had analysed the white light of day. Elucidation can destroy mystery.

A primrose by a river's brim
Dicotyledon was to him
And it was nothing more

was a parody popular in my youth. Indeed, it is not inspiriting to look on surf or fountain as an arrangement of H₂O. And yet some scientific knowledge can be an aid to contemplation. Understanding of the ancient weather which has carved hills and valleys, of the cold volcano which once violently raised a mountain, can enliven our inward vision when we relish the intrinsic beauty of a landscape. With some vague sense in our minds of their purpose, the spectacle of fire-flies becomes something more than the sight of innumerable fleeting sparks. What is the display of beasts but a germinal art? And what is human art but a display by the highest of the primates?

The fire-fly does not give out a continuous light. In its movement separate sparks appear and vanish, succeeding one another, on and off, rapidly, along a thin line in the darkness. I have sometimes caught a fire-fly and watched its flashing in my hand. This quenching and renewal of tiny lights adds immeasurably to the wonder of the performance.

Long have I sometimes looked from my window, out into the blackness of the deep valley, and across to where forested slopes climb up steeply to cliffs. Now in one place, now in another, the fire-flies will dance more vividly than elsewhere. Among the darkness of the brown-limbed lemon trees they will suddenly appear in their white incandescent brilliance; then across the black depths of the valley the far-off woods will begin sparkling. Wherever the gaze wanders, tiny flashes become visible over large distances. Wall and road, lemon and vine, wild trees of the woodland — all are filled momentarily with grains of clear light, flashing and vanishing, each in a fresh place. Biological causes are forgotten; we can only be aware, watching entranced, of grace and pure beauty, of magical, cool, fleeting, tiny fires, flashing in the magnificence of the shadowed valley. No solemnity of thought intrudes as at the sight of the patient, laboriously enduring dung-beetle. At least, none has ever come to me.

CHAPTER XV

The Miracle of the Manna

In Constantinople, after its infamous conquest by the crusaders, that great benefactor of Amalfi, Cardinal Pietro Capuana, discovered, almost by chance, where was preserved the body of St. Andrew, for long venerated as the patron saint of Amalfi. Visiting the church of the Holy Apostle in the company of some Amalfitans, he was shown where, in that very church, lay the relics of the saint. 'He took them secretly' — so says the account which I have read, prettily euphemising a pious burglary. He kept them hidden in his lodgings until the time came for his return to Italy. He carried away with him the body not only of St. Andrew, but of St. Luke as well. Other relics in his baggage included the head of St. James the less, the hand of St. Philip, the arm of St. George, and many little bones of the Innocents. I do not know if he brought any other of the eminent relics listed by Pansa, which included milk of the Virgin, and wood from the cross of the penitent thief. Not everything was for Amalfi cathedral. His new monastery, now the Hotel Cappuccini, was enriched with many holy remains.

The head of St. Andrew, as I have told, was kept in the stone casket, still visible in the cathedral. Doubters may be a little troubled by a gold reliquary, formerly in the Vatican, reputedly containing the head of St. Andrew and which was lately restored by Pope John to its original home in a Greek monastery. This, I have been reassured, contained only the face bones; it is the cranium which is preserved at Amalfi.

The remains of St. Andrew gave great merit to Amalfi. Many pilgrims, and among them St. Francis, frequented the shrine. A voice from heaven said to St. Bridget of Sweden: 'Go to Amalfi, and visit my apostle St. Andrew. I have made him in that city a repository of my grace.'

On November the twenty-fourth, 1304, an unknown pilgrim, prostrate before the shrine of St. Andrew, rose abruptly and said to a priest nearby: 'What is this that has taken place? Have you not seen it?' The priest paid no attention; but when Mass was over, and the unnamed pilgrim gone, the priest, with others, looked, and were amazed at what they saw. The bones had been enclosed in the substance of the altar, much as the bones of S. Felice were disposed of at Nola (as I have mentioned in the chapter on the miracle of the blood). In the hollow underneath was a silver vessel, and none could tell by what means it had come there. In the vessel was liquid, and on its surface floated a gummy substance like manna.

Guide-books say that the bones of the apostle exude the 'manna', which miraculously liquefies on the vigil of the saint, November the twenty-ninth. In a tablet, recording the embellishment of the crypt by Spanish kings, mention is made of the 'holy dew'. For a period during the sixteenth century, owing, it was supposed, to contemporary sinfulness of the citizens, the miracle failed. In the next century morals would seem to have improved, for on November the twenty-fourth,[1] 1686, the miracle happened again. A record of the times declares that an abundant effusion was looked on as a normal event.

One year I arranged a visit so as to witness the miracle. On the evening when, as several of my local friends put it, they 'make the manna', I made my way to the cathedral. I first went into the crypt where, in a nineteenth-century reliquary of rococo style, the skull of the apostle was exposed on the altar. It consists, as I have said, only of the cranium with, in part, the back of the head. The authenticity of ancient relics must always be doubtful. Yet one thing is certain: for some fifteen hundred years and more this skull was reverenced as the veritable organ which enclosed the

---

[1] It will be noticed that the miracle was first observed on November the twenty-fourth and that, in the seventeenth century it recommenced on the same day. This may be due to an error of transcription. If it be correct, I do not know when November the twenty-ninth became the habitual date of the wonder.

thought of St. Andrew, brother of St. Peter, and first called of all the apostles. In face of such antiquity of faith, only a mean and trivial spirit could feel nothing of veneration.

There is a liturgy for the vigil of St. Andrew, and this was being celebrated in the cathedral overhead. I attended about half of the service and then, to be sure of a good view, I went back to the crypt. I got as close as I could to the altar, in front of which, defined by benches, was an open space for the clergy. A series of invocations to St. Andrew is printed for the use of the devout. A woman was reading it, and the people spoke the responses. That a woman should conduct any sort of service is, so Roman Catholic friends have told me, a most unusual occurrence. Women are associated with the miracle of St. Januarius in Naples. I have sometimes wondered if these miraculous lique-factions may not derive from antique ceremonies with which priestesses were associated.

Inside the altar is a large cupboard-like space, a baroque equivalent of the opening in Romanesque altars; this is called the Confessio, and relics were enclosed in it. Various vessels are there, but no relics are visible. The enclosing grids were now open. The space was lit inside.

The crypt became very full, and at last the archbishop came down with his attendants. He knelt before the altar. Prayers were said. At intervals a priest looked inside. The congregation recited the Creed, and then the *Ave Maria*. Suddenly the priest brought out from under the altar a small glass jug, covered by a wide and shallow funnel. The jug had glass legs and a slender spout.

'The miracle has happened!' proclaimed the priest and, tipping the jug, revealed a small amount of clear liquid. The jug was put on the altar, and the congregation sang the hymn of St. Andrew. Then the priest began to distribute pieces of cotton-wool dipped in the manna (this must have been from an earlier miracle). People jostled forward until a child knocked over and broke a glass lamp with a candle in it.

'I shall not give you any more,' said the priest and then, relenting, continued his largesse from a place where careless folk could do no damage.

Outside, another ceremony was going on. People were ascending the cathedral steps, on each of which they paused to say a prayer. Disguising my curiosity as best I could, I stood close to one of the devout. She was reciting the *Ave Maria* and this, I suppose, was the practice of all. Speed of speech got some to the top in shorter time than others. I do not know if this act of devotion incurs defined benefits. Many carry it out and, until late at night, the slow, devout, murmurous ascent of the stairs is going on.

Peculiar local legends have gathered about St. Andrew. He seems to be a testy saint but this, as with the severe S. Trofimena of Minori, has not one whit diminished the affection for him of the Amalfitans. Some of these stories are most odd. St. Mark came from Venice — I presume osseously — to visit St. Andrew in Amalfi. St. Andrew was given to understand that the visit must be courteously repaid, but this he was very unwilling to do. When the time came for his journey, he called up so tremendous a storm that the venture became impossible; indeed, the tempest drowned a number of fishermen, of whom he is the especial protector. At another time some alteration displeasing to him was made either in the ceremony or in the ordering of the next day's procession. When his effigy was being carried out of the cathedral, there fell such a deluge of rain that the procession had to be given up. Once he quarrelled with his brother St. Peter, protector of Cetara, some ten miles to the east. The effigies of the two saints were taken by boat and, meeting at sea, half way, the saintly brothers were reconciled. These bizarre stories illustrate, first, how real a person is St. Andrew to the Amalfitans: secondly, the living fecundity of that country in the creation of legend.

In the performance of his miracle, he is not so complacent as S. Pantaleone at Ravello. I have been four times to the ceremony, and twice he failed. On the first such occasion the priest said: 'Since the miracle has failed, we must pray every day until . . . "such and such a date," . . . and especially we must pray for the Pope.' That evening I told a cynical friend about it. 'That is because the demochristian vote has dropped,' he said. 'The Pope must have written to St. Andrew, telling him not to do the miracle.' On the second defective occasion, when I had brought friends, the priest contented himself with pointing out that the failure of the miracle had no bearing on things of the spirit; St. Andrew was none the less a presence among them. At one moment looking — guiltily as we thought, though I dare say mistakenly — in our direction, he said: 'It is not a spectacle!' After these failures people sang as heartily as when the miracle had happened, the hymn of St. Andrew. Next morning the procession was magnificent as ever, and just as enthusiastically attended.

A band waits in the cathedral square. Advance guards assemble in the portico. Banners appear, one with the image of the nymph Amalphi; others bear the city arms, with its Maltese cross. The bearers and attendants are most of them clothed in long red garments. Some wear on chains large medallions with the image of St. Andrew. When a canopy appears in the portico they get into order, some on the steps, some below. Then through the bronze doors appears the great silver image of St. Andrew. Metal fish dangle from his arm; a miniature boat is beside him. He is carried slowly down the steps. The archbishop follows, mitred, and with attendants holding his garments. Lesser clergy come behind. The cavalcade turns and disappears north towards the Valle dei Molini. Intermittent explosions indicate pauses of the invisible saint. After a while he returns in the direction of the sea. At this moment a display of fireworks starts up from the mole. It would be wonderful, if only we could see more than smoke with bright sparks in it. Rockets shoot up, first a few at a time and then, finally, a long, echoing, deafening cannonade. The mole thunders, the mountains roar, as though lifeless nature were shouting its homage to the saint. St. Andrew is then carried to the beach and set down close to the waves, where he blesses the sea and the fishermen. I have been told that once the organisers of the procession decided to omit this part of it. Some of the wronged fishermen accordingly seized the image and carried it themselves to the verge of the sea (this must have been with the connivance of the proper, appointed bearers, or else a most indecorous scene would have resulted). After the second failure of the miracle, this diversion would have been impossible. Huge waves were roaring ceaselessly up over all the shingle. The apostle had indeed been disobliging.

At my first sight of it, after the procession had returned from the sea to the road, I met a friend. We chatted for a while, and then he said: 'Shall we watch St. Andrew going back into the cathedral?' and we went into the Piazza Duomo. The precedent partakers in the procession, red-robed, went up the steps. St. Andrew remained below, while the archbishop and attendant clergy ascended and solemnly entered the cathedral. St. Andrew was lifted, and I noticed, behind the bearers, a scrum of men, each with his hands out, to push his fellow in front of him. They began to run. Swiftly, unpausingly, the great figure of St. Andrew rushed up the steps to the portico, while the crowd loudly applauded; he rested a little, and then entered his abode.

I have told how the bearers of the Madonna run up the steps at Maiori. In the procession of St. Matthew at Salerno, the apostle is accompanied by many lesser saints. These, on their return to the cathedral, are carried up the aisle at a trot. Slowly, solemnly, St. Matthew follows after them to the altar.

What does this hurrying signify? St. Mary at Sea chose Maiori for herself. St. Andrew, it is true, arrived at Amalfi as holy loot; yet he was content enough in his Italian resting-place to honour it with miracles, and to save the city from Saracen invasion. Let me recall the story of his unwillingness to quit Amalfi, even though it was to honour St. Mark. May it be that among the petty, local, friendly little gods whom the saints displaced, there were some in particular repute for love of the land they protected? Well might such a spirit, after outward display, hasten back, like St. Andrew, to his shrine.

A fitting protector, St. Andrew, for a maritime community. Under his care, the republic prospered for long with her far-wandering merchant fleets. From some disasters he preserved the city. And today he is invoked there for so many benefits that I sometimes wonder how he has time for the affairs of my native country, Scotland. Some of his southern duties are enumerated in his hymn:

The Miracle of the Manna

O protector of Amalfi, St. Andrew our leader, shed a ray of thy brightness to lighten our spirit. Hurl a dart of thy love into the breasts of thy children and, in a flash, fire all with the flame of charity. As innocent babes, from the cradle, we cried to thee; today our vows and our love still are turned towards thee. Be enthroned upon the prows of Amalfitan ships; bring back in safety from far-off shores every steersman. Fisher of Galilee, bless each morning both net and shore, both bark and fishermen. Assuage tempestuous seas, keep away sickness and rain-fall and thunder, at the sweet sound of thy name, O most noble protector.

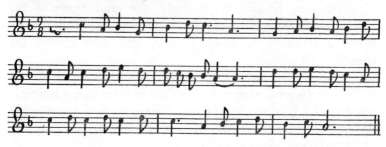

Epilogue

A little inland from Minori, on eastern slopes of the valley, is an ancient church tower. Of the church itself nothing seems to remain. That tower, which I have never troubled to visit, stands up for me now like a finger, beckoning to future discoveries and, at the same time, admonishing me for many indolent failures. If fullness be a duty, there must always be ahead of me, in the pleasures of new searching, the uneasiness of a troubled conscience. 'In this I have failed,' I will say to myself as already, since this work was apparently ended, I have heard and seen things which appeared, though ever so slightly, to magnify the vision.

In a lifetime of thought and reading and enquiry I have become certain of one thing, the extent of my own huge ignorance. Over twelve years and more I have explored the territories of Amalfi, I have read and talked of Amalfi. Always I am discovering something fresh: in a mill, the great stone wheels pulping olives before the all but sacramental process of pressing out the oil; in the press itself, the ooze of oil trickling glitteringly down like an amber-green varnish; and, concerning a weather-cock in Amalfi, the unkind saying of several neighbouring towns: 'When the cock crows, Amalfitans will speak the truth.' The foot-square hole at the base of a vine-terrace, with a serpent inside which comes out once in a hundred years, in weight a hundred quintals, and with a head as large as a small room (I have not discovered the date of its last appearance).

My intention has been to present, as they have become known to me, the face and spirit of Amalfi. Until a man is dead we cannot conceive his full character. Until my last visit is over, revelations will come to me whose omission I shall rue. Yet, although actions of friends the most intimate will at times surprise us, we do not therefore conclude that we haven't known them. In the incompleteness of our knowledge we each of us see, in the same person, to some degree, a different character, and the difference depends upon the perception of our own years.

I have drawn as best I could the portrait of my Amalfi — the city and all the lands of the dead republic — drawn them as they have bewitched my enwrapt spirit. Could new legends, new explorations, or works of art undiscovered still, alter for me, although they might enrich, that inward vision, the vision I have attempted to impart? Would it not rather be a filling-in of blank spaces in a map I already know. My eyes, and my enquiring mind have their preferences. The given picture and character of the country are what I have, in a way, chosen to see. Others may find for themselves a different Amalfi; what I have offered here is my own.

28. Below S. Maria dei Monti, to the north (page 201)

29. Léttere: the castle and old cathedral tower (page 207)

APPENDIX I

Dates significant in the history of Amalfi

———————

Many of these, even down to the Norman times, derive from early and unreliable chronicles and traditions, and cannot be taken as reliable; yet they are at least roughly true, and the chronology is probably accurate.

100–150 Probable date of the Roman villa at Minori.

328 Founding of Constantinople.

339 Supposed year when the traditional founders of Amalfi set sail.

400–500 (roughly) Period of Barbarian invasions, and the epoch when probably the Amalfitan community was founded in Scala.

553 Teias, last king of the Goths, defeated near Léttere by the army of Justinian, and Amalfi becomes formally part of the Byzantine empire.

571 Lombard duchy established in Benevento.

596 First mention of a bishop of Amalfi.

Eighth century. Amalfi, for a while, in association with Naples.

Early ninth century. Naples seized by Sicone, Lombard prince of Benevento, and Amalfi becomes independent, subject to the shadowy overlordship of Constantinople.

838 Amalfi seized by Sicardo, Lombard prince of Benevento and Salerno.

839 Amalfi frees herself and
The first prefect established as elected head of the state.

849 The fleet of Amalfi, with those of Naples and Gaeta, defeats a Saracen fleet threatening Rome.

Appendix I

897 Amalfi defeated by Sorrento in a war at sea.

914 The first judge, Mastolo I, installed as head of the state.

958 Judge Mastolo II murdered and Sagio chosen as first of the doges.

981 Mansone, doge of Amalfi, seizes Salerno and assumes the style of prince.

983 Loss of Salerno.

987 Amalfi becomes an archbishopric.

1003 Arrival of Normans in south Italy, some of whom in
1016 help to raise a Saracen siege of Salerno.

1030 Rainulph the Norman invested as count with the city and territories of Aversa, the first such achievement by a Norman.

1059 Robert Guiscard invested by the Pope at Benevento with the duchy of Apulia, with Calabria and with Sicily.

1073 Amalfi taken and sacked by Robert Guiscard, who now adds to his other titles the style of Duke of the Amalfitans.

1096 Amalfi revolts, and elects the last of her doges. Roger Borsa, son of Robert Guiscard, besieges the city, which is saved by the sudden departure to the first crusade of many besiegers.

1101 Final subjugation by the Normans of Amalfi, which retains certain autonomous rights.

1130 Roger, nephew of Robert Guiscard, anointed king of Sicily.
Revolt of Amalfi on Roger's plan to extinguish her last republican privileges.

1131 The revolt defeated.

1135 and 1137 Sack by Pisans of Amalfi, Atrani, Ravello, Scala, Minori and Maiori. Pandects of Justinian stolen, and a colony of 'Africans' settled in Atrani.

1193 Accession of Frederick II as king of Sicily and Emperor.

1250 Death of Frederick: the kingdom ruled by his natural son Manfred.

1258 Manfred crowned king of Sicily.

1266 Manfred being deposed by the Pope, Charles of Anjou is crowned king of Sicily. Manfred dies in battle. During these wars Charles was supported by Amalfi, and Manfred in revenge planted a colony of Saracens in Atrani (but see page 276).

1268 Conradin, grandson of Frederick II, attempting to recover his kingdom, captured by Charles of Anjou, and beheaded in Naples. During these troubles Maiori and Minori sacked by Pisans.

1282 Sicilian Vespers and political separation of Naples and Sicily.

1443–1458 Sicily and Naples united during his reign under Alphonso of Aragon.

1461–1468 Piccolomini dukes of Amalfi. The second, Alphonso, who died in 1498, was married to Joanna of Aragon, Webster's Duchess of Malfi.

1502 Naples seized by Spain.

1552–1707 Naples and Sicily ruled by Spanish viceroys.

1738 Don Carlos recognised as first Bourbon king of Naples.

1806–1808 Joseph Bonaparte king of Naples, succeeding the Parthenopean republic set up after the French conquest.

1808–1815 Murat king of Naples.

1861 Francis II, last king of Naples, surrenders Gaeta, and his kingdom is absorbed into the kingdom of Italy. There followed a long period of misery and disturbance in the south when Bourbonist resistance, allied with bandits, troubled much of the country.

　　Under fascist rule Atrani was joined administratively to Amalfi. With the return of democratic government, their integrity was restored.

APPENDIX II

The Maritime Republic: a short history of Amalfi

On an early visit to Amalfi, while the ship I had travelled on was making fast in the harbour, I saw a strange sight. Up the eastward rising road was travelling slowly a large, archaically designed boat. On shore, I asked about it. There had just been held in Amalfi the annual regatta of the four ancient maritime republics, Genoa, Pisa, Venice and Amalfi. What I had seen was the Genoese boat starting out on its long overland journey home. During the festivities Amalfi had been celebrating the magnificence of her ancient independence, and the times when her rivalry with those other sea-faring communities had involved graver matters than the racing of picturesque boats.

Old histories of Amalfi begin with legends to account for the name. A Roman lady called Amalphi, according to one story, enchanted by the many delights of the coast, founded a town to settle in, and gave it her own name. More poetic is the story of a beautiful nymph Amalphi living here, with whom, after killing Cacus, robber of cattle, Hercules fell in love. The name of Amalphi is not to be found in Smith's great dictionary of Greek and Roman antiquities. Nevertheless these most doubtful traditions have left one certain mark on the place; to this day a municipal banner bears the image of the nymph (or lady) Amalphi.

The traditional founding of Amalfi is too Virgilian to be true, and too good to be passed over. Although feeble with improbabilities the story may well embody something of historic truth.

In the year 339, so the story goes, certain noble Romans, in five ships, set sail for the newly founded city of Constantinople.

Storm-beset in the Adriatic, they were driven ashore at Ragusa. Although kindly received, they became uneasy within three years, having incurred the distrust of the inhabitants. They set off again and landed a little to the north of Palinuro, on the Tyrrhenian sea. They built a settlement there beside a river named Molfia or Melfa (other variations are Molfa, Malfa, Malfia and Melfia). From this they came to be known as Malfitani or Amalfitani. Their situation being insufficiently fortified, and too much exposed to barbarian incursions, they removed to Eboli. Here they abode for some considerable time. Eboli did not seem secure enough, and finally they settled in easily defended Scala, occupied then only by a people of aboriginal stock (Pansa records a tradition that Piacenza, having supported Hannibal, was destroyed by the Romans, and the inhabitants eventually settled in the mountains of Amalfi). From here, increasing in numbers and riches, they eventually founded and fortified the city of Amalfi, giving it the name they had acquired for themselves near Palinuro.

The first puzzling improbability is the course which they followed. It is difficult to conceive how voyagers from western Italy, with whatever perversity of the winds, could have been driven on to the Balkan coast near Ragusa. And if they had come from coasts of the Adriatic, why did they voyage to Palinuro, with its beautiful but uncouth inland of the Cilento mountains? They would either have continued to Constantinople, or returned home. There was no thought at the time of barbarian invasions, whether from land or sea. Italy was safe in the fourth century.

Having got them to the Tyrrhenian coast, their movements are still difficult to explain. Even a hundred years later, the danger was rather from land than sea. Their abode near Palinuro was a more hopeful refuge than Eboli, standing as it does so close to the vulnerable plain. It would seem that we have here several traditions blended rather clumsily into one. Yet plausible conclusions may be drawn. The name Amalfi might well come from a settlement on the variously named river. (The founders of Positano are said to have come from another part of the same region.) The probability is this: When Italy began to be devastated by barbarian invasions, many people fled from dangerous places to the security of obscure mountains. The tradition must put the settlement at too early a date. Barbarians did not appear in Italy until the fifth century. Our best analogy is Venice which, for the same reason, was founded among waters and marshland, and where the earliest church is traditionally said to have been consecrated in 432; it must have been at some such date that many people fled to the mountains of the Sorrento peninsula and established a community which was to grow into the flourishing and splendid republic of Amalfi. Never was it to be conquered or ravaged by pagan barbarians — unique in this among the Italian cities, except for Venice.

It should be remembered that the state was initiated while the western empire, though tottering, was still in existence. The founders were Roman and, for seven hundred years, an islet of the classic empire was to survive on the bay of Salerno.

About the constitution of the earliest settlements we know nothing. Since, even after the establishment of Lombard principalities in Campania, the republic of Amalfi practised Roman law, it is likely this Italian settlement was administered as were the municipalities of the Roman empire.

Huns, Vandals and Goths invaded and devastated Italy. Amalfi, among her mountains, remained immune. There is no evidence of its becoming in any way subservient to the Christian Gothic kingdom, under which Italy prospered. In the sixth century Justinian, emperor in Constantinople, reconquered so much of the western empire as lay around the Mediterranean — North Africa, Italy, Spain and much of France (according to one tradition, Ravello became populated by immigrants during the long course of these wars). Amalfi, while owing a nominal allegiance to Byzantium, remained in fact a self-governing state. Even the legal bond was very tenuous. In relations with the Lombards, in making war or peace, there was no mention of her formal overlord, the emperor in Constantinople. At their greatest the territories of Amalfi extended along the coast from somewhere beyond Positano to Cetara. Westward they ended at the borders of Sorrento, which was subject at times both to Naples and

Salerno, and was also for long periods independent. Northward, beyond the mountains, they included Gragnano and Léttere, and probably touched the river Sarno, which debouches into the bay of Naples north of Castellammare; eastward they marched with the confines of Cava, a city subject to the Lombard princes of Salerno.

In the year 596 — the first exact date in her history — a Primemio or Primenio is mentioned as bishop of Amalfi, proving her to have become by then a city of some importance. Many cities of south Italy were at that time under Byzantine rule. When the eastern grasp on them lessened, they established themselves as autonomous republics, Naples being the first to do so. In 568 the Lombards invaded north Italy. Penetrating southward, they founded the great duchy of Benevento. Their domination in the south lasted almost five hundred years, until their conquest by the Normans. They never established a secure dynasty, and these southern territories were at times divided into the three duchies or principalities, often mutually hostile, of Capua, Benevento and Salerno. In these cities they have left to this day some notable monuments as, for example, the campanile in Capua, the church of S. Sofia in Benevento, and the aqueduct in Salerno.

During the eighth century, Charlemagne imposed himself on Italy by force, inaugurating the Holy Roman Empire which, as the Austrian empire, lingered on into the time of many of us who are alive today. The Lombards acknowledged themselves as feudatories of the western emperor; Amalfi remained formally loyal to Byzantium. Immune from those troubles and wars, she built up a fleet, both military and commercial, and the trade began which was to make her rival to Pisa, Genoa and Venice. For a while she seems to have been associated with the duchy of Naples, her sole declension in early times from independence; yet such evidence as remains indicates an association closer to alliance than to subjection. Her fleet was her own; her conduct of affairs was that of a sovereign rather than a servile state.

In the early ninth century, Sicone, Lombard prince of Benevento, subjugated Naples, and stole the relics of St. Januarius. It

was then, evidently, that Amalfi assumed indisputable independence. A little after 830 Sicone was succeeded by his more overbearing son, Sicardo (at this time the Saracens began their
conquest of Sicily). Sicardo was then undisputed lord of Benevento and Salerno. There was the possibility that he might have
established a large, enduring realm, as the Normans were to do
some three centuries later. Many Amalfitans settled under his rule
in Salerno. In 838 Sicardo besieged and, aided by traitors,
captured Amalfi. At the time there were fortifications towards
the sea. Various tempests are recorded which destroyed large
parts of the city, and there must once have been flat inhabited
land where now there is water. It was the seaward defences which
were treacherously opened to Sicardo. After sacking the town, he
withdrew.

Sicardo's outrage infuriated even the Amalfitans who had made
themselves subject to him in Salerno. In the autumn of 839,
profiting by the absence in the country of many citizens at work
on the harvest and vintage, the Amalfitans of Salerno, having
asked for ships from their compatriots, rose and, after sacking the
town much as the Israelites spoiled the Egyptians, returned to
Amalfi.

The year 839 is supremely important in the history of Amalfi.
The citizens resolved to establish a new and firm constitution.
They set up a prefect as head of the state. The system was electoral,
and the post intended to be yearly. This was the beginning of
Amalfitan greatness, which lasted until 1101, when the state
was finally subdued by the Normans.

The records of Amalfi are meagre; the names and dates of
rulers are in many cases known only from their appearance in
civil contracts. The chronicles are no more than annals, and
lack altogether those lively trivialities which make the reading
of history enjoyable. The election of prefects was carried out, it is
said, by the worthies of Amalfi and Atrani; there is no record of
other communities of the republic having any say in the proceedings.

The prefects would seem to have lacked absolute power, yet
they were leaders of a state growing in importance, and whose

help was sometimes called for in affairs of great consequence. It is perhaps significant that they were first created in the year when Sicardo died by assassination. Radelchi, his treasurer, was elected in his place as prince of Benevento. Siconolfo, younger brother and rightful heir to Sicardo, was imprisoned in Taranto. The Salernitans, resenting the rule of Radelchi, and forgetting their late implacable fury against Amalfi, asked for her help in the rescue of Siconolfo. Ships were required.

In darkness the Amalfitans landed at Taranto, and wandered around crying: 'For the love of God, give us shelter this night.' The only lodging available was in the castle where Siconolfo was, and there they were hospitably received. They invited the keepers to sup with them, and offered heavy wine, which they themselves drank watered. When the guards had become drunkenly insensible, the Amalfitans took their weapons and liberated the prince. He, though close prisoner, had been well treated and free to roam about the castle. His evenings he had enjoyed in the embraces of a young Grecian woman of rare beauty. Although the record says nothing of it, we must hope that he took her faithfully away with him.

This apparently chivalrous act by Amalfi may have been not without cunning. In Salerno, Siconolfo was proclaimed prince of Benevento, with the accord of some from that city, and also from Capua. Anarchy and civil war followed, weakening the most dangerous neighbour of Amalfi.

Their fleet was often prayed for, in most cases as aid against the Saracens. In the ninth century they twice came to the rescue of Rome from a fleet of Saracens. Of one such occasion, in 849, Gibbon wrote: 'A fleet of Arabs and Moors . . . cast anchor before the mouth of the Tyber, sixteen miles from the city; and their discipline and numbers appeared to threaten, not a transient inroad, but a serious design of conquest and dominion. But the vigilance of Leo had formed an alliance with the vassals of the Greek empire, the free and maritime states of Gayeta, Naples and Amalphi; and in the hour of danger, their galleys appeared in the port of Ostia under the command of Caesarius the son of the Neapolitan duke, a noble and valiant youth, who had already vanquished the fleets of the Saracens. With his principal companions, Caesarius was invited to the Lateran palace, and the dextrous pontiff affected to enquire their errand, and to accept with joy and surprise their providential succour. The city bands, in arms, attended their father to Ostia, where he reviewed and blessed his generous deliverers. They kissed his feet, received the communion with martial devotion, and listened to the prayer of Leo, that the same God who had supported St. Peter and St. Paul on the waves of the sea would strengthen the hands of his champions against the adversaries of his holy name. After a similar prayer, and with equal resolution, the Moslems advanced to the attack of the Christian galleys, which preserved their advantageous station along the coast. The victory inclined to the side of the allies, when it was less gloriously decided in their favour by a sudden tempest, which confounded the skill and courage of the stoutest mariners. The Christians were sheltered in a friendly harbour, while the Africans were scattered and dashed in pieces among the rocks and islands of an hostile shore. Those who escaped from shipwreck and hunger, neither found nor deserved mercy at the hands of their implacable pursuers. The sword and the gibbet reduced the dangerous multitude of captives; and the remainder were more usefully employed, to restore the sacred edifices which they had attempted to subvert. The pontiff, at the head of the citizen and allies, paid his grateful devotion at the shrines of the apostles; and, among the spoils of this naval victory, thirteen Arabian bows of pure and massy silver were suspended round the altar of the fisherman of Galilee.'

Salerno also benefited from the maritime aid of Amalfi. Some of her warlike activities were less momentous. In 897 there was war at sea with Sorrento, the latter perhaps aided by Naples. Amalfi was defeated, and her prefect captured. He was ransomed, but died from heart-break and humiliation within a few days.

The last of the prefects, Mansone II, had associated with himself, in the year 900, his son Mastalo I. This is the first record of such a practice in Amalfi, though not necessarily the first time it occurred. Mansone was following the imperial Roman custom, when the emperor, the Augustus, elevated an associate to the rank of Caesar who, if he survived, inherited the supreme power. Since the Caesar was often son of the Augustus, a dynasty was thus established within a system which was nominally electoral. Mansone died in 914, and Mastalo, succeeding him, was given a new title, judge, with the prefix 'most glorious'. He reigned until 952. During his time Slav invaders harassed the Adriatic parts of Italy. Mastalo constructed inland fortifications, and in particular a castle near Gragnano, called Castello di Pino. There is reason to think that he was associated in the government, at least formally, with his mother Androsa (or Drosa). On her husband's death she had married one Adalferio. Mastalo II succeeded his father as judge. In 958 he was murdered by, or at the instigation of, one Sergio. In less than sixty years the system of judges was over. Sergio was chosen as first of the doges. His election, it is said, was carried out, *sine aliquo scandalo*, without any scandal. However reprehensibly begun, the system inaugurated the golden age of Amalfi.

The doges, like the briefly established judges, followed the old Roman practice in appointing their successors. Until her ultimate subjection by the Normans, Amalfi was ruled henceforward by members of a single family. The form remained republican, but the doges were, in practice, absolute sovereigns. The law was Roman. A priceless possession of Amalfi was an ancient manuscript, the Pandects of Justinian, who codified the imperial law.[1] At some time, Amalfi drew up a system of maritime laws, known as the *Tavola Amalfitana*. This exists only in late manuscripts, and the date of its compilation appears to be unknown. It is reasonable to suppose that these laws were drawn up during her days of independence.

[1] 'The Pandects . . . have escaped with difficulty and danger from the common shipwreck, and criticism has pronounced, that *all* editions and manuscripts of the West are derived from *one* original. It was transcribed at Constantinople in the beginning of the seventh century, was successfully transported by the accidents of war and commerce to Amalphi, Pisa, and Florence, and is now deposited as a sacred relic in the ancient palace of the republic'. Gibbon: *Decline and Fall*, chapter XLIV.

Appendix II

A tenuous connection was kept up with Constantinople. A doge formally announced his accession to the emperor and was frequently honoured by him, many doges being granted the dignity of imperial patrician, and other Byzantine titles.

Sergio was succeeded in 966 by his son, Mansone III, greatest of the doges (his predecessors of that name had been a prefect and a judge). Amalfi had grown in power and prosperity under Sergio; its magnificence increased under Mansone III. A city of merchant adventurers since the ninth century, Amalfi established trading colonies in many towns of the east, among them Alexandria, Syrian Tripoli, Beirut, Jaffa and Cairo. In this she anticipated both Pisa and Genoa. In Constantinople her merchants had privileges as vassals of the empire. It has been said of Amalfi that her imperialism was commercial and, unlike her rivals', Venice and Genoa, not territorial. Her traders benefited the cities they settled in, and they were welcome in many towns of Italy.

Vestiges of one such a colony I have seen. I was travelling with friends in Apulia, and we went to the coast town of Monopoli, in order to see a church called S. Maria Amalfitana. With such a name, I should in any case have wanted to see it; but there are intrinsic merits in the church, a good Romanesque building, with fine sculpture on the exterior of the apse. It was a happy venture, enlivened by an antipast of mild exasperation. The open space round the church is mostly enclosed by railings, of which the gate was locked. A group was sitting at a door. On our asking how we could get to the apse, a man, with one hand in plaster, said he would find the key. He did better, bringing the key of the church as well. After we had looked round, he took us down to the crypt. We found remains of frescoes in Byzantine style with Greek inscriptions; in one corner of the floor was a rectangular tank. Our friend told us that the water seeped in from the sea, at whose level we were standing. He gave the traditional reason for the naming of the church. An Amalfitan ship was driven on to the rocks here; passengers and sailors vowed that if they came safe ashore, they would build a church in honour of the Virgin. It was, he told us, the crypt which they built; this probably dates from the eleventh century, or a little earlier. The story of the shipwreck may well be true, but this was clearly the church of an Amalfitan community in Monopoli. It stands in the Via Amalfi, a name which must indicate a foreign quarter in the town, as Lombard Street does in the city of London. Our friend, although out of work as a result of his injured hand, refused a tip.

From Arabs and Persians, the Amalfitans acquired cloves, cinnamon, nutmegs of Ceylon, indigo and perfumes of Java, ivory, skins, gems, ambergris, pearls, silk stuffs, and Persian textiles. In return they exported amber, coral, rose-water, iron, timber, hemp, oil, metals and corn. At times they carried on a lucrative trade in slaves.

The duchy of Amalfi matched in miniature the larger countries of Europe; the constituent communities — Ravello, Scala, Positano, Tramonti, Léttere, Maiori, and Minori — resiled continually from a central domination (little political activity is recorded from Capri). Atrani alone remained closely and loyally linked with Amalfi. We may be sure that under the strong rule of the doges these other towns, whatever their municipal patriotism, regarded themselves as ingredients of a powerful and prosperous state.

Mansone had brave ambitions for his country. In 981 a prince of Salerno died and, troubles succeeding, his son could not securely maintain himself. Mansone invaded the city and established himself as its ruler, styling himself prince of Salerno. Indignantly the emperor Otto II seized the town. Mansone, revealing something of his character, pacified the emperor, had promise of his support, and remained in power there for almost three years. On the death of Otto in 983, Mansone was deprived of his princely glory.

The Salernitans may have lamented their revolt. The successor was a cruel and licentious prince who used to say to his companions that he would enjoy after his death the pleasures which he had enjoyed during his life. One night the news came to Salerno that Vesuvius was in eruption. 'For sure,' said the prince, 'some wicked and powerful man is to die soon, since hell has opened to receive him.' In the morning he and a concubine were found dead in his bed, strangled in their sleep, it was affirmed, by demons. For this reason he was called by many John the Accursed.

Mansone lost not only the principality but also, for a time, the duchy of Amalfi. His brother Adalferio, in 984, organised a revolt and deposed him. Adalferio's wife, Androsa, mother of the last judge, Mastalo II, had become by this marriage daughter-in-law to her son's murderer. Mansone, after nearly two years' imprisonment, returned to power and reigned until 1004. Adalferio was exiled to Naples, where he appears to have lived in pomp and consequence.

In 987, at Mansone's request, the Pope elevated the see of Amalfi to an archbishopric, and initiated suffragan bishoprics at Scala, Minori, Léttere and Capri — evidence of population and importance. Amalfi under Mansone III was wealthy and powerful; her ships covered the Mediterranean, enriching her with silver and gold, till she came to be regarded as the Tyre of southern Italy. Her merchant colonies were scattered around the coasts of meridional Europe, Africa, Palestine and Asia Minor; she traded in goods from India, Africa and Arabia. In her was abundance of gold, silver, pearls and precious oriental silks. She was the rival of Venice.

In 1003 there befell a small event of fatal import to Amalfi, and to the Byzantines and Lombards of south Italy. Some Normans sailed from the Holy Land in Amalfitan ships, and landed at Salerno where they were bravely entertained by the prince. They returned home with stories of splendour. In 1016 a Saracen fleet from Sicily attacked Salerno. The siege had lasted for a month, when other Norman pilgrims arrived in Amalfi. Their help was implored by the Count of Avellino; they consented and, with a large company of men from Amalfi, Avellino and Nocera, marched on Salerno. After bloody fighting, the Saracens were driven off. The prince of Salerno, hoping to keep such paladins in his service, made them generous offers. The Normans declared that all they had done was only for the glory of God; they were resolved to go home. The prince sent ambassadors to accompany them, with large stores of apples, citrons, almonds and other exquisite fruits. He added sumptuous saddle-cloths, and mantles stitched in gold. Like the spies of the Israelites, they brought back to their people certain evidence of a rich and fertile country. Early in the eleventh century, Normans returned to southern Italy. The appeared first as professional soldiers in the employ of Lombard princes, much like the *condottieri* of northern Italy, who traded their services to the highest bidder. Norman aid was often decisive in perilous cases, but the Lombards, all unknowing, had traded for present survival their freedom in the future. Fatal in the end to the Lombards were the progeny of Tancred de Hauteville, a small squire of Normandy. First they acquired estates, then territories, until at last under a king, entitled King of Sicily, they ruled the whole of south Italy.[1]

In 1030 Normans had attacked Saracen-held Sicily. By 1046 much of Byzantine Apulia was in their hands. Robert Guiscard was appointed as leader. In 1063, the Saracens suffered a grave defeat in Sicily. In 1071, Bari surrendered. Lord of a great part of Apulia, Calabria and Sicily, Robert resolved on seizing Amalfi. In 1073 it was taken and sacked. Robert now called himself, with his other titles, Duke of the Amalfitans. After violent defence, Ravello and Scala were taken, and suffered fearful destruction. Many discontented aristocrats were seized, and transported to Sicily.

For all his brutality, Robert was a wise ruler. Having captured the duchy of Amalfi he restored its fortifications, and confirmed the inhabitants in their ancient customs and freedom. At the same time it was covenanted that none of his troops should come into the territories of Amalfi. The citizens were to have charge of their defences. His position was much like the Czar's in the Baltic provinces; he was their sovereign, but they did not consider themselves as part of the Russian empire.

Robert Guiscard died in 1085 (his cruciform reliquary, which held a fragment of the true cross, is in Salerno cathedral). He had all but united southern Italy, and made possible the kingdom

---

[1] The complicated epic of this Norman conquest has been lucidly and admirably told by Lord Norwich in *The Normans in the South*. Here I am narrating no more than is needed to understand the history of Amalfi.

which, save for a period under Spanish viceroys, was to last into the second half of the last century. His powers and possessions were assumed by his brother, Roger, Great Count of Sicily.

It is evident that at this time the duchy of Amalfi had much independence; surviving Amalfitan documents from 1093–1095 do not mention Roger. In 1096, the Amalfitans occupied their castles, renounced allegiance to Roger, and elected a doge — the last of all the doges of Amalfi — Marino Pansebaste.

Enraged at the news, Roger called his newphews, Bohemond, the famous crusader, and Roger Borsa, son of Robert Guiscard. The fortresses stood; the sea-defences held, in spite of a fleet carrying, it was said, twenty thousand Saracens from Sicily. Citizens of neighbouring towns came to the help of Amalfi. Six months the siege had lasted, when news came that a French army of crusaders had arrived in Apulia. Bohemond, with his epic cousin Tancred, cut purple cloaks into crosses for their soldiers. For the most part, the troops of the two Rogers followed their example, crying out: 'It is the will of God! It is the will of God!'

The freedom of Amalfi was soon to be benighted, but the sunset, with the glow of this all but miraculous rescue, was glorious. In 1101, Roger recovered Amalfi. The story of his triumph has never been told. One chronicle, called the *Cronica Cavense*, records laconically: 'The year 1101, Duke Roger besieged Amalfi and took it.' An Amalfitan document of January 10, 1102, bears the name of Roger, and of Guiscard, his son associate, and dates it as the second year of their reconquest. It is curious that the little duchy of Sorrento was not incorporated until 1135.

Amalfi was the first to fall of the great republics. Her metropolitan bounds were too narrow; her population was scattered abroad in trading colonies. Had Mansone III succeeded in his conquest of Salerno, a larger, more powerful and more enduring state might have been set up. Yet could she have ever defended herself successfully against the Normans? Venice herself would probably have fallen, like Saxon England, before such conquerors.

Norman rule was not, at first, oppressive. There remained an Amalfitan fleet. A mint, founded in 957 under the prefects,

continued in use until it was abolished by the emperor Frederick
II in 1222. The citizens kept their laws and customs. They
manned their own fortresses. There was still, although Norman,
a ruling duke of Amalfi. Yet how could they be content? Loss
of freedom is always a heavy loss, aggravated in this case by a
most bitter mortification. The Amalfitans looked on themselves,
and with truth, as Romans. To them the Normans must have
appeared as uncouth as did crusaders to the courtiers of Byzantium. To acknowledge such louts as their lords must have
meant a humiliation all but insupportable.

Roger I, dying in 1101, was succeeded by his six-year-old son,
Roger II, who, in 1129, claimed the title of king, in which he was
confirmed by the antipope, Anaclete. In 1130 he was anointed
by an antipapal delegate. Robert Guiscard's work was complete.
Roger immediately set about making his rule secure. Following
this plan, he resolved to abolish utterly the republican status of
Amalfi. He demanded control of the fortresses. The citizens
bravely and resolutely defied him.

He ordered the Sicilian fleet to be brought against Amalfi,
under the Admiral George of Antioch (to whose piety we owe
the mosaics in the Martorana, in Palermo). Troops were sent
into the mountains. Yet Amalfi, with other fortified towns, held
out for almost a year. Then fell the fort in the Siren Isles: then
Capri: then Tramonti together with Ravello, in which the
Amalfitans had put their chief hopes. Scala fell next and the
remoter Castello di Pino. This tale, so brief, of castles illustrates
both the bravery and the hopelessness of that heroic defiance.

On February 17, 1131, Roger himself appeared at Amalfi,
with a large Sicilian fleet. That night, it is told, he awoke to the
sound of his name, softly uttered. He saw a man with an axe,
ready to kill him if he called out.

'Who are you,' said the king, 'an angel or an evil spirit?'
'I am a man like yourself and, as you see, master of your life.'
'Where do you come from, and what do you want of me?'
'I am from Amalfi, and I ask the freedom of my country.'
'What is your name, and who sent you on this errand?'
'I am Pietro Alferio, the fifth of six brothers, who are decided,

as I am, to remain free, or to die. They have chosen me as the bravest of them.'

'Very well, Pietro Alferio!' cried Roger, starting up in a dreadful manner, and seizing his adversary by the throat, 'Tell your five brothers that Roger, naked and out of his sleep, threw down the bravest of the citizens of Amalfi. Tell them, too, if they submit, that they will have less to lament of the past than you, in that you dared to waken King Roger.'

Amalfi fell. Next day, peacefully, the gates were opened. Roger, true to his word, confirmed their laws, their municipal customs and even their own coinage. He demanded only their fleet and their armed men for the subjugation of Naples (dog was very ready to eat dog in those days). But Naples capitulated without a struggle. Her example was followed by almost every rebellious city of the new kingdom. Roger had shown a wise leniency at Amalfi. But henceforward her history was to be bound up, often unfortunately and sometimes all but disastrously, in the history of Italy.

After the Norman conquest, Amalfi lost all shadow of vassalage to the Byzantium emperor, and was accordingly deprived of some trading privileges in Constantinople.

Pisa was then loosely allied with Genoa. There was enmity with Roger. They had begun to harass and brutally frustrate Amalfitan traders. Under fierce threats from Roger, all citizens of Pisa, summoned by the sounding of trumpets, swore on the four gospels that they would respect the rights of Amalfi. Nevertheless, in 1135, when troops and ships were at Salerno in defence of that city, a large Pisan fleet attacked Amalfi and Atrani and neighbouring towns, sacking and inflicting outrageous damage. Roger came late to the rescue and, although the Pisans were utterly defeated, Amalfi was crippled. Two years later the Pisans returned. This time the damage was worse. Atrani was devastated, and most of the inhabitants were removed to Amalfi; their town was repopulated with immigrants from Africa — probably, it is said, Alexandrines — but whether Greek or Arab is not recorded. During those raids many documents were destroyed, and the Pandects of Justinian carried away. Later, when Florence conquered Pisa, the manuscript was deservedly lost to the conquerors. It is now in the Laurentian library. At the same time the Florentines carried away the great chain which was drawn across the river for defence. The chain was later given back to Pisa, and can be seen today in the cloisters of the Campo Santo. Nobody seems to have considered returning the Pandects to Amalfi.

Constance, sister of Roger, was a nun, but was absolved of her vows in order to marry the emperor Henry VI. The Norman male line ended with the death of Roger's grandson. The empress Constance was legitimate heir, but the throne was seized by an illegitimate grandson of Roger called Tancred. The emperor did nothing until the death of Tancred in 1194, when his son acceded to the throne. Henry, in a war of unusual ferocity, took the Norman kingdom, and reigned, in his wife's right, as king of Sicily. In 1197 he died, and was succeeded by his infant son Frederick, who had been born in 1193. This child was to become the most famous emperor, Frederick II, *stupor mundi*. During his reign, Amalfi was first disturbed by divisions between Guelphs and Ghibellines.

It was a calamity of history that the kingdom of Sicily and the Holy Roman Empire should have had at this time the same ruler at their head. This was a period of enormous papal pretensions, the pontiff claiming to be the disposer of kingdoms. The Pope was determined, as a temporal monarch, that never should southern and northern Italy be in the same hands. Frederick, who died in 1250, withstood him, but finally the Pope triumphed over his family.

Frederick was succeeded in power, though not at once on the throne, by his natural son, Manfred. In 1266 the Pope formally deposed Manfred, and proclaimed Charles of Anjou king of Sicily and the mainland territories. Manfred was defeated by Charles, and died in battle. In 1268, Conradin, last prince of Norman blood, fighting for his kingdom, was defeated and captured by Charles, and publicly beheaded in Naples. But for the fatal imperial connection, the Normans might well have established a settled kingdom, lasting, like the kingdom of

England, into modern times. Had there been a strong, able and lasting dynasty in Naples and Sicily, the history of modern Italy would have been different. Indeed, the neglected south might have been faring better than it does today.

Amalfi had its unwilling share of consequent troubles. The Pope had resisted with arms and excommunication the successors of Frederick, whose own long terms of excommunication imposed interdicts on Amalfi. When Manfred fought as king of Sicily, he punished Amalfi for having taken the Guelph or papal side, by settling a thousand Saracens in Atrani.[1]

The Angevins were incompetent rulers, from whom Amalfi suffered greatly. From the beginning, ancient privileges were taken away, and intolerable taxes imposed; according to a contemporary writer, not only money was taken from the people, but their very marrow and blood as well. Rights of Amalfi were confirmed from time to time, and as often violated. During the schism when there were pope and antipope — and once three popes at a time — ecclesiastical life was sometimes confused by the appointment of two archbishops. The rulers, occupied in civil strife, were unable to protect the land. The coast of Amalfi was exposed to raids by Saracens, Pisans, Genoese and Sicilians (after the Sicilian Vespers, the island was at enmity with Naples).

During these continuous troubles, the disintegration of the duchy was miserably demonstrated by some towns taking one side, some another, so that at times Ravello and Scala, for instance, were at war with one another. The very towns were divided in themselves; once two castles in Amalfi were held by different factions.

Nature increased the miseries of the land. On November 24th, 1343, a storm of tremendous violence struck the Mediterranean; the city of Amalfi is said to have been diminished by a third. A few years later came, calamitously, the black death. Yet such was the resilience of the people, worthy of their Roman forebears, that

---

[1] It is curious if this peculiar outrage was twice inflicted on the same town. It may be that chroniclers have made two incidents out of one. Mansi, mentioning only one such plantation, says that it was carried out by Pisans at the behest of Manfred.

prosperity continued. During the thirteenth century Pisan and Genoese outrages had deprived them finally of their eastern trade; after, they confined their activities, very profitably, to the western Mediterranean. Politically, Amalfi was allowed many of her ancient rights and customs; her dukes, however, were little more than feudal lords, who profited by many dues and taxes which formally went to the benefit of the state.[1] One ducal family must be of interest to every literate Englishman.

Pius II, Aeneas Silvius Piccolomini, is, to men of today, perhaps the most attractive of the great Renaissance popes. Diarist, poet, writer, humanist, he is probably best known from the dazzling frescoed history of his life painted by Pinturicchio in the cathedral library at Siena: and to some by the exquisite, miniature town of Pienza which he caused to be built at his birth-place in Tuscany. He adopted his sister's son, Antonio Todeschini, and made him take the name of Piccolomini.

Alphonso V of Aragon became — by the will of Joanna II — king of Naples, as Alphonso I. Being hereditary king of Sicily, he united the two countries under one crown for the first time since the Norman rule. Though the union did not last, this was the foreshadowing of the kingdom of the two Sicilies. On his death in 1458, he bequeathed Sicily to his brother, king of Navarre, and the Italian mainland to his natural son Ferdinand. Pope Calixtus III, having been at enmity with Alphonso, refused to confirm Ferdinand, alleging him to be the supposed and not the true son of Alphonso, a declaration which encouraged rebellion in the kingdom. (Calixtus introduced to Rome his nephew Rodrigo Borgia, later to become Pope Alexander VI.) Calixtus died and Pius II, succeeding him, declared that the kingdom had reverted to the church. After negotiations and various conditions accepted, Pius and Ferdinand became reconciled. Ferdinand was crowned by a papal legate. We must favour him, at least for a while, since, on their request, he immediately confirmed the municipal rights of Amalfi and Atrani.

---

[1] Mastalo II, the judge, granted to Amalfi cathedral the rights of Maiori beach: and to the church of S. Trofimena, in Minori, the rights of the beach there. Mastalo's grants were evidently munificent.

Many supported, as rightful king, John, son of Renato of Anjou, a representative of the deposed dynasty. The communities of Amalfi, except for Ravello and Tramonti, declared for John. For some time the Angevins prevailed until Ferdinand, desperately besieged in Naples, begged help of Pius, who sent an army under the command of Antonio Piccolomini. Ferdinand triumphed, aided in the east by an Epirote prince. He rewarded Antonio with the hand of his natural daughter Maria, and endowed him with the duchy of Amalfi. Maria died young, leaving three daughters.

In 1493 Antonio died leaving, by a second marriage, a son named Alphonso as duke of Amalfi. Alphonso married Joanna of Aragon, a niece of Ferdinand. In 1498 he died, leaving his wife pregnant. The posthumous child was a boy, also called Alphonso. During his minority she administered the duchy.

She had a steward named Antonio Bologna. He is described as a fine and handsome gentleman. She fell in love and so, it would appear, did he. They were secretly married. A boy she gave birth to undiscovered was named Frederick, and was sent away to be brought up and educated in safety and undetected. A girl followed, and the brothers, one of them a cardinal, became suspicious. Bologna seeing this, and believing himself to be suspected and in danger of assassination, escaped to Ancona with the children. The duchess, pregnant by him a third time, resolved to follow, and declared that she had a vow to fulfil at Loreto. She followed Bologna to Ancona and there, to her household, told of her secret marriage, ending: 'I would rather live privately with my husband, than remain duchess.'

Her brother, the cardinal, hearing of this, had them banished from Ancona. Bologna fled to Siena, and thence to Padua, where he was eventually killed. The duchess, with her children and maid, was captured and imprisoned in a tower on the Amalfi coast, where they were all murdered. This tower, as I have told, is believed by many to have been the Torre dello Ziro, which still overlooks Amalfi. The story — of the Duchess of Malfi — inspired Webster to uncouth additions and alterations, and to great poetry:

Appendix II

'Cover her face; mine eyes dazzle; she died young'.

The Piccolomini possessed Amalfi for a hundred and thirteen years. It is said that they ruled the duchy mildly and with kindness. The last duke, Giovanni Piccolomini, died in 1584, leaving enormous debts. His mother and guardian, Donna Maria d'Avalos, resolved to sell the duchy to a princess of Melfi, for the agreed price of 212,697 ducats, with which she could satisfy her son's creditors; but the Prince of Stigliano raised the offer to 216,160, a sum he could not immediately raise. The citizens of Amalfi intervened, and guaranteed security with an office of the royal domains. They were successful and, having paid what was owing to the Prince of Stigliano, they gained, within six months, by the sale of many domains, a sum of about 946,000 ducats.

All was over. The proud duchy of Amalfi, the magnificent and intrepid republic, the immemorial treasury of Roman blood and ways, had become no more than a property on the market. Indeed, she had not even a king of Naples or Sicily for overlord. The kingdom had been seized by the Spaniards in 1502. After that, until 1552, a period of confusion followed. Then, until the coming of the first Bourbon king in 1738, Amalfi, once a splendid and autonomous vassal of the Byzantine empire, was to be ruled by a Spanish viceroy in Naples.

Index

To avoid confusion with people and places named after saints, the names of churches are printed in italics

Adalferio, usurping doge of Amalfi, 270
Agérola, 28, 192
Allium neapolitanum, 120
  pendulinum, 119–20
  roseum, 120
  triquetrum, 119
Alnus cordata, 128–9
Alphonso I of Aragon, king of Naples, 159, 166, 259
Alyssum maritimum, 115, 130
Amalfi, 25, 39–62, 108–13, 210, 248–254, 255
  Arsenal, 62
  Cathedral, 42–46, 51–58, 90
  Chiostro del Paradiso, 59
  Crocifisso, 42, 44, 59–60
  Hotel Cappuccini, 61, 248
  Hotel Luna, 61
  Piazza Duomo, 42
    Flavia Gioia, 39–41
  S. Maria Maggiore, 61
Anacletus (Antipope), 75, 273
Andrea da Salerno, 66–68, 84, 92, 160
Anemone apennina, 117
  hortensis (stellata), 117
Antonello da Capua, Angelo, 164–166
Aragon, Joanna of, Duchess of Malfi, 259, 278
Archangeli, giovanni: *Flora Italiana*, 216, 220
Aristolochia species, 199
Artemisia camphorata, 128

Athanasius, Bishop and Duke of Naples, 210
Atrani, 62–70, 71, 109–11
  Carmine, 71
  Festa of the Magdalen, 187, 189
  Maddalena, 65, 66, 68
  S. Maria del Bando, 69–70
  S. Salvatore, 48–9, 63–65
Attwater: *Penguin Dictionary of Saints*, 138–9
Augustariccio, Archbishop of Amalfi, 60
Avington (Berkshire), 205

Bari, 140
Barisano da Trani, 76, 77, 87
Battenti, procession and hymn of, 110–11
Bayeux Tapestry, 44
Behrens, Timothy, 81
Benevento, 50
  Cathedral and doors, 50
Berenson, Bernard, 30, 36, 48, 59, 214, 237
Berkeley, Lennox, 110
Bernini, Pietro, 56, 57
Bisceglie (Apulia), 136
Blake, William, 177
Blythburgh (Suffolk), 49
Boccaccio, 30
Bohemond, Prince of Antioch, 49, 272
Bologna, Antonio, 278
Bologna, Ferdinando, 227
Bologna, Archbishop Michele of Amalfi, 52, 53

Index

Bonaparte, Joseph, 259
Borsa, Roger, 258, 272
Breakspear, Nicholas, *see* Hadrian IV
Browning, Robert, 22, 211–12
Buonaventura of Potenza, Blessed, 88
Byron, Lady, 89

Cacciapuoti, F., 92
Calixtus III, Pope, 277
Camera, Matteo, 13, 16, 103, 166
Campanula fragilis, 121–3
  isophylla, 122
Campidoglio, 100–1
  Annunziata, 100
  St. John the Baptist, 101
Canosa (Apulia): tomb of Bohemond, 49
Canterbury Cathedral, 55
Capo d'Orso, 25, 150
Capri, 21, 25, 115, 150, 210, 212–28, 270, 273
  certosa, 224
  Faraglioni, 150, 213, 218
  S. Costanzo, 86, 223
  S. Michele, 225–6, 227
  S. Stefano, 223–4
Capua, 226
Capuana, Archbishop of Amalfi, 52
Capuana, Cardinal Pietro, 44, 52, 57, 61, 248
Carlos, Don, first Bourbon king of Naples, 259
Carucci, Arturo, 189
Casanarella (Apulia), 54
Caserta Vecchia, 43, 81
Cassella, 213, 215
Castellamare, 38, 192
  Antiquarium, 153–4
  Grotto of S. Biagio, 153
  Roman villas, 144
Castellano, Guiseppe, 52
Castello, 204–6
Cava dei Tirreni, 157, 263
Cefalù (Sicily), 151
Cetara, 26, 115, 154, 251, 262
Charles I of Anjou, king of Sicily, 97, 258, 275

Chiunzi, Tower of, 28, 158, 196
Cilento, 25, 116, 150, 226, 261
Colchicum *alpinum*, 127
  corsicum, 127
  neapolitanum (?), 127, 199
Conca
  Convent of S. Rosa, 163
Connochia, La (near Capua), 43
Conradin, 275
Constance, wife of the Emperor Henry VI, 275
Convolvulus cneorum, 121
Corbet, Richard, 185–6
Coronilla emerus, 115
Corpo di Cava, Abbey, 67, 81
Cosmatesque work, 54–55, 79, 81–84, 92, 102, 162, 206
Crivelli, Protasio, 194
Crocus imperati, 73, 116–17, 199
  corsicus, 117
  etruscus, 116
  suaveolens, 116
  versicolor, 116–17
Cyclamen neapolitanum, 123–5, 204
  repandum, 118–19, 195

D'Afflitto family, 90, 102
Dalton, O. M., 36
D'Amato, Giovannangelo, 66
Dell'Asta, Andrea, 52
Desiderio, Abbot of Montecassino, 46
Desiderio, Marziano, 223
Douglas, Norman, 75, 139–140, 212, 213, 222
Doyle, Sir Francis, 89, 139
Dragone, River, 25, 62, 70, 105, 128, 245
Dung-beatle, 242–5

Eboli, 261
Erchie, 26
Erica multicaulis, 122–3
Euphorbia dendroides, *see* Tree spurge

Fairfax, Edward, 129
Fanzago, Cosimo, 57

Index

Ferdinand, King of Naples, 277
Ferula communis (giant fennel), 120–1, 241
Fire-fly, 245–7
FitzGerald, Edward, 238
Fondi, 81
Fontana, Domenico, 56, 57
Forster, E. M., 90
Francis II, King of Naples, 259
Fraxinus ornus (flowering, or manna ash), 128–9
Frederick II, Emperor, 60, 61, 258, 275
Furore, 103, 164–70
  S. Elia, 165
  Vallone di Furore, 168

Gaeta, 78
Galli, *see* Siren Isles
Gargano, 116
George of Antioch, 273
Gibbon, Edward, 31, 191–2, 265–6, 267
Gilmour, John, 221
Gioia, Flavio, 40
Giordano, Luca, 68, 157
Gladiolus species, 119–20
Glastonbury Abbey, 85
Gragnano, 191, 202, 203–4, 263, 267
  Corpus domini, 203
Gregory VII, Pope, 47
Grimthorpe, second Baron, 90
Grotto di Smeraldo, 25
Guglielmelli, Arcangelo, 53
Gull, Mediterranean, 241

Hadrian IV, Pope, 75
Hall, Joseph, 39

Iffley (Oxford), 205

John of Procida, 60
John the Accursed, 270
Justinian, Emperor, 191, 262

Knights of Malta, 99

Lacaita, Carlo, 89, 235

Landor, Walter Savage, 22
Lanfranco, 68
Lattari Mountains, 21, 240
Lawrence, D. H., 90, 245
Leopardi, Giacomo, 128, 182
Lesser periwinkle, *see Vinca minor*
Léttere, 191, 203, 206–9, 257, 263, 270
Lieto, Giuseppe di, 207, 235, 238
Lithospermum purpureo-caeruleum, 120
  rosmarinifolium, 121, 217
Lone, 160–1
Ludwig II, Emperor, 210

Mackenzie, Sir Compton, 213, 222
Madonnina (Rock), 168
Maiori, 25, 147–54
  Festa of the Assumption, 182–4
  S. Maria a Mare, 148–9
  S. Maria de Olearia, 150–3, 168
Malagno (Lazio), 78
Malato, Enrico: *Vocabularietto Napoli-tano*, 158
Manfred, 65, 258, 259, 275, 276
Mansi, Luigi, 14, 134, 137–138, 143, 157, 276
Mansone II, Prefect of Amalfi, 266
Mansone III, Doge of Amalfi, 258, 268, 269, 270
Marina del Cantone, 22
Marinetti, 213, 215
Massaniello, 70
Massine, Léonide, 211
Mastolo I, Judge of Amalfi, 258, 266, 267
Mastolo II, Judge of Amalfi, 258, 267, 277
Matteis, Paolo de, 226
Mauro, son of Pantaleone of Amalfi, 46
Medici, Giovann di, Pope Leo X, 205
Minori, 25, 143–7, 253, 270
  'Moorish' Fountain, 146–7
  Roman Villa, 34, 144
  S. Trofimena, ex-cathedral, 144–5
Mintorno, 78, 81
Minuto, 102, 150
  Annunziata, 102–4

Index

Monopoli (Apulia), 268–9
  S. Maria Amalfitana, 268
Monreale (Sicily), 76, 102
Montecassino, 46
Monte Cerreto, 27, 197, 201
Monte S. Angelo (Apulia), 48
Monte S. Angelo a Tre Pizzi, 27
Monte Vergine, 55
Morra, La, 188–9
Morra, Umberto, 36, 237
Morrell, Ottoline and Philip, 90
Murat, 259

Naccherino, Michaelangelo, 56, 57, 224
Naples, 210
  Carmine, 65
  Cathedral Baptistry, 34
  Gesù Nuovo, 226
  Immacolatella Fountain, 57
  Neptune Fountain, 56
Narcissus aschersonii, 126, 216, 218–21
  poeticus, 198
  tazetta, 125–6
Newman, John Henry, 140
Niccolo di Bartolomeo di Foggia, 79
Nocera Inferiore, 28
  Cathedral, 227
Nocera Superiore: *S. Maria Maggiore*, 32
Nola, 139
Norwich, John Julius: *The Normans in the South*, 271

Oderiso da Benevento, 49
Oman, Charles, 95
Ophrys fusca, 117
  lutea, 117–18
  scolopax, 117–18
Orchis italica, 118
  purpurea, 118
  simia, 118
Orsino, Raimondo, Prince of Salerno and Duke of Amalfi, 159
Orvieto, 95
Ostia, 55
Otto II, Emperor, 269

Paestum, 25, 38, 54, 150, 162
Pagani, 28, 68
Palermo, 86
  Capella Palatina, 82
Palinuro, 261
Pandects of Justinian, 258, 267, 274–5
Pansa, Francesca, 13, 16, 83, 193, 208
Pantaleone of Amalfi, 45
Pantaleone, the younger, of Amalfi, 48
Picard, Gilbert: *Living Architecture: Roman*, 34–5
Piccolomini Dukes of Amalfi, 259, 277–9
Pimonte, 193–4
Pino, G. di, 14
Pino, Marco, 203
Pirri, Pietro, 14
Pius II (Aeneas Silvius Piccolomini), 277
Pius V, 208
Pogérola, 91, 187, 208, 242
Pompeii, 38
Pontone, 101, 104–7, 245
  Carmine, 104
  S. Eustachio, 101–2
  Montagna, 71, 104, 117, 241
  St. John the Baptist, 104
  S. Filippo Neri, 104
Positano, 22, 28, 161–3
  Assunta, 162
  Chiesa Nuova, 163
Pozzuoli, 138
Praiano, 161
  S. Caterina, 161
Punta Campanella, 22, 211

Radelchi, Prince of Benevento, 265
Raffaelino del Garbo, 59
Ravello, 25, 28, 70–91, 136, 273
  Annunziata, 86
  Castiglione, 71
  Cathedral, 67, 76–80, 208
  Hotel Caruso, 84, 90, 102
  Hotel Palumbo, 90
  Madonna dell' Ospedale, 87
  Marmorata, 71, 136
  Palazzo d'Afflitto, *see* Hotel Caruso

Index

Palazzo Rufolo, 33, 89, 147, 235
Piazza della Fontana, 83, 146
St. Cosmas and St. Damian, 190
S. Francesco, 88
S. Giovanni del Toro, 83, 84, 88
S. Maria in Gradillo, 86
S. Maria Maggiore, 89
S. Martino, 88
Villa Cimbrone, 90
Ravenna, 31, 32
  S. Appolinare in Classe, 32
  S. Appolinare Nuovo, 32
  Bapistries, 32
  S. Vitale, 33, 208
Reid, Neville, 89
Robert Guiscard, 75, 271
Roger I, Great Count of Sicily,
  brother of Robert Guiscard, 272–3
Roger II, first king of Sicily, 75, 258,
  273–4
Rome
  Pantheon, 33
  S. Costanza, 31
  S. Paolo fuori le Mura, 46–47
  Spanish Steps, 57
  Terme Museum, 85
Rosemary (Rosmarinus officinalis), 115–6
Ruggero da Melfi, 49
Runciman, Sir Stephen: History of the
  Crusades, 98–99
Ruskin, John, 246

Sabatini, Andrea, see Andrea da
  Salerno
Sagio, Doge of Amalfi, 258
St. Andrew the Apostle, 121, 248–54
  Hymn of, 228, 254
  Miracle of, 232, 249–52
St. Bridget of Sweden, 248
St. Francis of Assisi, 61, 97, 248
St. Januarius, 138, 139, 250, 263
St. Louis, 97
St. Matthew, 121, 253
St. Nicholas of Bari, 76, 83, 140
St. Paul's (London), 208
St. Walburga, 140
Salerno, 38, 147, 253, 258, 269

Cathedral, 49, 79, 80, 83, 85
Cathedral Museum, 189
  S. Giorgio, 67, 69, 227
Salvia glutinosa, 193
Samaritani, 12, 151, 167, 168, 169, 170
Sanbuco: La Madonna della Pumice,
  187–8
S. Agata sui due Golfi, 69
S. Alfonso de'Liguori, and the order
  of the Redemptionists, 100, 194
S. Angelo in Formis, 43
S. Catarina, 195
S. Egidio di Monte Albino: Maddalena,
  68
S. Felice, 139
S. Gennaro, see St. Januarius
S. Maria Capua Vetere, 53
S. Maria dei Monti, 28, 100, 194, 197–
  200, 240
S. Maria dell' Avvocata, 143
S. Pantaleone, Festa, miracle and
  legend, 131–42, 251
S. Trofimena, 145–6, 251
Sasso, Gerardo, and his family, 98–99
Scala, 28, 91–100, 270, 273
  Cathedral (S. Lorenzo), 92–97
  S. Pietro in Campoleone, 97–98, 195
Schiavo, Armando, 14, 43, 164
Scilla bifolia, 117, 199
Scott, Geoffrey, 36
Sergio, First Doge of Amalfi, 267, 268
Sergius, Duke of Naples, 210
Sessa Aurunca, 78, 81, 82
Sicardo, Prince of Benevento and
  Salerno, 146, 257, 263
Sicone, Prince of Benevento, 257, 263
Siconolfo, Prince of Benevento, 265
Simon of Syria, 45
Siren Isles (Galli), 22, 23, 150, 211–12,
  273
Solario, Antonio (Lo Zingaro), 59
Solimena, Angelo, 227
Solimena, Francesco, 68, 225, 226–7
Sorrento, 129
  Museo Correale, 78
Spanish Broom, 23, 128
Spartium junceum, see Spanish Broom

Index

Sperlonga, 222
Stauracio da Scio, 47
Stromboli, 128, 241

Talbot-Rice, David, 36
Tasso, Torquato, 129
Tavola Amalfitana, 267
Teano, 81
Teggiano, 64, 79
Teias, last king of the Goths, 191–2, 257
Termini, 22
Tern, Black, 241
Terracina (Lazio), 81, 82
Teucrium fruticans, 116
Tiberius, 222
Torella, 143–4
Torre dello Ziro, 106, 235, 236
Tovere, 163–4
Tramontana (Wind), 159
Tramonti, 154–9, 167, 273
  Cesaranno, 156
  Figlino, 156, 159
  Pocara, 157–8
  Polvica, 155
Trani (Apulia), 76
Tree Spurge (*Euphorbia dendroides*), 127–128
Trevelyan, Robert, 90
Troia (Apulia), 49, 51
  Cathedral, 49

Turner, Reginald, 213, 214, 215
Tuscania, 189

Ugolino di Vieri, 96
Urginea (Scilla) maritima, 123

Vaccaro, Domenico Antonio, 42, 225
Valle dei Mulini, 105
Valle del Dragone, *see* Dragone
Vallerano (Lazio), 141
Vasari, 67
Venice: St. Mark's, 47, 85
Verlaine, Paul, 228
Vesuvius, 28, 32, 158
Véttica Maggiore, 161
  S. Gennaro, 161
Vettica Minore, 161
Vietri, 26, 66, 147
Vignola, 141
Vinca minor (Lesser periwinkle), 120
Viola lutea, 201
Vulture, Black, 241
  Griffon, 241

Wagner, Richard, 89
Warbler, Cetti's, 241
  Savi's, 241
Webster, John, 106, 259, 278
Westminster Abbey, 44, 55
William, King of Sicily, 75